NEPAL AND CHINA

A HISTORICAL PERSPECTIVE

NEPAL AND CHINA
A HISTORICAL PERSPECTIVE

Niranjan Bhattarai

ADROIT

ISBN: 978-81-87392-89-7

Published by
ADROIT PUBLISHERS
4675/21, Ganpati Bhawan, Ansari Road,
Daryaganj, New Delhi-110 002
Phones : 011-23266030

Distributors
AKHIL BOOK DISTRIBUTORS
e-mail: akhilbooks@yahoo.com
akhilbooks@hotmail.com

Printed in India on behalf of M/s Adroit Publishers
by Arpit Printographers • E-mail: arpitprinto@yahoo.com

Preface

Nepal and China are neighboring countries. The cultural contact between the two countries spans to over two thousand years. The story of the birth of Buddha reached China in 2 B.C. Commencement of this communication is regarded to be the beginning of contact and also the beginning of Nepal-China relations. Since then Buddhist teachers like Buddhabhadra of Kapilavastu. Nepal visited China and Chinese Buddhist scholars like Seng-tsai, Fa-Hsien (Fahian), Hsuan-Tsang (Huentsang) and others visited places related to the life of Buddha in Nepal. They also collected Buddhist Sutras and other materials concerning the teaching of the Lord. Ever since then, mutual visits by the Buddhists of the two countries have continued. Exchanges of opinions and experiences among them have helped to spread Buddhism in China. Thus Buddhism became the guiding force of development of relations between Nepal and China.

Formal and official contacts between the two countries were established in the seventh century. Emperor Tang Tai Chong Li Shimin had sent an official Mission headed by General Li Yipiao with gifts to present to King Narendra Deva of Nepal and Emperor Harshabardhana of India. In 643, the Mission visited Nepal then went on to India. King Narendra Deva in return sent a Mission headed by his son Prince Priyajeeva with gifts to present to the Emperor of China in 646. These contacts between the two neighboring countries are regarded to be the beginning of official relations between Nepal and China. However, after the demise of the Tang dynasty, the official visits paused for some time

The fourth chapter is devoted on the mythical story of the birth of Bodhisattva Manjushree, who is equally revered and worshipped in Nepal and China. Since historical times in Wu T'ai Shan and his visit to Nepal and draining the water of the Kathmandu Valley and making it habitable is traditionalized.

The well-known traveler Hsuan Tsang who visited Lumbini, Kapilavastu and other places of Nepal in 635 and had mentioned a brief introductory account of Nepal in his famous book Travels to Western Countries in Tang Dynasty.

Then Arniko visited Tibet and China during Yuan Dynasty and made contributions in fulfilling the wish of Emperor Kublai Khan by giving concrete shape and visible form, to the concepts of Buddhism by constructing Chaityas, Stupas, Temples and Monasteries and images of Buddha to draw attention of the Chinese people to Lord Buddha and his teaching. This way on the one hand he helped the Emperor to establish peace in the newly established Empire and on the other provided the people with an object to adhere to and express their devotion. For these invaluable contributions Araniko earned great respect and was the most admired person in that period of time. So his life is described in detail.

During the Ming Dynasty exchanges of official Missions were initiated again and in response Nepali side also sent their Missions to China. The life of two eminent Buddhist scholars Sahaja Shree and Shree Sariputra who visited China during that period and helped the Emperors enhance their understanding of teaching of Buddha and also played guiding role in performance of the Buddhist rituals including in their Coronations are also noteworthy.

Nepal's relations during the period of Ch'ing Dynasty were marked by war between the two neighbors and its conclusion by signing agreements and exchanges of Missions.

These expressions of mutual regards also continued when China became a Republic.

After the emergence of the People's Republic of China, the two ancient civilizations have renewed their traditional relations by establishing formal diplomatic relations in 1955 on the basis of the principles of equality, peaceful- coexistence and mutual benefit. Since then it is developing to the mutual satisfaction of both the countries.

The event during these two thousand years are not yet systematically studied and fully utilized for further enhancement of mutual interests of Nepal and China. This book is a humble attempt in this direction. The objective of preparing this work is to let general readers know our relations in the past, encourage them to study the process of development of relations between the two ancient civilizations and utilize the knowledge to understand the new China, flying high in recent times, and help also to promote it further.

Archives in China and Tibet are well organized, but not yet open to foreign scholars. So it is difficult to reach scientific conclusions concerning the studies of the developments taken place in this area in such a long-time.

Most of the information furnished in this book is from the published books and articles in Chinese, English, Hindi, Nepali, Sanskrit and other languages mentioned in footnotes, in the list of reference books and in other ways. I had an advantage to contact and learn from Chinese academicians, professors and other distinguished scholars about Nepal-China Relations when I was in China while studying there Chinese language for two years and serving two terms in the Nepal Embassy in Beijing. But as foreign diplomats had no easy access to the Chinese libraries, my information from Chinese unpublished resources remained limited. Regarding Tibetan resources, it is limited to some distinguished Tibetan professors' scholarly advices, information and verbal translations of some relevant Tibetan documents and books translated into Chinese, English or other languages.

Nepal's socio-economic and cultural relations with Tibet are thousands of years old. Nepal worked as entrepot for trans-Himalayan trade between parts of China and India.

In recent times relations between Nepal and Tibetan Autonomous Region of China have flourished. Socio-cultural intercourse and trade are developing continuously. After the Araniko Highway was constructed connecting Nepal and the TAR it has become a very effective instrument in promoting trade between Nepal and Tibet on the one hand and other parts of China on the other.

A brief account of the relations between Nepal and People's Republic of China based on the principles of equality and mutual benefits are presented. Mutual visits of the leaders of the two countries during more than fifty years period of time and the main objectives achieved on those occasions and their impact on bilateral relations are described. A brief account of the continued developments of cultural and economic relations and progress in trade and commerce with updated data are added.

Nepal and China both consider Buddhism has laid a solid foundation of their bilateral relationship. This relationship based on the principles of peaceful coexistence has made significant contributions for the development of good neighborly relations between the two countries. In this context the story of Buddha, and glimpses of his life in the Kingdom of Kapilavastu, before and after his enlightenment, development of Buddhism in Nepal, Nepal's contributions to introduction and to develop Buddhism in Tibet and spread of Buddhism in China are highlighted. These descriptions are added at the end of this book as appendix 8, to facilitate the readers who like to study in a bit more.

A collection of photos of Deities worshipped both in Nepal and tombs of Buddhabhadra and Shri Sariputra, and architectures and other works constructed by Nepali architects and artists and treaties and agreements signed in the early period after establishment of diplomatic relation and photoes of Nepali and Chinese leaders who exchanged visits in the last sixty years are added in the book.

I hope the readers will find this book informative and useful.

Niranjan Bhattarai
Sanepa, Lalitpur

Foreword

I feel very happy to know Mr. Niranjan Bhattarai's scholarly book entitled **Nepal and China: A Historical Perspective** is coming out very soon. Mr. Bhattarai, well trained in diplomatic career, is the author of two books entitled **China Ra Tyasasita Nepalko Sambandha (1961) and Nepal-China Sambandha (2001),** which are the books on the subject and **Collection of Tenzing Sherpa and other Songs and Poems.** His inclination on the scholarly aptitude must be appreciated.

As a student of history, I would like to request all those experienced persons like bureaucrats, politicians, diplomats and others to come forward with the publications of their experiences and thoughts. Such efforts will not only enlighten the posterity but also help in determining or adopting the right step for the better future in the right perspective. The concerned foreign rulers and diplomats will also be enlightened by such expressions in the form of the books. They will learn what impression the author has gathered during his tenure as an ambassador. Such contributions will be eye-openers to the posterity.

Mr. Bhattarai must be appreciated for his most meticulous research work on Nepal-China relations. As a student and Deputy Chief of the Mission (the Nepali Embassy) to China from Nepal for about ten years he has first-hand contemporary information on Nepal-China relations. Moreover having a scholarly aptitude he collected many authentic source materials on the subject to write the book. Writing on the subject a scholar may differ with that of a person with diplomatic career. The first one will be more theoretical whereas the second one more practical and realistic.

Mr. Bhattarai has very meticulously explained the spread of Buddhism in China from the beginning. Nepal's pride of being the birthplace of Lord Buddha has its own important contribution in Nepal-China relation. This aspect is well presented by Mr. Bhattarai. He has also explained the contributions of Arniko in the Nepal-China relation and the role of various missions at different times. He has rightly pointed out the religio-cultural aspects also, which cemented the Nepal-China relations strongly.

Mr. Bhattarai has also well explained the political relations between the two countries based on his own personal experience. Such expression by a scholarly person like him with long diplomatic career will help us understand the reality on the subject. This sort of academic work will be of much value to the scholars, academicians and the decision-makers. Hence I express my earnest congratulation to Mr. Bhattarai for his noble work. I wish he would come forward with more valuable academic works in future also.

Professor Dr. T. R. Vaidya
Former Head
Central Department of History
Tribhuvan University Nepal

Acknowledgements

I am indebted to Mr. Bhuban Lal Pradhan for allowing me to quote references from his published and unpublished books on Buddhism in Nepal. I express my sincere appreciation for it.

I express my sincere gratitude to Dr. Chen Hansheng, Professors Liu Tanian and Ma Yong of the Academy of Social sciences of China for their guidance in research work on the history of Nepal-China relations.

I am highly obliged to Professor Dr. Tulasi Ram Vaidya for sparing his precious time to review the book and making significant suggestions to give final shape for publication.

My grateful thanks are due to Mr. Jan Sharma for his kind cooperation to go through the whole book, to refine the language, and make valuable suggestions to make it useful.

It would be a great injustice if I do not mention my sons Anoop, Atul and Amal for their sincere assistance in every respect from A to Z of all the requirements regarding the publication of this book.

I feel highly obliged to the writers of the books, articles and other works I have referred and quoted in this book, the owners of the photos published in this book and also to those who have helped to make this book useful.

Niranjan Bhattarai
Sanepa, Lalitpur

Contents

List of Illustrations

Photo Gallery

Lushan Mountain in Dungling, where Pagoda temple of holy relcs of reverend Buddhasbhadra are enshrined are located

Princess Bhrikuti clay status in Potala

Status of Princess Bhrikuti
at a temple at Lhasa

Statue of Princess Bhrikuti
made of wood

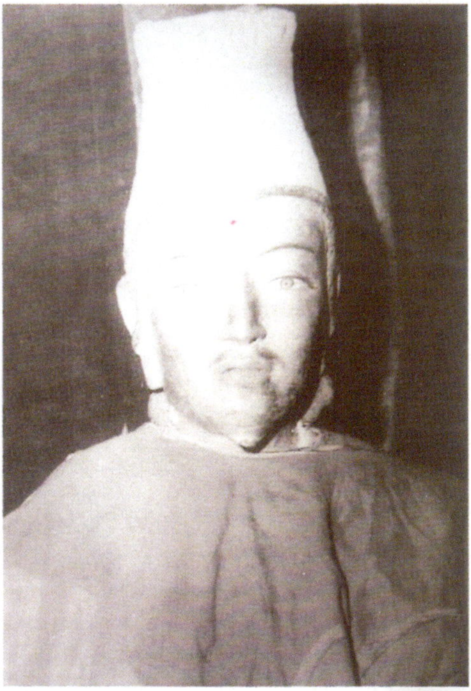

Mgar Tochan who came Nepal to beg Princess Bhrikuti to marry with Tiben King Srongtsan Gampo

Clay sculpture of Princess Bhrikuti as Harita Tara Sculptured by Tibetan artist Asanga in Araniko style

Princess Bhrikuti as Harita Tara in blessing poster

Maitreya, the future Buddha (Painting of image carried by Princess Bhirkuti while going to Tibet)

Postal stamp issued by Nepal government in honour of Princess Bhrikuti in 2007.

MANJUSHREE
AT WU TAI SHAN

Image of Manjushree in Pho Guang Shi Temple at Wu Tai Shan

Image of Manjushree in a Temple at Cheng Teh

Image of Manjushree in
Nan Chang Shi Temple
at Wu Tai Shan

Image of Manjushree riding
on a lion enshrined in
a Temple in China

Metallic image of Manjushree made by Araniko

Golden Chaitya Made by Araniko at Shakya Monastery

White pagoda in Wutaishan where the hairs of Manjushree are said to preserved

A Stupa at Shakya Monastery
made by Araniko

An Arch with Nepil-scripts made by Araniko at Bataling, Beiging

A painting of Buddha made by Araniko

A painting at Shalu Monastery in Tibet in Araniko's style

A Portrait of Genghis Khan in traditional style.

Portrait of Kublai Khan presumed to be Araniko in Nepali style

Clay sculpture of MAHAKAL, The Guardian Deity of Kublia Khan

Beijing city in earlier days
where the Bai Ta stands Tall

Postal stamp issued in honour of Araniko in 1972

Sardar Gunjaman Singh, Principal adviser and Ambassador Yuan Zhangxian signing an agreement to establish Diplomatic Diplomatic relations between Nepal and China 1955

Chairman Mao And Premier Chou Enlai wearing Nepali cap presented by Balachandra Sharma, leader of the Nepali Cultural Delegation during their visit to China in 1956.

Chairman Mao receiving Prime Minister Tanka Prasad Acharya 1956.

Prime Minister Tanka Prasad Acharya with Premier Chou Enlai

Prime Minister Tanka Prasad Acharya and Premier Chou Enlai signing the Agreement for Economic Cooperation between Nepal and China in the presence of Chairman Mao during Acharya's official visit, Beijing September 1956.

Premiere Chou Enlai being received in Kathmandu during his first visit to Nepal, 1957.

Chairman Mao receiving Prime Minister Bishweshwar Prasad Koirala during his official visit to China, Beijing March 1960.

Prime Minister Bishweshwar Prasad Koirala And Primier Chou Enlai signing the Nepal-China Treaty of the Peache and Friendship during Premier Zhou's visit to Nepal, April 1960.

Chairman Mao receiving King Mahendra and Queen Ratna during their State visit to China, October 1961.

King Mahendra and President Liu Shaoqi Signing the Nepal China Boundary Treaty during King Mahendra's State visit to China, October 5, 1961.

Author with Premier Chou Enlai at Nepal Embassy Beijing, 1970

Chairman Mao receiving King Birendra and Queen Aishwraya during their state visit to China, December 1973.

King Birendra receiving Deputy Premier Deng Xiaoping during his visit to Nepal February 1978.

Deputy Premier Deng Xiaoping being received in Lalitpur during his visit to Nepal, February 1978.

King Birendra with Vice Premier Deng Xiaoping in Beijing 1979.

King Birendra and Queen Aishwarya welcoming President Li Xiannian and
Madam Lin Jiamei at a banquet hosted in their honor
during their visit to Nepal March 1984.

King Birendra receiving Premier Li Feng during visit to Nepal 1989.

President Jiang Zemin receiving Prime Minister Girija Prasad Koirala during his visit to China 1992.

President Jiavg zemin receiving Prpme Minister Manmohan Adhikari in Beijing 1995

President Jiang Zemin receiving Prime Minister Sher Bahadur Deuba during his official visit to China, 1996.

King Birendra and President Jiang Zeminafter signing of agreement during the President's visit to Nepal 1996

King Birendra receiving Premier during his visit to Nepal, 2001

Prime Minister Girija Prasad Koirala receiving Zhu Rongji during his visit to Nepal 2001

President Hu Jintao receiving Prime minister Pushpakamal Dahal Prachanda in Beijing 2008

A Pagoda built by Araniko's disciple Liu Yuan at Bei-hai Beijing

Sarira Pagoda built by Araniko and Temple of Manjushree au Wu Tai Shan

Statue of Araniko (1244-1306), at White Pagoda-Premises, Beijing, China

Ashoka Pagoda built by Araniko at Wu T'ai Shan

Yuan Zhao Pagoda in Wu T'ai Shan, where relics of Revered Bhikshu Shree Sariputra (1335-1426) of Nepal are enshrined

Tooth Relic Pagoda, Beijing

Ashoka Pagoda built by Araniko at Wu T'ai Shan

Chapter 1

Birth of Buddha

Story of Birth of Buddha

The story of Birth of Buddha, which took place in 563 B.C., in Lumni Guo (Lumbini state) had reached China in 2nd year B.C., the time of the reign of Emperor Ai Ti (6 B.C.1 B.C.) of Western Han Dynasty.

According to the reference of the story in "San Guo Zhi" Ching Lu, the son of the scholar of Imperial Court met with Yi Chun-an ambassador of a Buddhist state Yueh-chih then located in the region of former Scythia, present Afghanistan and Northern India.

"The Ambassador verbally recited some of the Buddhist Sutras, described the event of the Birth of Buddha at Lumni Guo (Lumbini State) and explained some aspects of Buddhism to the scholar Ching Lu. Ching Lu conveyed his conversation with Yi Chun to his other friends and scholars at the Imperial Palace."

The conversation between Yi Chun and Ching Lu was the first instance of the narration of the story of the Birth of Buddha and hence the introduction of his preaching in China.

As their conversation mentioned Lumbini, Nepal, it is regarded to be the first point of contact made between Nepal and China.

According to other references, in the same book, in this context "Buddha was born from Maya Devi, the Queen of King Shuddhodana of the Kingdom of Lumni Guo (Lumbini state). At the time of birth the colour of the body of Buddha was yellow. His hair was black and soft like silk. He also had hair on his chest. The color of his eyes was red as that of copper. Queen Maya Devi had seen a white elephant in her dream when she became pregnant. Buddha was born from the left armpit of the Queen Maya Devi. When Buddha was born he walked seven steps immediately."

"Sariputra was a disciple of Buddha. Among other disciples, there

Fig. 1 : Maya Devi giving Birth to Siddhartha Gautama, Lumbini, Nepal

were Upashaka, Sramana, Bappa, Sumana, Bipashwi Bhikshu and Kaudinya."

From then on, communication between Nepal and China developed regarding Buddha and Buddhism, which brought the two countries closer. The exchange of visits of Buddhist scholars enhanced friendship and understanding which later became the basis for further development of relations between the two countries.[1]

Buddhism in China

During the reign of Han Emperors Huan Ti (147-167) and Ling Ti (168-189), Buddhism became so popular in China that statues of Buddha were even established and worshipped in the Palace, while equal respect was paid to Buddha as to Huang Ti (Yellow Emperor) and Lao-tse, the traditional Chinese saint. In the following years, Buddhist monks were invited from India and other places to Luoyang where they joined the translation work of Buddhist scriptures into Chinese language along with their Chinese colleagues, marking the beginning of the most magnificent translation venture seen in the history of cultural exchange between China and other country. With successive visits to China by many Buddhist scholars from India, Nepal and other countries, the theories of Buddhism began to be introduced more extensively in China, while Chinese scholars also began their studies of Buddhism.

During the 400 years from the second half of the fourth to the mid eighth century, the search for and collection of Buddhist scriptures in Sanskrit continued with growing enthusiasm in China. Such noted monks Kumarjiva and Buddhabhadra went to China. Sheng -Tsai Fa Hsien, Dao Tai, Zhi Meng, Bao Hsien, Hsyan Tsang, Yi Jing and Bu Kong traveled to India, Nepal and China respectively one after another with the objective to promote understanding of Buddhism in China. Hsuan Tsang was most successful in collecting 657 volumes of Sanskrit scriptures including Mahayana scriptures and Mahayana Theories.[2]

Spread of Buddhism

Buddhist monasteries first appeared in China during the Eastern Han dynasty but it was only after the Western Tsin dynasty (255-316) that Buddhism began to spread in this country and flourished in the Southern Dynasties. At its heyday in the Northern Dynasties, Buddhism boasted thirty thousand monasteries and over two million monks and nuns throughout the country.

The propagation of Buddhism and translation of a large number of Buddhist scriptures exercised a great influence on the culture of China. Buddhist scriptures embody the culture of ancient India and Nepal including knowledge about nature, views on human life, as well as their historical records. They also contain beautiful literary works, such as tales, fables, long poems and songs. These constituted a rich source of inspiration for the science, philosophy and literature of China. It was also to the influence of Indian and Nepali art, architect, sculpture and painting that Chinese art owed its unique style.

At that time, there were three famous Buddhist translators: the Venerable Tao An (312-385) a Chinese, Kumarajiva (343-413), an Indian; and Buddhabhadra (358-429) a Nepali who spent many years in China and translated more than three hundred volumes of Buddhist scriptures.[3]

By the first half of the sixth century, everywhere in north and in south China temples and pagodas were built and Buddhist statues sculptured, cast and molded. These works of art are a tribute to the great achievements in the field of art made by the people of the time.

In Northern Wei it took more than one hundred years to complete the many grottoes and temples on Yun kang Hill (near Tatung, Shansi Province). An image of Buddha carved of stone is still intact. It is 50 feet tall and is in a grotto measuring 70 feet wide and 50 feet deep. The Buddha sits on a pedestal measuring 50 feet across and is surrounded by four smaller Buddha's.[4] The pedestal, column and walls are richly carved. There is also a big image of Manjushree seated on a lion carved in the mountain.

This process continues till today. And thus China has become a prominent Buddhist country equipped with a great collection of Buddhist script, sculptures, arts and architects. Like in other areas it has also become a source of Buddhist matters for which scholars and artists from different countries solicit their cooperation.

Tooth Relic of Buddha

The Holy Tooth Relic of Shakyamuni Buddha is enshrined in a new pagoda constructed by Buddhists of China. The pagoda is located at the original site of the Ling Kuang Monastery, at the western hills in the suburbs of Beijing. This Holy Tooth Relic has been preserved in China for more than fifteen hundred years.[5]

After the establishment of the Peoples Republic, the Tooth-Relic was brought to Kuang-Chi Shi monastery in 1955, where the Tooth-Relic was enshrined in a golden stupa embedded with seven kinds of jewels kept in the Sharira Pavilion, for the worship of Buddha by the devotees both at home and from abroad.

On June 25, 1964, the Buddhist Association of China performed in a solemn way the inauguration Ceremony of the newly built temple when the Holy Tooth was enshrined for Tooth-Relic Pagoda. Buddhist delegations from Cambodia, Ceylon, Indonesia, Japan,

Laos, Mongolia, Nepal, Pakistan, Vietnam attended the ceremony. The Buddhist delegates of these countries expressed their pleasure and praise for the significant occasion in the history of Buddhism in China.[6]

Thus it could be seen how the Chinese people appreciated Buddhism as an agreeable way for mental peace and also for harmonious social relations. This popular opinion helped Buddhism to secure an important place among the guiding principles of Chinese

Fig. 2 : Tooth Relic Pagoda, Beijing

life like Taoism and Confucianism. This concept remains till today to be a special characteristic of Chinese life.

In the early period of introduction of Buddhism in China, when devotion to Buddha and Buddhism had become already a part of reverence of Chinese devotees Sheng -Tsai was the first to visit the places related to the life of Buddha in Nepal and India in Tsin dynasty (265- 420). There - after, Fa Hsien together with some of his fellow students set out from Chang-An in 399 to India, Nepal and Sri Lanka. When he returned back home he carried books and other materials on Buddhism collected during his visits. During the visit he had heard about Buddhabhadra and expected to meet him and translate the books and materials into Chinese language with the help of the Nepali scholar who was already working in China.

Buddhabhadra had arrived in China in 409 and was helping Chinese people to understand teaching of Buddha in Nanjing. After arrival in China Fa Hsien met with Buddhabhadra and requested him for assistance to translate the materials he had brought from his visit to the western countries into Chinese language. Both devoted Buddhist scholars together worked for many years to translate the materials. Fa Hsien died in 410 and Buddhabhadra continued working till he died in 429 in China.

Because of the vital roles Fa Hsien and Buddhabhadra have played by contributing to the solid foundation for institutionalizing Buddhism and initiating the whole process of spreading Buddha's teaching, they are regarded by the Chinese and Nepalis as great pioneers and immortals.

End Notes

1. 24 History Books of China, Beijing, Wei Lue, Xizhang, 3rd Part 30th Zuan, Zhong Hua Shu Zhu, Xin Hua Shu Dian, 1975, pp. 859-60
2. Kenneth Ch'en: Buddhism in China. A Historical Survey: Princeton and New Jersey: Princeton University Press, 1973. pp. 31-32
3. An Outline History of China: Foreign Languages Press, Beijing, China 1958, pp. 98-99
4. Ibid, pp. 99-100
5. The Buddhist Tooth Relic Pagoda, Beijing: The Buddhist Association of China, 1969, pp. 5-6.
6. Ibid, pp. 8-10

Chapter 2

Two Eminent Buddhist Scholars Fa Hsien and Buddhabhara

Fa Hsien (Fa Xian or Fahian) and Buddhabhadra (Zue Hsien)

Fa Hsien was born in 338 in Ping Yang of Shahxi. Fa Hsien's original name was Kung. He was admitted to the Buddhist order at the age of three and was given the religious name Fa-hsien, meaning Law Manifest. He was already sixty-two when he left for his travels and was seventy-six by the time he finally made his way back to China. In 414, the year after his return to China he wrote the record of his travels and later, by request, added certain material to make an improved version, which we have today. Title of his book is 'A Record of the Buddhist Countries also known as the 'Travels of Fa Hsien'. It gives a complete description of his journey and is the earliest comprehensive account we possess of the customs, geography and history of the countries located in the area of present Central Asia, India, Nepal and the Indian Ocean. This is a great travel book comparable only to the later Record of Western Region by monk Hsuan-Tsang (Tripitaka) of the Tang Dynasty.

The famous monk Fa Hsien, together with some nine or ten of his fellow students, left Chang-An, and set out for India, Nepal and other places of Buddhist pilgrimage. On his way to the West he passed the Tarim Basin and Climbed over the Pamirs.[1]

His team, and another team of scholars led by Pao Yun moving towards west with a similar objective of studying Buddhism and convey back home the Buddhist scriptures and organizational aspects of Samghas, happened to meet at Chanpe. The two teams then traveled together for some distance and were separated from a place called Kucha (Quici), now in the Autonomous Region of Xinjiang.[2]

Fa Hsien's objective

Fa Hsien's objective was to visit the birth place of Buddha in Nepal's Lumbini, and other places of pilgrimage in Nepal, India and Sri Lanka, study and understand organizational aspects, rites and rituals of Buddhist Samghas, collect Buddhist Sutras and related literature, carry them back to China and promote preaching of Buddhism in China.

The Team of Pao Yun

The team of five Buddhists – Pao Yun, Chi Yen, Teng Shao and other two – intended to visit a monastery, learn teaching of Buddha and invite a Buddhist scholar to go to China so that Chinese Buddhists could enhance their understanding of Buddhism and also get answers to their problems concerning the teaching of the Lord in China itself. The team of Pao Yun took the route to Kashmir where there were Monasteries and other institutions to teach Buddhist philosophy.

The Team of Fa-Hsien and Pilgrimage

The team of Fa Hsien moved towards the East to go to India on the way to Lumbini, the Birthplace of Buddha in Nepal and other places of Pilgrimage around the area. Some extracts from his records are presented below.

The Town of Napika, the City of Kapilavastu and the Garden of Lumbini

"Traveling twelve yojanas (1yojana is approximately 8 miles) Southeast from the city of Sravasti, they arrived at a town called Napika, where Krakuchchhanda Buddha was born, and entered Nirvana. Monasteries and stupas have been built at these places. Less than one yojana to the north they reached where Kanakamuni Buddha was born and entered Nirvana. Stupas and Monasteries have also been built at all these places.

Less than one yojana to the East they reached the city of Kapilavastu. This city has neither king nor citizens, and looks completely deserted; only some monks and a few dozen families of the laity live here. Among the ruins of the palace of King Suddhodana is an image of the prince's mother Mayadevi showing the prince riding on a white elephant, coming to enter his mother's womb. A stupa has been built over the spot where the prince, having left the city by the East Gate, saw a sick man and ordered his charioteer to drive back to the palace. Here too are the places where Asita observed the marks on the prince, and where the prince with Ananda and others brought down a wild elephant. An arrow shot from here entered the earth thirty li (1 li is 500 meters) to the Southeast, causing a fountain to spring up; and the people made a well from which wayfarers might drink water. Stupas have also been built at the following places: where Buddha returned to see his father after attaining Buddhahood; where the earth quaked six times when five hundred men of the Shakya clan saluted Upali after renouncing their homes; where the Buddha expounded the Law to devas while the four celestial kings guarded the four gates of the hall so that his father, the king, could not enter; and where Buddha sat facing East under a Nyagrodha tree which is growing to this day and where Mahaprajapati offered him robe. Here also can be found the stupa built at the place where King Virudhaka slaughtered the descendants of the Sakya clan, who had all attained to the first stage of sainthood. A few li to the Northeast of the city is the royal field where the prince sat under a tree to watch men ploughing in the field. Fifty li to the east of the city there is the royal garden called Lumbini. It was in this garden that the queen entered the pond to bathe. After bathing she came out from the Northern side of the pond, walked for about twenty paces and holding the branch of a tree and facing east, gave birth of a princely son. As soon as the prince was born, he took seven steps. He was bathed by two dragon-kings. A well has been made at that bathing place, and monks often drink the water from it as well as from the pond.

Four places are already preordained in advance: where Buddha's shall attain Buddhahood; where they shall begin to preach; where they shall expound the Law and refute heretics; and where they shall descend from the Trayastrimsat Heaven after having preached to their mothers. Other places are chosen according to circumstances.

The country of Kapilavastu is deserted and few people travel its roads for fear of the white elephants and lions there. One cannot journey without taking real precautions.[3]

The Country of Ramagrama

Five yojanas East of Buddha's Birthplace lays the country of Ramagrama. The king of this country obtained a share of the relics of Buddha, and upon his return home built a Stupa named Ramagram. Beside this Stupa is a pond in which lives a dragon that keeps constant guard over the Stupa and worships there day and night. When King Ashoka was living, he determined to demolish eight stupas and built 84,000 new ones; and having pulled seven, he came to raze this country of Ramagrama. But then the dragon appeared and took him to its place, where it showed him all the vessels it used in worship.

"If your vessels are better than mine," it said to the king, "then destroy the Stupa and take it away, and I will not quarrel with you."

Knowing that the dragon's vessels were not of this world, King Ashoka had to go home.

Since this place was completely deserted, there was no one to sweep and water it. But a herd of elephants would often come with water in their trunks to water the ground, and they offered fragrant blossoms of many kinds here. A monk who came from another country to worship at this Stupa was terrified at the sight of the elephants, and hid behind a tree. But when he saw these beasts presenting offerings in the approved manner, he was deeply moved to think that there were no monks here to look after this Stupa and that it was left to the elephants to keep it clean. He there upon gave up his status as a fully ordained monk to take up the duties of a novice, cutting the weeds and brambles himself and leveling the ground, till all was in good order. This done, he urged the king to build a monastery there, and volunteered to be the abbot of it. There are monks now living there. This occurred recently, and the abbot of this monastery has always been a novice since that time.

Three yojanas east of this is the place where the prince dismissed Ch'andaka and his white horse. A stupa has also been built here.

Traveling East again for four yojanas, they arrived at the Ashes Stupa, where there is also a monastery.[4]

The City of Kushinagara

Twelve yojanas further East, they reached the city of Kushinagara. It was North of this city, between two trees beside the Hiranyavati River, that Buddha entered Nirvana with his head towards the North. Here are stupas and monasteries which were built at the following places: where Subhadra, Buddha's last disciple, entered the order; where the Blessed One, lying in a golden coffin, received homage for seven days; where Vajrapani laid down his golden mace; and where the eight kings shared the relics of Buddha. This city is almost deserted, with only a handful of monks and a few laymen as its inhabitants.[5]

The Last Farewell of the Licchavis to Buddha

Traveling twelve yojanas to the Southeast they reached the spot where the Licchavis, (the community residing in nearby state called Vrijji) wished to follow Buddha to the place of his Nirvana, but could not get his consent. Out of affection for him they would not go away: so Buddha made a deep ditch appear which they were unable to cross. He then gave them his alms-bowl as a relic, and sent them home. A stone pillar with inscriptions was erected at this place.[6]

Pao Yun reaches Kashmir

The group led by Pao-Yun reached to the monastery called "Mou Thian Tho Lo" in Kashmir where Buddhabhadra happened to be teaching Buddhism.

Buddhabhadra (Zue Hsien)

Buddhabhadra (358-429) was born in the Shakya family of Kapilavastu in Na Ali Cheng of Nagarhara state of a Buddhist kingdom at that time at the location of Present Afghanistan. Na Ali Cheng, the city of Jalalabad at that time, was a famous center of Buddhism and also a market place of objects related to Buddhism and other goods of daily use. An enterprising man also a Buddhist, Buddhabhadra's grandfather (mother's father), had moved from Kapilabastu with his family, wife, daughter and son-in-law to Jalalabad for business and better livelihood for his family. Buddhabhadra was born there in 358 A.D. He was bereaved of his father when he was three years old and mother when five years. Because of this sudden and tragic incident, Buddhabhadra's grandfather together with his wife and grandson came back to Kapilabastu. After some time, both the grandfather and grandmother of Buddhabhadra died in Kapilabastu and Buddhabhadra did not have anyone to look after him. He grew up under the attention and care of his relatives and neighbours in Kapilabastu.

Buddhabhadra was intelligent and studious. At the age of 16 or 17, he had already acquired a substantive knowledge of Buddhism. His teachers were impressed with his understanding and good character. Because of his speedy progress in learning and understanding, he had already become known in the area. It appears that he became a Buddhist under the guidance of a local Buddhist priest at that time. As he was liked by everybody and had already become famous to the Buddhist world at the time, he went to Kashmir and joined the Monastery called "Mou Thian Tho Lo" to teach Buddhism and continue his meditations according to the Buddha's instructions and methods.

It was in this Monastery where the Chinese group led by Pao Yun arrived to study. After the group completed their studies, they requested the Chief of the monastery to recommend a teacher who could go to China and help Chinese Buddhists understand the preaching of Buddha and Buddhist Sutras, explain and answer their questions and lead them to enlightenment. The chief of the monastery recommended the name of Buddhabhadra on the basis of his belonging to Shakya clan and also being a direct descendant of Buddha's uncle Amritodana and had come from the Kapilabastu in Lumbini (the Lumni Guo) state where Buddha was born.

The Chinese students petitioned to him accordingly; Buddhabhadra accepted their sincere request and went to China. It took three full years from 406 to 409 for this group to reach China via Chiao Tse (the present Vietnam). They went from Shang Tu to a monastery in Chang-An, where every body welcomed them and after making necessary arrangements they started working there as planned. But because of some difficulties created by the miscreants there Buddhabhadra left Chang-An in 410. With more than forty students he moved to Chang-Jiang river valley (present Hubei Province). On the way to his tour he arrived at Lushan Mountains. Hui-Yuan, a noted Chinise monk scholar warmly welcomed the Nepali Buddhist scholar there for his reputation as Dhyana (Zhan) Master. Later on, Buddhabhadra, along with his disciples continued his journey and went to Nanking. After arriving there he maintained his teachings and helped Chinese devotees to understand Buddhism in the way Buddha had explained to his disciples after his enlightenment.[7]

Fa Hsien and Buddhabhadra meet

When he was in India, Fa-hsien had already heard about Buddhabhadra's sojourn in China, so he went directly to Chang-An in 412 to meet the Nepali scholar who had come from Kapilabastu. But after arriving at Chang-An, he learnt that Buddhabhadra had moved to Nanking. So Fa Hsien also went to Nanking and met him there. Both the Buddhist scholars Fa Hsien and Buddhbhadra were delighted and elated at meeting each other.

In Nanking the two great scholars from Nepal and China made a plan to work together. They translated and compiled many

Fig. 3 : A Pagoda at Dungling, Lushan Mountains, Jiangxi Province, China where holy Relics of Reverend Buddhabhadra (358-429) of Kapilavastu, Nepal are enshroned

Buddhist scriptures and Sutras. The works they completed during that work-period were divided in 107 roles (zhuan) and 15 collections or volumes. Among them there were also the famous Avatamsaka Sutra, Samadhi Sutra, Vaipulya Sutra, Garva Sutra, Maha Parinirvana Sutra and Jnana Sutra. Fa-Hsien died in 420. After the Nirvana of Fa Hsien, Buddhabhadra continued their work till 429 when he also achieved Nirvana in China.

The tomb of Buddhabhadra was discovered recently at Dong Ling Temple, in Lushan Mountains, Jiangxi Province of China and renovated. This occasion was celebrated in a grand scale. Many distinguished Buddhists from all over China including Beijing had attended the ceremony.

Fa Hsien was one of the first Chinese Buddhist to visit Kapilabastu, Lumbini, Kushinagar and other places of pilgrimage related to Buddha's birth, growth and his activities. He wrote a book on his journey, "A Record of the Buddhist Kingdoms", and described and narrated events during the journey and also about the countries he had visited. This book provides valuable references about the places related to Buddha in Nepal, India and other countries.

In the same way, Buddhabhadra was the first Buddhist scholar to visit China, live there for 20 years (409-429), help Chinese people to understand Buddhism, co-operate with Fa Hsien in translating and compiling the Buddhist scriptures in Sanskrit and Pali languages into Chinese language and facilitate Chinese Buddhists to study Buddhism in their own language.

Both scholars were devoted to popularize Buddhism and Buddha's preaching and dedicated their whole life for this objective. Therefore they are regarded to be the first distinguished personalities laying the solid foundation for the growth of Nepal-China relations.[8]

End Notes

1. Fa Hsien, *A Record of the Buddhist Countries*, Translated by Li Yong Shi, Kathmandu: Tiwari's Pilgrims Book House, pp. 7-9
2. Niranjan Bhattarai. *Nepal Chin Sambandha (Nepal China Relations), Lalitpur,* Sajha Prakashan, 2058 B.S, p. 87
3. Fa Hsien, p. 49
4. Ibid, p. 52
5. Ibid, p. 53
6. Ibid, p. 54
7. Bhattarai, pp. 86-88
8. Ibid, pp. 89-90

Other References Books:

Shen Fuwei. *Cultural Flow between China and Outside World Throughout History*: Beijing: Foreign Language Press, 1997. Pp. 103-104

Fa Hsien Yatra Vivaran (Travel Description of Fa-Hsien), Banaras, India: Nagari Pracharini Sabha, *(in Hindi Language*), 1961. pp. 48-50

Records on life of Fa hsien, Buddhabhadra Hsuan-tsang Iching, Inning and other eminent Buddhists could be found in *Gao Sheng Zhuan* published in China (collection of life stories of eminent Buddhists) and *Encyclopedia of Buddhism*, Published in Japan.

Zhue Hsien Zhuan: compiled by the disciples of Buddhabhadra could be found in Beijing University Library, China.

A record of Buddhist Countries by Fa Hsien is also translated and published by Foreign Languages Press, Beijing, China.

Chapter 3

Nepal-Tibet Relationship

Lha Tho-tho-ri Receives Karandabyuha Sutra

After the establishment of the Kingdom in Tibet, eighteen generations after Podekungyal, a son of the Royal line named Lha Tho-tho-ri (Lha Tho-tho-ri Nyantsen) was born in 173.[1] He ascended the throne, and became the twenty-eighth King according to the Tibetan Annals. It is said that when Lha Tho-tho-ri was sixty years of age, he received, while living in the palace of Yambula Kang, a casket fallen from heaven which contained the book of Buddhist scripture called Karandavyuha Sutra, Karma Shataka (the 100 precepts on cause and effect) and a golden chaitya.[2] He could not read the book because it was in the Sanskrit language and at that time, there was no one in Tibet who could read Sanskrit. The King called the books and chaitya, "Nyenpo Sangwa" (the sacred). They were revered by the King and were kept secret for many years. The King told his ministers that it had descended from the heaven and only after four generations some body will be able to read and understand the book because the Bonpas believed any thing sacred to come down from the heaven.

This event marked the initial introduction of Buddhism into Tibet. Since Buddhism was introduced during the reign of Lha-Tho-tho-ri, the Tibetans regarded this King as incarnation of Samantabhadra Bodhisattwa. This event was regarded to be of such an importance that Tibetan currency notes are dated from the year of that introduction, 233.

Birth of Srongtsan Gampo (Slon-brtsan-Sgam-po)

Four generations later, in 617, Nyatri Srongtsen, the 32nd king, had a son named Tride Songtsen who is better known, now as Srongtsan Gampo. His birth took place just one year before the founding of

Tang Dynasty, when Kao-Tsu became Emperor in 618. Srongtsan Gampo ascended the throne at the age of 13.[3]

Some Western scholars including Luciano Petech maintain the view that these Buddhist scriptures belong to a much later period. However, it is very difficult to be precise about these dates particularly the Karandavyuha Sutra, which occupies an extremely important place in Nepali Buddhism.

Karandavyuha Sutra could have been the early works of Mahayana Buddhism similar to Sukhavati Vyuha Sutra. It gives us a hint of some sort of early missionary activities of the Buddhists of Nepal or India in Tibet. The text Karandavyunha Sutra describes vividly the visit of a group of merchants, headed by Simhasarthavah to Tibet for the business of jewels and gold they found in the land of Tibet. If we believe this legend we can infer that there were Nepali merchants who used to travel to Tibet in the early century of Christian era. Local Nepali tradition gives much credit to this legend. These books, which had received from heaven by the King Lha-Tho-tho-ri, it is considered, actually brought to Tibet by Pandit Buddhirakshita (blo-sems-tsho) and translator Li-The-Se. Since the Tibetan king could not read and understand the meaning of the books in Sanskrit, the Pandit and translator returned.

The second phase of this diffusion of Buddhism in Tibet commenced after the marriage of Nepali Princess Bhrikuti to Srongtsan Gampo with the establishment of many Temples, Jokhang, Ramoche and others, and also the original two-structured Potala Palace connected with a bridge at the red mountain.[4]

At that time, Tibet, divided into autonomous ethnic principalities and groupings, was in the process of unification. The central authority was not yet developed. Bonpa-philosopy and the tradition prevalent at that time, it appears, were considered not capable enough to provide the people with essential guidance for unification and necessary development of Tibet. This notion of the new generation might have necessitated introduction of a new approach to life and an objective to strive for. This situation seems to have created an atmosphere to welcome Buddhism, which had flourished in India, had already become agreeable to some sections of peoples of Nepal and China and was moving towards Tibet through Nepal with new ideas, contents and components suitable for all the countries.

Buddhism also brought other religious, cultural and social customs and manners developed in Nepal and India to the land-locked and nearest of the northern neighbors Tibet. China was the other close neighbour of Tibet. The Tibetan people also received impacts of ideas and ideals similarly developed in China.

Nepal also was the main route in the south for communication, trade and transport of goods from Nepal and India to Tibet. Tibet exported salt, wool, yak tail, musk, dust gold, hides and other commodities to Nepal and via Nepal to India and other central Asian states. Actually it was not only Buddhism and spiritual or social aspects of life, but also other views and concepts, which were useful for daily necessities and social life, finding their way into Tibet from or through Nepal.

Srongtsan Gampo

This was the situation in Tibet when Srongtsan Gampo was born in 617 in Yambula Kang Palace in Tibet. When Srongtsan Gampo reached the age of maturity by local standard, and could understand state- affairs as well as the spiritual and social environment developing around his country and nearby states, he might have started to consider consolidating the unification of his country.

He was intelligent and deep in his thinking. His bravery was well known and recognized around the neighboring countries like Nepal, India, Central Asian states and China. After appropriate arrangements he moved at once to consolidate the unification of the country, opened 18 mountain passes around Tibet, and established a viable route from Lhasa to Chang An, the Capital of Tang Empire of China on the one hand, and Lhasa to Kathmandu and via Kathmandu to Magadha, the Capital of Emperor Harshavardhana of India on the other. Thus the emergence of King Srongtsan Gampo and a unified Tibet opened a viable and comparatively secured-route from Chang An via Lhasa and via Kathmandu to India and beyond. This opening-up of the new land route through Nepal facilitated the communications and commercial transactions among the people of India to China and vice versa.

He seems to have understood and recognized the usefulness of Buddhist concept to be the guiding principles of state affairs and objectives and also of social life in Tibet. He also seems to have decided to replace Bonpa by Buddhism. He was declared the incarnation of Avalokiteshvara and assumed the authority for legitimatization of his rules and orders. To materialize this idea to promote Buddhism and also to find knowledge developed in closest neighboring countries like Nepal, India and China, he, according to Monikabom, thought it expedient to marry the princesses of Nepal and China, Bhrikuti and Wen Cheng respectively and expected that they would bring with them the images and icons of Buddhist deities, the scriptures, the Buddhist scholars who could translate and explain Buddha's preaching to Tibetan people. He also seems to have hoped that the knowledge of achievements in different areas of life in those countries could be most useful for making a new Tibet. This as he envisioned, helped him to consolidate the unification of the country, stabilize his administration, establish peace and lead the people to prosperity. He wanted to let the people know what he had conceived to do for their good.

Besides scholars like Shilamanju and other Chinese scholars like Huo Shang who accompanied princesses Bhrikuti and Wen Cheng from their respective countries to promote Buddhism in Tibet, the King invited many scholars from India who were famous for their scholarship and known to Thommi Sambhota or other Tibetans who went to Nepal or India before them. He wished sincerely that the people of Tibet should understand the subject and encouraged them to grasp the letter and spirit of Buddhism.

The King as Orator

The King was also a good orator and could speak eloquently and clearly. According to the King the qualities of speech should be bold as a lion, gentle and soft as a hare, impressive as a serpent, pointed as an arrow and evenly balanced as a dorje held by its middle (literally- its waist).

The four relations of speech- the question should first be stated, the arguments should be duly connected, the later with the earlier. Essential points should be repeated and the meaning should be illustrated by examples.

Religious King Srontsan Gampo according to the Moni-kah'bum, as quoted by Waddel, had said that speech should float freely forth like a bird into the sky and be clothed in charming dress like a goddess. At the outset, the object of the speech should be made clear like an unclouded sky. The speech should proceed like the excavation of treasure. The arguments should shoot forth nimbly like a deer chased by fresh hounds without hesitation or pause. This shows how meticulously he thought things in their detail.

Fig. 4 : Princess Bhrikuti, Potala Palace

Srongtsan Gampo in Mythological Interpretation

As it is said in mythological way, the marriage of Srongtsan Gampo with Princess Bhrikuti and Wen Cheng were preordained and the Trinity of the King, the incarnation of Avalokiteshvara and his two consorts, Bhrikuti and Wen Cheng, the incarnations of ShwetaTara and Harita Tara respectively were to extend all their divine attributes to make Tibet a Buddhist state in every respect.

The king, for this purpose, seems to have thought it necessary to have understanding of the Buddhist faith, efficient application of it for consolidation of the unification and development of Tibet. He expressed his opinion to his ministers and asked them to go to Nepal and China and beg the King and the Emperor, the hands of their princesses Bhrikuti and Wen Cheng to marry with himself. So that he could have profound knowledge of how Buddhism is used in those countries and apply it for the benefit of his own country and the people.[5]

Minister Mgar Tontsan visited Nepal and China, begged for their princesses to marry with the king and succeeded in fulfilling his mission to bring Princess Bhrikuti and Princess Wen Cheng to Tibet and got them married with his king.[6]

Fig. 5 : King Srongtsan Gampo and Princess Bhrikuti

The first important item the Princesses of Nepal and China Bhrikuti and Wen Cheng brought to Tibet was Buddhism in its well-established forms in India, Nepal and China. The second one was the visit of the scholars like Shilamanju and Huo Shang accompanying the Princesses. They taught Buddhism to Tibetan people and helped them to translate Buddhist scriptures in Tibetan language. In the third place, the Princesses introduced to Tibet religious rites and rituals, culture of social behavior, customs and manners, administrative systems established and developed in their respective countries. Beside these, other important aspects of life which were useful and King Srongtsan Gampo wished to get them through their scholars and officials from Nepal, India and China, were the methods and ideas prevailing in these countries which could also be useful for the purpose of organizing the newly unified country, stabilize peace, and enhance the well being of the people of Tibet. The association and interaction among the personnel who went to Tibet with Princesses Bhrikuti and Wen Cheng, like scholars, administrative staff, ladies who could manage household affairs, experts on industry and agriculture, artists and architects who provided innumerable and invaluable help to develop a Buddhist Tibet as the King had visualized.

The sculptures of King Srongtsan Gampo, Queens Bhrikuti and Wen Cheng minister Mgar Tontsan, Thonmi Sambhuta and other important persons who were in the king's court at that time can be seen at the Chogyal Drupung Cave (meditation cave) of the king at Potala Palace.

Srngtsan Gampo's help to Narendra Dev

On the political side, King Srongtsan Gampo helped the brother of Princess Bhrikuti Prince Narendra Deva who had gone with his father Udaya Dev in exile in Tibet. King Udaya Dev died when in exile. Tibetan King then helped Narendra Dev to come back to Nepal and restore his throne, occupied by his uncle Dhruva Deva earlier.[7]

Chinese Imperial Mission to King Narendra Deva and Emperor Harshavardhana

Chinese Emperor Tang Tai Chong Li Shimin had sent a Political Mission headed by General Li Yipiao and accompanied by General Wang Hsuan-chi to Nepal and Kannauj, India to present gifts to the King Narendra Deva and Indian Emperor Shiladitya

Harshabardhana in the first half of the 7th Century (643). This was one of the first visits of Chinese officials by land route from China via Tibet and Nepal to India. The Mission came to Nepal on the way to Kannauj, India. King Narendra Dev welcomed and extended warm hospitality to the Mission. They presented the gifts sent by the Emperor to the King. Among the gifts there was a small image of Manjushree. The king took them around the valley and showed them a hot water pond called Achipomi (Agnibhumi) called Achipoli (Ankhen pokhari) or By Hsuan-tsanng and now called as Nagadaha or Nagahrada at Dhapakhel in the Lalitpur or Patan District at present. General Li Yi-piao visited the Swayambhu Chaitya, prayed the Buddha there and offered Khada to his image.

In India, as the Emperor had already died, Arunashwa (A lu na shyun), the Governor of Magadha, without knowing the purpose of the visit, presentation of gifts from the Chinese Emperor to the Indian Emperor Harshabardhana, confiscated the gifts they had brought and opened hostilities against the Mission led by General Li Yi-piao. They managed to escape from Magadha and came back to Nepal. General Wang Hsuan-chi, the second in command, with the help of Nepal and Tibet, went again to Magadha and fought against the hostile Governor, defeated him and took the governor and his family with him to China.[8]

First Official Contact between Nepal and China

On his way back to China General Wang came to Kathmandu Valley (then known as Nepal-Mandal), thanked the King and requested him to send his Mission along with him to China. King Narendra Dev, agreeing to the proposal, sent a Mission to China and established friendly relations with the Emperor in 646. According to Jnanmani Nepal, this Mission was led by his son Prince Priyajeeva.[9] This mission is regarded to be the first official mission from Nepal to China and also the first official contact between Nepal and China.[10] According to D.R. Regmi, "King Narendra Deva had sent a mission to China to offer homage and presents in 651." [11]

In the opinion of another historian Baburam Acharya there were three missions sent from Nepal to China at that time and the first son of the King Prince Skanda Deva had led the third mission.[12]

It is said description of the events was recorded in the memoir (or Story of Travel) of General Li Yi-piao. This work is not available now. Some scholars are engaged in compiling the extracts or references they could gather from different historical source materials and to compile these information contained in the book by Li Yipiao.

References about Nepal and lifestyle and social system are recorded in the Xin Thang Shu[13] and Jiu Thang Shu. They provide vivid descriptions of the Royal Palace and the country in general as well as observations of the two generals during their stay and on the occasion of the King's audience to them. [14]

With these accounts of inter-action it can confidently be said that the two princesses Bhrikuti and Wen Cheng lived in the Palace of King Srongtsan Gampo amicably and harmoniously, and were effective in promoting friendship and understanding between Nepal and China. Their contributions are remembered and regarded to be very helpful to lay a strong foundation and enhance friendly relations between Nepal, Tibet and China.[15]

Cooperation between Princesses Bhrikuti and Wen Cheng

Standing high in the Lhasa Valley, the Potala Palace was built on Red Hill by Srongtsan Gampo for Royal residence. It used to be called Kukhar Phodrang. It had thirteen stories and was built mainly of mortar, stones and timber according to the scheme and plan designed by Nepali architects and artists on behalf of Nepali Princess Bhrikuti.

Fig. 6 : Princess Bhrikuti and Princess Wen Cheng

It is said that she built for her a nine-story palace called Jalachi Siang Liang. There was a silvery bridge to join it with the King's Palace. It was destroyed later by natural causes. But there are still two rooms left to commemorate Srongtsan Gampo's Chogyal Drupung cave inside the Potala Palace, which dates back to the early seventh century on the Red Hill. The palaces were decorated with arts, sculptures and architectural designs of Nepali, Chinese, Indian and indigenous Tibetan character.

Another Temple the King ordered to be built was Ra Sa Phrul Nang Tsuklakhang Temple now known as Jokhang which is situated at the heart of the capital City Lhasa to enshrine the images of Akshovya Vajra, Maitreya and Tara which Princess Bhrikuti had carried with her when she was going to Lhasa to get married with King Srongtsan Gampo. When Chinese Princess Wen Cheng got married with the king, she constructed another Temple, Ramoche, to enshrine the image of Jovo Shakyamuni, which she had brought with her from China, nearby the Jokhang Temple.

But because of the fear of its destruction by hostile elements, the Chinese princess, with the consent of Nepali Princess, took the image of Jovo Shakyamuni out of the Temple Ramoche and hid it in a corner of Jokhang Temple and built a wall around it. Then the image of Akshyovya Bajra was transferred to the Ramoche Temple where it could be seen till today.

The image of Jovo Shakyamuni hidden in a corner was discovered in the Jokhang Temple after Princess Chin Cheng, who was married with King Tride Tsungtsen, a descendant of King Srongtsan Gampo, inquired about the image. The image of Jovo Shakyamuni was discovered and enshrined at the prominent place constructed for the main image in the Jokhang Temple.

Postal Stamp in Honor of Princess Bhrikuti

As Princess Bhrikuti who was grown up in congenial atmosphere of Nepal, agreed to live in the comparatively difficult environment of Tibet and enlilghtened the people with the teaching of Buddha, she earned their deep respect. Because of her great contribution in awakening the society with the message of Buddha she is remembered with due respect and honor in Nepal and Tibet even after thirteen hundred years till today. Recognizing this devotion of the Princess, the Postal Department of Nepal Government issued a postal stamp of five Rupee denominations with the photo of her statue in her honor belatedly in 2007.

Fig. 7 : Akshovya Bajra in Ramoche Temple, Lhasa

With Potala, Jokhang, Ramoche, other Temples, Stupas and Monasteries and their prominent features reflecting Nepali architectural style and structures, Lhasa looked like another Kathmandu, the people there used to observe.

End Notes

1. Tsepon W. D. Shakabpa. *Tibet A Political History.* New York: Potala Publications, 1976. p. 24.
2. Min Bahadur Shakya. *Princess Bhrikuti Devi.* New Delhi: Book Faith India, 1997. pp. 31-33.
3. Shakabpa, p. 25.
4. Niranjan Bhattarai. *Nepal Chin Sambandha.* Lalitpur: Sajha Prakashan, 2058 B.S. p. 97.
5. Ibid. pp. 98-100.
6. Gyanamani Nepal. *Nepal Bhot Chin Sambandhaka Kehi Samskritik Paksha.* Kathmandu: Royal Nepal Academy, 2045 B.S., pp. 7-8.
7. Bhattarai, p. 113.
8. Ibid, p. 114.
9. Gyanamani Nepal: *Nepal Bhot Chin Sambandhaka Kehi Samskritik Paksha,* Kathmandu Royal Nepal Academy, 2045 B.S.
10. D. R. Regmi. *Ancient Nepal.* Calcutta: Firma K. L. Mukhopadhyay, 1960, p. 178.

11. Baburam Acharya: *Cheen Tibbat Ra Nepal*, Kathmandu: Shree Krishna Acharya, 2003, p. 29.
12. Ibid, p. 117.
13. Ershisi Shi. *Twenty-four History Books of China* (*Xin Thang Shu*). Beijing: Zhong Hua Shu Zhu, Xin Hua Shu Dian, Lezhuang 146 Shang Xizhang p. 6213.
14. Ershisi Shi. *Twenty-four History Books of China*, (*Jiu Thang Shu*). *Beijing:* Lezhuang, 148, pp. 5289-90.
15. Bhattarai, p. 118.

Chapter IV

Maha Manjushree in Nepal and China

Manjushree

Manjushree is a divine incarnation. He is one of the two great Bodhisattwas like Avalokitesvara. He belongs to the Amitava family. He is regarded to be the propounder of Mahayana school of Buddhist philosophy, the origin of Saddharma Pundarika and Prajnaparamita. They were the result of his meditation, it is said. His name Manjushree suggests that his origin was in India. He was equipped with all attributes that are regarded to a wish-fulfilling divinity. It did not take much time for the story of his omnipotence to reach nearby country China and inspire the Chinese people to revere him in all his manifestations.

According to legends he was born in Wu Thai Shan of China and came to Nepal. He is worshiped as a deity of knowledge and wisdom. Because of the profound knowledge attributed to him, he is revered as a Budhisattwa who could bestow blessings to any devotee to fulfill his wishes. Therefore his popularity spread far and wide.[1 and 2]

The Lake of Nepal or Kathmandu Valley

According to Swayambhu Purana, Manjushree came from China to Nepal to pray and worship Swayambhunatha.[3 and 4.] At that time of his visit, Kathmandu valley then known as Nepal was submerged into deep water, as a deep lake it was therefore uninhabitable. When he saw this situation he placed his two consorts, Varada and Mokshada at the safe places of Fulchoki and Champadevi Hills respectively, cut a gorge at the place called Chovar and let the water flow into the Bagmati and find an outlet to the sea. Manjushree, after making the valley habitable, asked Raja Dharmakar to rule the country. Thus Nepal Valley became a habitable and suitable place for living, development of culture and civilization. Nepali people devoted to him still believe this story and dedicate all credit for making the valley habitable to him. They also take distinguished

Fig. 8 : Manjushree in Wu T'ai Shan

guests from China, supposed to be the birthplace of the deity, to show the gorge, which was considered as cut by Manjushree.

Some people in Nepal think that when Li Yi-piao, general of the Imperial forces of Tang Emperor visited Nepal via Tibet, he had brought an icon of Manjushree together with other valuable gifts to King Narendra Dev of Nepal. The people regarded this event to be the occasion of the visit of divine personality called Manjushree. From then on, Manjushree became the Deity of reverence and worship. The act of letting the water flow to Bagmati, making the valley habitable and preaching Mahayana philosophy of Buddhism to the Nepali people all were attributed to him. As the image of Manjushree had come from China the Nepali religious people here accept the story as historic and that Manjushree himself in person had come to Nepal and helped it to prosper. Therefore he was considered to be the historical personality.

The people of the valley have constructed a Stupa at a hill called Go-shringa Prabat Mountain nearby Swyambhunath to commemorate the event and worship the Bodhisattva. There is a stone-plate at the base of the Chaitwa engraved the footprint of Manjushree on it. The people offer their respect and worship the footprint. Buddhists of Nepal worship him as a Bodhisattwa and Hindus as Saraswati, the Goddess of Knowledge. Both the communities regard him as an incarnation of knowledge and wisdom. They visit the shrine every year on the fifth day of bright fortnight of the month of Magha, the tenth month of the year according to the Nepali Solar calendar, and offer flowers, fruits and other objects of worship. Both the Hindu and Buddhist youngsters light hand-made cotton threads with charred butter produced from milk of cow on that occasion.

The young boys and girls start their education by learning the alphabet of their language on that day. Before they start the learning the teachers, their parents ask them to pray Manjushree as "Namo Bagishwaraya" for Buddhists and "Saraswatyai Namha" for the Hindus.

This day, "Shree Panchamee" (the last word 'shree' of the name of Manjushree is added to honor the deity) and "Basanta Panchamee" (as traditionally called) is observed as the first day when spring season begins and celebrated with highest pomp and show in Nepal. The kings of Nepal used to listen songs and music recited by the priests in celebration of the beginning of the Spring Season on this day. It is organized in a state courtyard called Nasalchok where the

Coronations of Kings are held. High-ranking officials also attend the ceremony. Thus, in great scale, Spring Season is welcomed and respect is paid to Manjushree in Nepal. This day used to be an official holiday till few years ago.

It is said the people of China also celebrate the beginning of the Spring Season as their New Year and observe the day as dedicated to Manjushree. It falls on the first day of bright fortnight of Magha four days earlier, corresponding with the first day of the month according to Chinese calendar.

Thus, Manjushree is revered in both Nepal and China and worshiped in the month of beginning of Spring Season and regarded as the Deity who bestows blessings for the happiness to the devotees.

The Lake Drained by Natural Process

The lake of Nepal Valley was drained by normal process of the outbursts triggered by natural events as landslides and floods. It took tens of thousands years to get drained at several intervals. The last bang occurred about 10,000 years ago. It was the natural process that made the valley habitable and not the divine power, which let the water, flow out by cutting one or more gorges at a time. This fact is based on the findings of the team of scientists numbering more than 20 from different Japanese Universities and four from the Tribhuvan University of Nepal. They were working since November 1999 on this research project. Dr. Tetsuya Sakai of Kyoto University and well-known Professor Tabata were among the leading figures of the team.[5]

Fig. 9 : Chaitya with Footprint of Manjushree, Swayambhu, Nepal

Wu T'ai Shan: The Holy Abode of Manjushree

The Ch'ing-Liang Mountain, popularly known as the Wu T'ai Shan, located in the northeastern part of Shansi province, is one of the four sacred mountains dedicated to Buddhism in China. Traditionally it is believed to be the religious center of Manjusree Bodhisattva. As there are five peaks that stand prominent, it is called the Wu T'ai Mountain (the Mountain of Five Terraces), and as the climate there is usually cold, it is also known as the Ch'ing-liang Mountain (the Mountain of Coolness). The main part of this mountain falls within the administration of Wu T'ai district, with some of its branches extending into the Fan-chih district of Shansi and Fu-p'ing district of Hopei.

The whole mountain comprises two principal ranges. The eastern range runs straight towards the southeast. Through its numerous precipitous steeps and rocks, flows the Ch'ing-shui River that cuts out a big valley of more than 200 Li(1Li = 500 metre) in length. The western range, which again branches off into the East and the West, and the Eastern Ridge forms the watershed between the Hu-t'o and the Ch'ing-shui Rivers. All along the range, many small ridges stretch out towards the south in winding and interlocking zigzags. Thus, with its endless chains of hills and peaks vying with one another in strange shapes and grotesque beauty within an area of more than

Fig. 10 : Manjushree in Yun Kang Mountain

500 li in circumference, this mountain makes up a realm of impressive loftiness, depth and pleasant coolness.

Four of the so-called five "terraces" of the mountain, the eastern, the northern, the central and the western ones, are peaks connected together by an undulating chain of hills running from the east to the west, while the southern "terrace" is a separate peak standing by itself. The T'ai-huai town, the center of this mountainous region situated at a distance of 120 li to the northeast of the city of Wu T'ai district, is the site of the famous Hsien-t'ong Monastery and the Great Sarira Pagoda, which was constructed by the famous architect Araniko of Nepal in 1301. The Central Terrace (also called the Ts'ui-yen Peak) is 25 li away to the northwest of the Great Pagoda. The Northern Terrace (also called the Yeh-tho Peak), 10 li away to the north of the Great Pagoda, is the highest peak of the Wu-T'ai Mountain. The Eastern Terrace (also called the Wang-hai Peak) is 25 li away to the east of the Great Pagoda. The Western Terrace (also called the Kua-yueh Peak) is 25 li away to the northwest of the Great Pagoda. The Southern Terrace (also called the Chinhsiu Peak) is 39 li to the southwest of the Great Pagoda. All these peaks have wide and flat tops. As regards to their shapes, and approximate description is found in the Record of the Ch'ing-liang Mountain, written in Tibetan by Lcan-skya Rol-pahli sdo-rje who, using the words of some masters in ancient times, compares the Central Terrace to a noble lion, the Eastern Terrace to a standing elephant, the Southern Terrace to a flying horse, the Western Terrace to a dancing peacock, and the Northern Terrace to a Jeevajeeva bird, which as referred by Hsuan Tsang in his book as Ming- ming, were seen or found in abundance in Nepal.

The area environed by the five terraces is called the T'ai-nei (or the enclosure of the terraces), which may be entered by four entrances. On the west is E-K'ou (a pass lying on the boundary line of Fan-chih and Wu T'ai districts); on the north is Hung-men-yen (by the side of the Eastern Terrace); on the east is Lung-ch'uan Pass (situated at a distance of 20 li to the east of the Ridge of the Great Wall) and on the south is the Szu-yang Ridge (near the Tsun-sheng Monastery). Before the opening of the Shi-t'ai and the T'ong-P'u Railways, visitors mostly reached the mountain by the eastern route; pilgrims from Mongolia mostly came by the western route. At present visitors to the mountain mostly take the southern route. One can go by train either by the Cheng-t'ai Railway or by the T'ong-p'u Railway to reach the Chiang Village. From here one proceeds with automobile

Fig. 11 : White pagoda in Wutaishan where the hairs of Manjushree are said to preserved.

to the Tung-yen Town. After passing the city of the Wu T'ai district, the Tou Village and the Chin-K'uo Monastery, one reaches the T'ai-huai Town. The highway has been repaired, broadened and made into a high-speed super highway recently up to the vicinity of the city. Public roads have also been constructed for the other three routes.

In the T'ai-nei area the climate is very cold. The ice does not melt until the 5th month and it begins to snow in the 8th month. The highest temperature at the T'ai-huai Town is 35 c., and the lowest is about 30c. below zero. At T'ai-ting (or the Terrace Top) the highest temperature is 20c. and the lowest is about 45c. below zero. The change of weather is very drastic. Storms and showers occur very often and sometimes hail too. From the Terrace Top, one commands a very broad scope of view enriched with the ever- changing clouds, which often give rise to strange visions on clear days.

Avatamsaka Sutra

The earliest scriptural basis or the consecration of the Wu T'ai Mountain to the worship of Manjushree Bodhisattwa appears in the

"Chapter on the abodes of Bodhisattvas" in the Tsin translation of the *Avatamsaka Sutra*, fascicle (bundle 29). It runs thus: "In the northeast there is an abode of Bodhisattvas called the Cool Mountain, where many Bodhisattvas of the past had dwelt. At present, Manjushree Bodhisattva is living there with 10,000 Bodhisattvas as his relatives, to whom he often preaches on the Dharma." (The corresponding passage is roughly the same in the T'ang translation of the same sutra, fascicle.45.) But the text has not explicitly asserted that mountain is the Wu T'ai Mountain in China. It is in the *Manjushree Dharmaratna-Pitaka-Dharani-Sutra* (translated by Bodhiruci of the T'ang dynasty in 710) that the Wu-T'ai Mountain is definitely declared to be the abode of Manjushree Bodhisattva. In the text of this sutra it is recorded that once Buddha, the world-honored one told Guhyopada Bodhisattwa, saying, "After my passing away Manjushree-kumara-bhuta will take up abode at a mountain called five peaks in a country named Maha-china situated in the Northeast of this Jambudweepa, where he will preach on the Dharma for all living beings."

In the Record of Investigations into the Hidden Meaning of the Avatamsaka Sutra (fascicle.15) and the commentary on the Avatamsaka Sutra (fascicle.47) composed by Fa Tsang and Ch'eng-kuan of the T'ang dynasty respectively, the Ch'ing-liang Mountain mentioned in the *Avatamsaka Sutra* is positively identified with the Wu T'ai Mountain in China. The commentary on the Avatamsaka Sutra further explains different names of this mountain in the following way: "Being ice-covered throughout the whole year and having snows even in summer, this mountain practically knows no hot season. Therefore it is called the Ch'ing-liang Mountain (i.e. the Mountain of Coolness). Again, because it has five peaks that arise high into the air without any trees on the tops, resembling so many earthen terraces, it is otherwise called the Wu T'ai Mountain (i.e. the Mountain of Five Terraces). The number of "five" signifies that the great Holy one has attained the perfection of the five wisdoms, the purification of the five eyes, the ultimate secrets of the five classes of the Teaching and the thorough understanding of the true origin of the five Skandhas. Therefore he wears the crown of five Buddha's with his hair divided into five top-knots to represent the five directions and with the full possession of the essence of the five vehicles, he extirpates the harms of the five impurities."

Annotations of Manual of Watercourses

The earliest Chinese work that has mentioned the Wu T'ai Mountain is the Annotations of the Manual of Watercourses (watershed) composed by Li Tao-Yuan of the Northern Wei Dynasty. The passage is missing in the present edition of this book, but has been quoted by Hui-Hsiang of the T'ang dynasty in his Record of the Ancient Ch'ing-liang Mountain. It runs thus: "It has five lofty peaks that overtop all other mountains. Hence it is called the Mountain of Five Peaks. In the 3rd year of Yung-chia (309) of the Tsin dynasty, more than one hundred families of the people of the Yen-men prefecture came to the mountain to seek for refuge from war and settled down in separate groups among the hills. Afterwards when people went up to see them, they were nowhere to be found. Hence this mountain was believed to be a dwelling place of "Genii."

The next work that has mentioned about this mountain is the "Biography of Pai Chien" in the History of Northern Ch'i, fascicle. 40, compiled at the beginning of the T'ang dynasty. It records that in the 3rd year of Ho-ch'ing (564) of the North Ch'i the people of the Tai and Hsin Prefectures brought several tens of thousands of horses to Pai Valley by the north of the Wu T'ai Mountain to hide them away from bandits. According to the above- mentioned quotation from the Annotations of the Manual of Watercourses we know that, up to the end of the western Tsin dynasty, the settlers at the Wu T'ai Mountain were still very few. With its scarcity of inhabitants and its abundance of medical herbs, the Wu T'ai Mountain must have become an attractive place for those people who believed in the Taoist idea of achieving material immortality through physical cultivation. This is probably the reason why it was regarded as a dwelling place of Genii. This idea of achieving immortality had even affected the eminent monks of later times at the Wu T'ai Mountain. For instance, T'an-luan of Northern Wei once traveled to the south of the Yang-tze River to learn the Taoist art of immortality from Tao Hung-ching and there are many records in the *Ch'ing-liang-Chuan* about the obtaining of *Ch'ang-sung* and other herbs for elixir.

Spread of Buddhism in Wu T'ai Shan

The spread of Buddhism to the Wu T'ai Mountain also had close connection with the translation of the *Avatamsaka Sutra*. Its situation in the northeast and the coolness of its climate, which agreed so well with the conditions described in the *Avatamsaka Sutra* about the abode of Manjushree, eventually established it as a holy place dedicated to this Bodhisattva and an object of pilgrimage for the students of the same sutra. In this way Buddhism was brought to this mountain.

The Earliest Buddhist Monastery

The earliest Buddhist monasteries recorded in the Record of the ancient Ch'ing-Liang Mountain were the Fokuang Monastery, the Ch'ing-Liang Monastery and the Great Fu-t'u Monastery (the present Hsien-t'ung Monastery) constructed during the Northern Wei Dynasty. An old saying circulating among the inhabitants of the Wu T'ai Mountain alleges that "First the Fo-kuang Monastery and then the Wu-t'ai Mountain." This may justify us to speculate that the development of the Wu T'ai Mountain into a Buddhist center probably took place after the construction of the Fo-kuang Monastery. Considering the distance of going up the mountain, the Fo-kuang Monastery must have been the first one to be constructed, the Ch'ing-liang Monastery the second, and the Great Fu-t'u Monastery the third. These three monasteries were all constructed during the reign of Emperor Hsiao-wen (471-499) of the Northern Wei Dynasty, when Buddhism was already considerably prosperous on the mountain. According to tradition, there were twelve courts around the Great Fu-t'u Monastery. The present Hsien-t'ung Monastery was the Shan-chu Court and the present Bodhisattva Top, the Chen-jung Court of those days. During the Northern Ch'i dynasty, the Wu T'ai Mountain was said to have more than 200 monasteries, which were maintained with the revenue collected from eight prefectures.

The Earliest School of Buddhism

The earliest school of Buddhism that flourished on the Wu T'ai Mountain was the study of the *Avatámsaka Sutra (School)*. Ling-pien of the Northern Wei dynasty wrote a Treatise on the Avatamsaka Sutra in 100 fascicles (of which 10 fascicles (bundles) are extant), and Liu Ch'ien chih of the Northern Ch'i dynasty also wrote a work with the same title. Ch'eng-kuan of the T'ang dynasty who composed the commentary on the Avatamsaka Sutra in the Great Hua-yen Monastery was bestowed with the title of the National Preceptor of Ch'ing-liang. It was during his time that the study of the *Avatamsaka Sutra* on the Wu T'ai Mountain reached the zenith of its prosperity. After him, many eminent monks of the Wu T'ai Mountain continued to practice Buddhism according to the teaching of the *Avatamsaka Sutra*. Cheng-shun of the Yuan dynasty even got the name of

"Avatamsaka Bodhisattva."

Next came the Pure Land School. T'an-luan of the Northern Wei dynasty composed the annotations of the Sukhavati-vyuhopadesha, and Fa-chao of the T'ang dynasty initiated the "Five ways of intoning the Name of Amitava Buddha."

Next to be related was the Vinaya School. It is said that Fa-ts'ung of the Northern Wei dynasty once lectured on the Four-division-Vinaya in the North Monastery on the Wu T'ai Mountain. In the 2nd year of T'ai-ho (828 A.D.) of the T'ang dynasty, a decree put the performance of Buddhist ordination under ban throughout the empire with the sole exceptions of the Ordination altar on the Wu T'ai Mountain and the Liu-li altar at Loyang. In the 5th year of K'ai-ch'eng (840) two disciples of the Japanese eminent monk Ennin received their full ordination on the White Jade Ordination Altar in the Chu-lin Monastery. This event shows that the Wu T'ai Mountain had famous ordination altars during the T'ang dynasty. Ju-hsing who revived the study of Vinaya during the Ming dynasty, received his ordination on the Wu-t'ai Mountain. His disciple Chi-kuang at first erected an altar for ordination in the Chi-hsiang Monastery on the Wu T'ai Mountain, and later constructed another ordination altar at the Pao-hua Mountain near Nanking, where he composed the Right Regulations for conducting the ceremony of Ordination, which is still in use today.

Among the eminent monks of the Ch'an School may be mentioned Chieh-t'o of the Fo-kuang Monastery during the Sui dynasty, and Mu-ch'a of the Pi-mo Rock, Yin-feng of the Vajra Cave, chin-kuang-chao of the Bodhisattva Top, etc., during the T'ang dynasty. Ts'ung-shen of Chao-chou, a well-known Ch'an-master of the late T'ang, had visited the Wu T'ai Mountain nine times. This will attest the prosperity of the Ch'anschool on the Wu Tai Mountain during the T'ang dynasty. Pao-chin and Ching-ch'eng, who revived Buddhism on the Wu T'ai Mountain during the Ming dynasty, were also prominent figures of the Ch'an School. During the Ming and Chin dynasties, most of the "black temples" on the Wu T'ai Mountain belonged to the Chan School. Those of the Litchi Sub-sect ranked the first in number, while those of the Ts'ao-tung Sub-sect the second. The sect of Kasyapa-Matanga and Dharmaranya knew the Hsien-t'ung and Kuang-tsung Monasteries as belonging to their sect, which was unique of the Ch'an School of the Wu T'ai Mountain.

The T'ien-t'ai school was also once prevalent on the Wu T'ai Mountain. In the 5th year of K'ai-cheng, Chih-yuan, Wen-chien and some others lectured on the T'ien-t'ai teachings in the Great Hua-yen Monastery. It was under the direction of Chih-yuan that Ennin of Japan studied the *Mo-ho-chih-kuan* (or the Great Calmness and Insight) and copied the commentary works of the T'ien-t'ai masters.

The Tantric School of Buddhism occupied a very important position on the Wu T'ai Mountain. The *Manjushree dharmaratna-pitaka-dharani sutra,* which explicitly mentions this mountain as the abode of Manjushree Bodhisattva, is itself a text of Tantric Buddhism. The things that the five terraces of this mountain are supposed to signify, such as the five locks of Manjushree, the five Dhyani Buddhas of the five quarters, the five kinds of wisdom, etc., are all ideas of Tantric Buddhism. Stone dhvajas (flag) inscribed with Buddhapala's translation of the *Usnisa-vijaya-dharani* have been erected almost everywhere on the mountain. The founding of the Chin-kuo Monastery by Amoghavajra further established this mountain as a stronghold for propagation of Tantric school. During the Yuan, Ming and Ch'ing dynasties, as this mountain had become a favorite resort for the state ordination preceptors, many new temples were built and old ones re-constructed for their uses. Following them came a large number of monks and lay devotees of minor nationalities, chiefly Mongolians and Tibetans. During the Ch'ing dynasty, 10 "black temples" were turned into "yellow temples" and at the same time the monks of the 10 "black temples" were also turned into monks of the yellow robe, whereby China began to have Lamas of the Han nationality. Since the time of Byams-chen chos-rje, all the Lamas of the Wu T'ai Mountain belonged to the Yellow sect, and the Buddhist followers of minor nationalities who settled down on the mountain were all devotees of this sect. The majority of the pilgrims who come to visit the Wu-t'ai Mountain every year are Mongolians and Tibetans. The Lamas who reside on the mountain include the five nationalities of Han, Mongolian, Tibetan, Manchurian and Tu.

Records of Travels

The Wu T'ai Mountain has been held sacred not only by Buddhists of different nationalities in China as the abode of Manjushree Bodhisattva, but also by Buddhists of other countries as one of the five holy places in Jambudweepa. After the *Avatamsaka Sutra* was introduced to China, Western monks from afar had traveled to this mountain on pilgrimage now and again. During the Northern Chou dynasty there was a foreign monk who came to China in search of the abode of Manjushree on the Ch'ing-liang Mountain (i.e. the Wu

T'ai Mountain). In the 2nd year of Kan-eng (667) a monk of Simhala, named Sakyamitra, who has a monastic age of 99 years, came to China and ascended the Wu T'ai Mountain. Buddhapala of Kasmira visited the mountain twice, first in the first year (676) and then in the fourth year (678) of the I-feng period. It was he who translated the *Usnisa-vijaya-dharani* in to Chinese, and there circulated a legend that he had entered the Vajra cave and never returned to the world again. During the reign of Emperor Tai-tsung, the celebrated Tripitaka-master Amoghvajra played an important role in propagation of Buddhism on the Wu T'ai Mountain. Cunda, the architect in charge of the stupendous construction work of the Chin-kuo Monastery, was from the Nalanda Monastery in India. In the 10th year of Chen-yan (794) Prajna of Kapisa visited the Wu-T'ai Mountain. In the 1st year of Tuan-kung (988) of the Sung Dynasty Dharmabhadra and two Indian monks, came to China and paid a visit to the holy mountain. Other western monks who had visited this mountain include Sundrasri during the Chin dynasty, Amarasri during the Yuan dynasty, and Nepali Monks Shri Sariputra and Sahaja Shri during the Ming dynasty. Of the pilgrims from the Eastern countries, there were Chin Tz'u tsang of Silla (Greece) and his disciples Seng-shih and others who came to China in the 10th year

Fig. 12 : Image of Manjushree found in Tibet

of Chen-kuan (636) and Ch'ung-chi of the Chin-shan Monastery of the same country. The Japanese eminent monks who came and visited this sacred mountain include Reisen (who assisted in the translation of the Mahayana Sutra on the Meditation on the original Mind-ground), Ennin (who wrote the Record of Travels in China to seek for the Dharma), Eiun and Soei during the T'ang dynasty; Chonen Jakusho and Jojin (who wrote a Record of visits to the T'ien-t'ai and Wu T'ai Mountains) during the sung dynasty; and Shogen and others during the Yuan dynasty.[6]

(Because of limitation of my resources I could not prepare a complete list of the persons who visited Wu T'ai Shan thereafter).

A Nepali Buddhist scholar Dharmaloka Mahasthavira had visited to pay homage to Manjushree in 1924 (Manandhar, 1936). Another person, a famous Nepali poet Chittadhar 'Hridaya' who was a member of the first Official Cultural Delegation from Nepal to China, visited Wu T'ai Shan in 1956. He had written a poem dedicated to Manjushree Bodhisattva.

A delegation of Araniko Society, Nepal, led by its President Anoop Ranjan Bhattarai, visited in 2002 and offered prayers to Manjushree Bodhisattva and also went to pay homage to the Sarira Chaitya and its builder Araniko, the Nepali architect.

Installation of new Image of Manjushree

The Araniko Society, Nepal has taken initiative to construct bronze image of Manjushree in traditional classical style. The image is two meter tall and weighs two metric tons. The society bore the cost of 1.35 million rupees for its construction and transport expenses. This gold plated bronze image was constructed in Nepal and carried to China and installed at the central peak of Wu Tai Shan on the occasion of the 50th anniversary of establishment of diplomatic relation between Nepal and China on the 4th of Bhadra 2062 B.S. (2005) in a grand ceremony attended by high-ranking Chinese officials, officials of Araniko Society, Buddhist Bhikshus and other distinguished guests.

Present Arrangement for Contact

At present, the Commission of Nationality and Religious Affairs of the Department of Civil Affairs of the Shansi Province have a branch office in a Monastery here to take charge of the Wu T'ai Mountain. The Buddhist Association of the Wu T'ai Mountain is also located here. It has a premise covering a total area of 120mu (1mu=3/5 acre)

Fig. 13 : New image of Manjushree enshrined by Araniko Society in 2006

and including more than 400 apartments of monastic buildings.

Wutai Shan Research Committee publishes a magazine called Wu Tai Yanjiu (Mt Wu Tai Researches Contents). The first issue was published in 1997. It could be obtained from China International Maps and Books Trading General Corporation, Beijing.

End Notes

1. Balachandra Sharma. *Nepalko Aitihasik Ruparekha (Historical Outline of Nepal)*. Baranasi: Krishna Kumari Devi, 2008 B.S., pp. 55-57.
2. Bhuban Lal Pradhan. *Nepalma Bhuddha Dharma (Bauddha Religion in Nepal)*. Kathmandu: Royal Nepal Academy, 2045 B.S., pp. 77-90.

3. Hem Raja Shakya. *Shree Swayambhu MahaChaitya.* Kathmandu: Swayambhu Bikash Mandal, 1977, pp. 9-12, 16-19.
4. Niranjan Bhattarai. *Nepal Chin Sambandha (Nepal China Relation).* Lalitpur: Sajha Prakashana, 2058 B.S., p. 136.
5. Kathmandu Post, March 22, 2002. (More information may be obtained from the Department of Geology, Tribhuvan University, Kathmandu, Nepal.)
6. This presentation on *'Wu T''ai Shan: The Holy Abode of Manjushree'* is based on an unpublished report prepared by a commitee for studies on Wu T'ai Shan.

Some Important Reference Books on Wu T'ai Mountain

A List of Buddhist Monasteries on the Wu T'ai Mountain, compiled by the committee of Nationality and Religious Affairs of the Department of Civil Affairs of Shansi Province, 1959.

Ennin: A Record of Travels in China to seek for the Dharma.

Hsu Chi-yu (Ch'ing dynasty): A New Record of the WuT'ai Mountain.

Jojin: A Record of Visits to the T'ien-t'ai and Wu T'ai Mountains. Both this and Ennin's works are included in the Encyclopedia of Buddhism in Japan.

Pai Huan-ts'ai: The Cultural Objects of the Wu T'ai Mountain, published by the Shansi People's Publishing House, 1957[6].

Bhattarai's reference: Manjushree Mulakalpataru, Trivendram-edition, 1920. P. 137.

Wu T'ai Shan Yanjiu (Mt Wu T'ai Research Containts) A Magazine published by Wu T'ai Shan Yanjjiu Hui (Wutai Shan Research Committee) 1st issue of 1997. Distributed by China International Maps and Books Trading Corporation, Beijing 1997, p. 40.

Chapter 5

A Renowned Buddhist Traveller

Hsuan-tsang (Xuan Zhuang, Sanzang or Huentsang)

Hsuan -tsang was born in 596 as a native of Yan Shi in Henan. His original name was Chen Yi and a Buddhist name was given to him as Tripitaka. He made a pilgrimage to India, Nepal and other countries related to the life and teaching of Buddha. He visited Lumbini, Kapilavastu, and other places of Nepal in 635. He wrote a book Ta Tang Xi Yu Ji ('Records of the Western Regions in the Tang Dynasty), about the countries, places, religions, cultures and social system prevalent at that time. While studying in Nalanda he had met with many students from different Buddhist countries including Nepal and Tibet.[1]

According to the available documents and records about his visit the book gave a categorized account of 110 countries, which he visited and other 28 countries, which he had heard about (because then the countries of the south asian sub-continent were not united). He does not seem to have visited Kathmandu, the capital of Nepal but it is said, (while in Nalanda he had opportunities to have association with Nepai studenets and learn about Nepal from them) when he was at Vaishali (present Mujaffarpur in India), he wrote a special note about Nepal. It was the first article of its kind written by any Chinese scholar. Hsuan-tsang mentioned Nepal by its name (Ni-po-lo) described the life of the Nepali people and introduced Nepali life, custom and manners to the people of China. For this reason, the Nepali people regard him with great respect.[2]

There are some differences of opinion about how Hsuan-tsang left China to visit India. According to Wu Cheng'en the writer of "Journey to the West" Hsuan-tsang was sent on his pilgrimage by Tang Emperor Tang Tai Chong. But Kenneth Ch'en in his recently published book "Buddhism in China" says "Hsuan-tsang had left the country stealthily in 629, for his petition to the court for permission to leave had been refused. Before his departure he was already interested in Buddhist philosophy, especially the idealism of Bajrabadin school, but many unsolved problems such as discrepancies in the texts bothered him, and it was to search for an answer to these problems that he set-out." Another writer Shen Fuwei in his book "Cultural Flow between China and Outside World Through out History" supports this view and says, "He left the western border post of the Yumen Pass without official permission, to begin a long pilgrimage to Nalanda Temple in Central India."

Whatever may be the source of inspiration, Hsuan-tsang started his journey to Nepal and India on his own determination to study Buddhism, get answers to the problems he felt, make pilgrimage to the holy places related to Buddha's life, growth, enlightenment and preaching and collect Buddhist scriptures and books to take them back home to China.

He started in 627 and returned 644. He like his predecessor scholar Fa-Hsien also wrote the Ta-Tang Hsi-yu chi (Records of the Western Regions) in 647. This book included the political and social systems, customs and manners of the people in states he had visited or heard about when he was in this side of the world for 17 years. This book has been of great value to historians and archaeologists for the data it contains.[3] A few days after his arrival at the Capital he had an audience with the emperor, who questioned him closely concerning the climate, products, peoples, and manners of the countries he had visited. The emperor was so pleased with the information that he wanted the pilgrim to take some official post. Hsuan-tsang preferred to remain a monk.

And for the remainder of his life he dedicated himself to the task of translating the rich stores of sutras he had brought back with him. It is said he carried back to China 657 items packed in 520 cases. Of these he translated only 73 items in 1,330 chuan. When Hsuan-tsang died in 664, out of veneration and respect the emperor canceled his audiences for three days.[4]

The following description about Nepal is found in his book Records of Western Region in the Tang Dynasty:

Nepal is situated in the lap of the Himalayas, has an area of 4000 square li, (1 li = 500 meters). The area of Capital is twenty square li. In the mountain range, grains and fruits are grown. The mines of red copper and brass are found in many places.

Yaks and Mingming

The Yaks and the birds called Mingming (Kunming or Jeevajeeva) are seen in abundance in Nepal. Yaks are found in northern Nepal in abundance even now. Regarding the birds Mingming or Jeevajeeva as they were also called, are found as migratory birds in Nepal. They come in early spring season to a place known as Kalikasthan in a village named as the bird it-self, "Jibjibe" in Dhaibung Village Development Committee area in Rasuwa District at the west of Kathmandu. Whether the birds called by Hsuan-tsang as Mingming are the same as called Jibjibe in the area, where they are seen in the season, is still to be affirmed. A decorative wood carved picture captioned as Jeevajeeva could still be seen at the Potala Palace in Lhasa.

Climate, Coins, Arts and Architects

The climate of this country is very cold. Coins are used in buying and selling in the markets. Arts and crafts look in primitive stage. They do not look well developed. The shapes of images look rough and not clear. People profess in one religion but also believe other religions. Temples, Chaityas and monasteries are innumerable. There are more than two thousand monks. Buddhism has two branches called Heenayana and Mahayana. People believe in one or both the vehicles. Besides these two main ones, there are other religions and their branches or sub-branches.

King Shatili (Kshatri) belongs to Lichchhavi family. The king appreciates knowledge. He has sincere intentions. He believed in Buddhist religion and respected other religions also. In modern times there was a king called Yan Shu Famo (Amshu Varma, whose picture, it is said, can be seen in the Potala Palace of Tibet). He used to be called Kuang Chou in Tang dynasty. He was efficient and had good understanding of politics and principles. He had written a book 'Sheng Ming Lun' (Swara Prakasha Vimarsha or discourse on sound) on sounds of words. He used to respect knowledge and knowledgeable persons. He used also to have great regards to the people who had high morals. His glory and fame had spread far and wide.

Fig. 14 : Jeevajeeva bird, Potala Palace

Achipomi or Achipoli

There was, in the southeastern part of the capital a small pond with hot water. The pond is still there at Dhapakhel in Lalitpur District, but the water is not hot now as it was described in those days. It is said that the water used to be so hot even rice could be cooked if packed in a piece of cotton cloth and put into the water. These ponds known as Achipomi (Agnibhumi) or Achipoli (Akhenpokhari) are popularly known as Nagadaha, Nagahrada or as Ankhe Pokhari these days. They are now under the conservation programme of World Conservation Union(IUCN). The IUCN and the USAID extend assistance to Nepali nongovernmental organization, the Nepal Environment Management Program, to look after the ponds and for their maintenance. The IUCN supervises the arrangement.[5]

Local people visit there every year on Naga Panchami, the fifth day of bright fortnight of the month of Sharaban (early August) and wrship the sarpent deities.

There is Fishuly (Vaishali) in the neighborhood of the kingdom of Nepal. There is Gaga River in the South of Vaishali and across the River there is Magadha, the capital of the Empire of Harshabardhan.[6]

Hsuan-tsang had started in August 627 from China to visit India, Nepal and other states to study Buddhism, travel holy places related to the life of Lord Buddha and carry scriptures and books back home. Tang Dynasty has just started at that time. Tang Tai Chong Li Shi-min was ruling the country. Hsuan-tsang had crossed Govi desert and via Taskand, Samarkand, Balkh, and Khotan reached Kashmir. From there onward he visited Mathura and arrived at Kannouj the capital of Harshabardhana. The Emperor extended warm welcome to the distinguished scholar monk from China. The traveler Hsuan tsang also was very much impressed by the Emperor who had great respect to Buddha and deep study of Buddhism.

From there he visited Sravasti and saw the stupas, monasteries and gardens. At the Southern side of the city there was the famous Jetabana garden. There he also saw the places and relics, which could freshen the memories of Gautam Buddha's preaching. At the Northwest of Jetabana there were other places and relics, which could remind one of the occasions of teachings of Kashyapa Buddha. Farther Northwest there was the birthplace of Kashyapa Buddha. There was a stupa where the relic of Kashyapa Buddha's body was enshrined.

Hsuan-Tsang Visits Kapilavastu

Moving southwards from there Hsuan-tsang arrived at Kapilavastu.The area of Kapilabastu was 4000 squire Li. (It is note worthy that the area, 4ooo square Li, of the two states Nepal and Kapilabastu, as mentioned by Hsuan-tsang were the same at that time.) Originally, there used to be one thousand villages. But at the time of Hsuan-Tsang's arrival many of the villages were already deserted. The area of the capital of Kapilavastu was 15 square Li. There could be seen the foundation of the palace of Shuddhodana surrounded by walls. In this ruin, a statue of the king was erected. In the North of the monastery there were also some old foundations and remnants of the inside room of Queen Maya Devi's apartment. At this place also a monastery was constructed. There was a statue of Maya Devi inside the monastery. There was another monastery nearby. Around the wall, there were engravings of the scene describing the event of entering the soul of Buddha into the womb of Maya Devi and the birth of Buddha.

At the Northeast of the city there was a stupa where the astrologer Saint Asita had made the horoscope of the Prince. At both sides of the city there were places where prince Siddhartha used to practice wrestling with Shakya wrestlers. There was also the place from where Buddha had left while going away from the city riding on horse. The guides had shown Hsuan-tsang the places outside the palace where Buddha had seen the old age, sickness, dead body of different persons and an ascetic which created disenchantment from world in his mind.

From this place east via five hundred Li of wild forests Hsuan-tsang reached Ramagrama. Density of the population there was thin. At the East of the old city there was about 83 yard tall stupa. After the Nirvana of Buddha the king of that place had collected the remains of the Buddha's dead body, brought them to this place and enshrined them in the stupa. Hsuan-tsang was also told that bright rays used to appear from this stupa and wild elephants offered water and lotus flowers to it. There was also a Samgharama (monastery) where Bhikhus used to live. After going again through wild jungles (forests) to East about 100 li, they reached a stupa constructed by Emperor Ashoka. At the time of leaving home Siddhartha Gautam had reached this place where he had given his royal dresses, jewelries and crown to his charioteer Chandak and shaved his head. To commemorate that event, a stupa was constructed by the order of Ashoka.

After crossing the wild forest one could reach the capital of Kusinara (Kushinagara). This place was also deserted and nobody could be seen there. At the Northern corner of the city, where there was the house of Chundakarmar. Ashoka had constructed a Stupa there and another stupa was built at the West-North bank of three or four Li's distance at a Shalabana near the Achiravati River bank, where the Buddha had achieved Nirvana. A monastery built at that time is still there. In side the monastery, there was a sculpture of the Buddha made after his death. Seeing the sculpture one could get the impression and feeling as if Buddha was in sleep. At a side of the monastery, Ashoka had constructed a stupa, which was about 66 yard tall and there was also a pillar inscribed the event of Nirvana of Lord Buddha. But the date was not mentioned. There, at the place, where the body of Buddha was cremated, a stupa was constructed. This way Hsuan-tsang after visiting the places of birth, activities of youth, leaving for meditation and Nirvana moved towards Varanasi (Benaras). He visited Sarnath, Mrigadavana the place where Buddha preached his Sermons for the first time after his enlightenment. Then he went to the kingdom of Lichchhavies, Vaishali (Mujaffarpur district of Bihar in India at present). At the time when Hsuan-tsang arrived, Vaishali was also deserted and in-ruin. After visiting Sangharama (Monastery) at those places he moved towards Magadha.

This way Hsuan-tsang toured North India, Central India, Ujjain and Balavi. His study at the Nalanda is also mentioned in the records of Western journey. While leaving India after departing from Emperor Harshbardhana, he went back to China again through central Asian route.

Hsuan-tsang had carried more than six hundred (657) books with him to China. It took more than twenty years to translate and compile the scriptures and books into Chinese language. There were 1,300 books thus translated and compiled. They are still preserved well in the temple made in the model of Bodhgaya, a five-story structure constructed at the time of Hsuan-tsang, and two more stories added later at Xee-an, China.

After this, records of the visits of Suan Chao, Tao Feng, Tao sheng and Suan Hui and other monks accompanying them via Tibet to Nepal are found in the history books of their time. The description that a group of 300 monks led by Chi-Hne, the distinguished and well-known monk, had visited Nepal in 1027 Sung Dynasty and stayed at Swayambhu shows the visits of monks and Buddhist scholars from China to Nepal continued from the beginning made by the team led by Seng-Tsai who wrote 'Wuo Kuo Shi' (Matters concerning the five countries as India used to be called then) in Tsin Dynasty, Fa Hsien who wrote "A Record of the Buddhist Kingdoms" and Pao yun who invited Buddhabhadra to go to China.

End Notes

1. Shen Fuwei. *Cultural Flow Between China and Outside World throughout History.* Beijing: Foreign Language Press, 1997. pp. 104-107.
2. Gyanamani Nepal. *Hsuan-tsang's Visit to Nepal,* Souvenir, Kathmandu: Nepal China Cultural Council, 1980. pp. 16-22.
3. Samuel Beal. *Life of Hsuan-tsuang*. Delhi: Munsiram Manohar Lal, 1973. pp. 94-98.
4. Kenneth Chen. *Buddhism in China: A Historical Survey.* Princeton, New Jersey: Princeton University Press, 1973. p. 238.
5. *A Report Prepared by The World Conservation Union,* Lalitpur: IUCN Office, 1998. p. 1.
6. Niranjan Bhattarai. *Nepal China Sambandha*. Lalitpur: Sajha Prakashan, 2058, p. 161.

Other Reference Books on Hsuan-tsang:

1. Wu Cheng'en (1500-1582) of Ming Dyansty *Journey to West* describes the travel in the form of mythological Novel. It is translated by W.J.F. Jenner and published by Foreign Languages Press, in three volumes in 1981 and gives a complete and dramatized picture of the Journey of the Master.
2. Hsuan-tsang: *The Records of the Western Region in the Tang Dynasty* or *Records of western Travels:* Foreign Languages Press, Beijing has published its translation into English language.

Chapter 6

Nepal s Cultural Emissary to China

Araniko: The Genius Artist and Architect

Araniko was born in Nepal (the valley of present Kathmandu) in 1244.[1] At that time, the Kathmandu Valley used to be called Nepal. It was Prithvi Narayan Shah, the King of Gorkha State who later in unified the small states and scattered principalities of this area in 1769, and created present Nepal with expanded territory.

The valley of Kathmandu or Nepal was at that period divided into cities –Kathmandu, Patan and Bhaktapur. According to the local people of Kirtipur there are official documents, which describe the city of Kirtipur as part of Patan. It was separated from Patan and included in Kathmandu later. Patan was developed, comparatively, to be a city rich with people who were proficient in works of arts, architects and artifacts since the beginning or before the Christian era. The developed center of the city at that time, it is estimated, was spread in some square miles of Patan.

It is also because of the concentration of efficient and experienced craftsmen in this area that King Shiva Deva of Lichchhavi Dynasty had constructed as early as in the seventh century a grand monastery called Omkuli Varna Mahavihar at the heart of the city. This Mahavihar decorated with splendid art works, which still stands tall there to exhibit the excellent skill of the local people. Perhaps this is the reason why the city is called Lalitpur, the city of fine arts.

So it is presumed if some people proficient in these arts could go to foreign countries to build stupas and temples and create arts and crafts there from this place and not from any other in the valley at that time. Therefore the belief of knowledgeable people in Nepal in general, is that it must be at Patan, where Araniko might have been born, brought up and trained in knowledge and skill to produce art works, which helped him to earn name and fame for himself and also for his country.[2]

Among the people of Patan there were, and are even now, such people who are skilled in traditional arts and crafts. It may be presumed that Araniko understood and had basic knowledge of architecture, traditional metal casting, including hollow casting, engraving stone and woodcrafts and painting. He was sent to Tibet at the age of seventeen years, as a member of the group of eighty craftsmen upon the request of Phag-pa Lodro Gyaltsen alias Matidwaja the Imperial preceptor and chief of the Shakya monastery of Tibet.[3]

Anige, Arnige, Anige with 'mu', or Anigel

In various books and research papers we find Araniko, as he is known in Nepal. But the word is spelled as Aniko (Arniko, Anige Arnige, Anige'mu', Anigel or Aneka). The names are written in Chinese characters differently in different Chinese documents AAnika or AArnika and also pronounced in different ways by the Chinese or foreigners in deferent parts of China or abroad.

Anning Jing, an American-Chinese scholar, has mentioned Araniko as Anige, Arnige, Anigemu and Anigel while writing about Araniko. Anige or Arnige with 'mu' at the end has Buddhist religious connotation. Even now while performing 'Charya' dances the singers of the 'Charya' songs sing the name of their favorite deity by adding 'mu' at the end i.e. when they sing Bagishwara they will sing Bagishwara-mu. In similar way, those who might have regarded the genius Araniko like a divinity while singing his qualities might have added 'mu' at the end of Anige and sang Anige -'mu'.

Anigel with 'el' at the end as Anning Jing has mentioned in his research paper could have been influenced by the grammar of certain Asian language where we get many names of localities with 'al' or 'el' at the end. In Nepal also there are names of localities which end with 'g' (a or e) before 'l' at the end, like Satungal Manigal, Kilagal Jaulakhel, Tundikhel (with a or e in between g or kh and l). The names Jawalakhel and Manigal of Patan city where Araniko was born, or Kilagal, Satungal or Tundikhel of Kathmandu city may be mentioned as examples. In its instance 'Anigel' also could be the name of a locality known in the name of Araniko. But I have not been able to find any tangible clue for it.

Aneka

A distinguished historian of Nepal Baburam Acharya in his book 'Chin Tibbet Ra Nepal' has suggested, as the name of the grand father of King Ananta Malla, who was contemporary to Araniko, was Aneka, so the family of Araniko might have given the name Aneka to express Royal lineage to their newborn. But we have not found any reliable historical evidence to support this argument.

Origin of the Word Araniko

Now in order to find the origin of the word Araniko, there is a possibility that the word Araniko was derived from the word 'Arani' a Sanskrit word added with letter 'ka'. The word 'Arani' in Sanskrit means a piece of wood (samidha). Two pieces of this kind of wood are rubbed with each other to produce fire, like a flint, for religious rituals. The fire thus created by rubbing two 'Aranis' is called 'Aranika'. This may be the origin of the word Araniko.

As no record of names of persons of the team of artisans sent to Tibet at that time, is available, the name of Araniko was not known earlier in Nepal till it came to be known to us from books written by foreign scholars who mentioned Araniko by referring to the history of Yuan Dynasty 'Yuan Shi'. Then we knew the name of Araniko as written by them according to Chinese characters as Anika.

Hindus and Buddhists regard fire to be a sacred deity and worship it. A reference is found in Chinese history, as Araniko had mentioned that there was a religion called 'Mi' in Nepal. Mi in Newari language means fire and there are people who still worship it and maintain the system in Nepal and other Hindu or Buddhist countries. It may be because of this religious feeling also that he was given the name 'Aranika', originating from Arani. Another reason why the Buddhist family might have given the newborn the name of Aranika was because the boy was as bright as the pieces of fire. This brightness of Araniko's character had been proved in his profession and later career.

Another reason why the name may have been derived from a Sanskrit word 'Arani' is because of their family traditions according to which the first letter of the name of the newborn is derived according to the congregation of the planets at the time of his birth. Later it is mentioned as first letter of his name in the horoscope, like A in Araniko. Later Araniko has given to all his sons their names beginning with the first letter A. These names were also derived from Sanskrit words with connotation of Buddhist religion. The only exception is a grandson of Araniko with a Chinese name Yong An (eternal peace). Female members of the family had Newari, Chinese or Mongolian names except Arniko's wife Chaitya Lakshmi and daughter Madan Lakshmi who have original Sanskrit names according to their family tradition.

Family members of Araniko

Araniko had one son, one daughter, two grandsons and one granddaughter from Nepali wife's side. The first son's name was Asank (Asanga) whose son was Achala. Araniko had five sons and six daughters from Chinese and Mongolian wives. The names of his sons like Achuk a (Ashoka), Ashula (Asura), Akhaiya (Akshaya), Apoka (Abhoga), Achila or (Achira) could also have Sanskrit origin. All the names of his sons from Asanga to Achala start with the letter 'A'. This shows Araniko had distinct religious or traditional influence in him, while giving names to his sons and adding Lakshmi at the end of the names of the daughter as in the names of many Nepali ladies.

The name of his grandfather was Mithir. This word could be a derived form of 'Mithil' from the words 'Mithila' or Maithil. The name of his grandmother was 'Sungti' a Newari word that is prevalent even now in the Kathmandu Valley. They have added a Sanskrit word 'Lakshmi' (Goddess of Wealth) to make the name complete and respectable in traditional way. The name of his father was 'Lakhana' could be a derived form of the word 'Lakshmana'. His mother's name was 'Sumakhachi', a Newari name prevalent to this day. The name of Araniko's wife could be 'Chaitya Lakshmi' which has two Sanskrit words composed together as it is done while giving a name to a member of traditional family. The name Chaitya Lakshmi is appropriate and also suitable to a member of Buddhist family. Some foreign writers like Luciano Petech have transcribed the Chinese characters (pronouncing Chaiyatha) used in writing the first name of Araniko's wife Chaitya Lakshmi as Jayada Lkshmi. He has transcribed the first character in the name as 'Chai' to be 'ja' which is not correct. In the same manner, 'tha' was put after 'ya' as it should not have. The word 'tha' should have been put before the 'ya' as in chai-t-ya. The Chinese who transcribe the Nepali word to Chinese word like this do it mistakenly but innocently or unconsciously. Actually the characters 'ya' and 'tha' after 'chai' used in her name put in correct position i.e. 'tha' before 'ya' make the word 'Chaitya' as it should be.

The name of his first son Asanka (ga) is derived from Sanskrit word Asanga meaning without any attachment. This name was and still is popular in Buddhist communities. There was a great scholar with the name Asanga in early period of Buddhist preaching. The name Asanga is also found in Sri Lanka even these days.

The name Araniko had given to his daughter was Madana Lakshmi – derived from Sanskrit word 'Madana' which means 'Kama' (desire) and Lakshmi is a second word added to a personal name of a respected lady. One of the two grandsons name Achara was derived from a Sanskrit word Achala meaning stable without any fluctuation of mind or mental position.

His second grandson had a Chinese name 'Yong An' (Eternal Peace). This name also has a connotation from Buddhist religion.

His granddaughter was called Ch'ou Thong – a Chinese nickname given affectionately to a girl-child.

The above-mentioned names given to his sons, daughters, grandsons and grand daughters from Nepali wife's side have strong association with Sanskrit words. It shows that Araniko fully adhered to the Buddhist tradition while giving their names to his children, even when he was in China, far away from Nepal.

Araniko married altogether ten Han and Mongolian women. He had five sons and six daughters from them. All of the names of the sons were derived from Sanskrit words beginning with the first letter A. i.e. Achuka, Aphoka, Achila, Asula and Akhaia. The name of the daughter Ch'anti could also be a word derived from Shanti a word in Sanskrit meaning peace.

Asanga and Ashula acquired succession to their father. According to Anning Jing, Araniko was succeeded by his son Asanga from Nepali wife and Ashula from a Chinese wife, called Man Shi. Asanga was main successor to his father in knowledge and skill, and given assignments to imperial position of his father. Ashula was also appointed to the high position previously occupied by his father in the Imperial government.

These family names of Araniko are inscribed in the stone plate attached to the chaitya near the tomb of Araniko. All the names, his and his sons start from the 'A' as first letter. This shows that all the names were derived from the Sanskrit words.

Family of Shakya and Buddhist Religion

The Shakyas of Kapilavastu migrated to Nepal on many occasions from the time even when Buddha was alive. The reasons for migration were feuds among the nearby states, attacks from the nearby bigger states on Kapilavastu for personal interest or others. They not only traveled to Nepal but also to other countries. Those Shakyas who came to Nepal might have joined the industrious community in Patan and other cities and lived amicably with the original residents. The ancestors of the family of Araniko could have been one of the migrant families from Kapilavastu. In these localities there were and are many Shakyas till today. Therefore it seems reasonable to consider that Araniko also belonged to the family of Shakyamuni.[4]

Araniko was brought up, educated, and trained in accordance with the Buddhist tradition. He joined the life-long profession of creating arts, architects and other Buddhistic objects. He agreed to enter Buddhist system as a Bhikshu when the Imperial Preceptor Phagpa suggested him in Tibet. When Emperor Kublai Khan advised him to lead family life and sent his officers to get Araniko's wife to China he changed his Bhikshu's robe joined family life after his wife arrived there again. But he remained as a devoted Buddhist even while living with the family. Last rituals, after his death, were performed by his family in accordance with the Buddhist traditions, cremated as instructed by Araniko himself before his death. Judging by all these occurrences, it may not be wrong to consider him belonging to a Buddhist family of Nepal and himself to be a Buddhist.

Childhood of Araniko

Araniko was a very intelligent child. An anecdote in the epitaph (memorial inscription written by contemporary Ching Jufu on the inscription of the tomb) has it that "one day his parents brought him to pay homage to the Buddha. Looking at the Stupa, the three-year old boy surprised the people around him by asking, "Who the makers of the various parts of Stupa were?" The parents were amazed to see the boy's inquisitiveness. The epitaph also mentions that at school he was so quick in learning that even his teachers had some times to feel a sense of awkwardness in them. He was already good in painting and could memorize treatises on arts as soon as he read or heard them.[5]

At that time education to the children were disseminated in neighborhood. Every family was considered to be a complete school with perfect curriculum for teaching the family profession to their children. The scholars and learned ones around the neighborhood used to depart knowledge to the youngsters willingly and free. The students had to go to the houses of teachers who taught different subjects in different grades. According to the system called Guru Kula (House of Teachers). The perfection in skill on the concerned subject itself used to be regarded as their real certificate.

The house of one's family in itself was the best school to disseminate knowledge acquired by their youngsters and students on their specific subjects. It also helped them to form their morale

Fig. 15 : Statue of Araniko (1244-1306), at White Pagoda-Premises, Beijing, China

and characters. The teachers in the workshops taught, designing to building and constructions of Temples, Chaityas, Monasteries and others, drawing and painting various types of Pictures, Thankas, Mandalas Portraits and Portraitures, engraving stone or wood, casting metallic, and making all kinds of statues and images and designing and making jewellery. The families used to teach all these arts to enhance the skill of the pupils. His own home and such workshops at nearby areas might have been the basic institutions where Araniko might have had his education and training for his future profession. Before leaving for Tibet he must have already acquired preliminary expertise on many of the above-mentioned subjects, which were the indigenous arts of Nepal.

Making these arts and artifacts had begun before the Christian era in Nepal. They were developed by the early second century, became matured by the fifth century and were in full bloom by the seventh century. From then on, Nepali craftsmen traveled to Tibet in the seventh century, and to China in the thirteenth century to build Temples, Stupas, Chaityas and Monasteries, statues, images, icons and other equipments for buildings and objects required for ritual purposes and objects of personal decoration.

Besides learning the academic subjects, Araniko might have, on his own, acquired vision, insight, natural capacity in organizing projects and lead the team of workers to the completion of the projects. Araniko's genius, talent, courage, aspiration for the leadership and ability to fulfill the obligations expressed in substantive form or concrete shape, in the later period, show that his family itself was the main school to train him. He had acquired such excellent qualities, which helped him to rise to the highest imperial positions in China and glorify his country and also earn honor and respect from China and the countries around. The glory and fame earned by him for Nepal remains for hundreds of years. Actually, the answers Araniko had given to the Emperor when asked by the Emperor about his special abilities saying that 'he learnt by keeping his heart itself as teacher' is hundred percent true. Araniko was a self taught man or in one word a genius. His deeds in Tibet and thereafter in China amply prove it.

Elective in his religions views, Emperor Kublai Khan ordered Phags Pa, the governor of Tibet, to build a golden chaitya in Tibet. Phagpa requested the King of Nepal to provide skilled craftsmen to build them.

Araniko Goes to Tibet

Araniko went to Tibet as a member of a team of eighty craftsmen. King Jaya Bhima Deva had sent them upon the request of the Imperial Preceptor and Chief of Shakya monastery Phagpa to construct a golden chaitya. They were also to build monastery for the Bhikshus to live together, learn scriptures and be instrumental for promoting Buddhism there.

Shakya

It may be relevant here to say a few words about the place called Shakyaa. According to Sharat Chandra Das Some Shakyas who were forced to flee from their countries Kapilabastu and other nearby states went to Tibet via Nepal and settled 160 Kilometers North of Sigatse. Some Nepali Shakyas and business people went after the marriage of Princess Bhrikuti with King Srongtsan Gampo and were living there. They had made some Buddhist Temples and monastery there and founded the colony in 1071. They had named their colony as Shakyaa.

A distinguished scholar, Shakya Pandita alias Ananda Dhwaj, grown there, with his untiring endeavor and perseverance rose to the high position of Sakya Pandita and earned fame around the area, was invited by the Mangolian Chief Khan, to China in the 13th century. The Emperor impressed with his knowledge and wisdom honored him as the religious teacher. Upon his suggestion Emperor Kublai Khan appointed his nephew named Phagpa equally well versed in esotericism and different aspects of Buddhism like his uncle as Imperial Preceptor. The Emperor advised Phagpa to construct Golden Chaitya and monastery in Shakyaa for further development of Buddhism there. For this purpose he had asked Nepali King to send some artists and architects to Shakyaa, Tibet. In response to the request, a group of artists and architects together with Araniko was sent to Tibet in 1260.

After arriving at Shakyaa, Tibet, no one in the team was prepared to accept the responsibility of the leadership of the team, which was to construct the Chaityas and Monasteries. But Araniko, the youngest of them all, announced that he could bear the responsibility. He told the people around that though his age was small, his heart was big and he can complete the assignments.[6]

Araniko and his team stayed in Tibet for about two years and completed the projects Imperial preceptor had assigned to them. They made golden Chaitya, and other buildings and images as planned.

After completion of the assignments there, Araniko wanted to return home and begged Phagpa for his permission. But Phagpa, highly impressed with his skill, courage and brilliance, suggested Araniko to accompany him to China and have an audience with Emperor Kublai Khan. Phagpa himself tonsured and performed other rituals to initiate Araniko to Buddhist faith and took him as his disciple to China.[7]

It is not known how many of the other Nepali accompanied Phagpa and Araniko, how many remained in Tibet for other works and how many returned back home.

Fig. 16 : Phag-pa, Imperial Preceptor, Potala Palace

Araniko Presented to the Imperial Court

After completion of the construction works in Tibet Phagpa took him along to the court of Emperor Kublai Khan. At the Imperial court, the Emperor observed him for a long time and asked, "whether he was afraid to come to the Great Empire?" Anege (Araniko) replied in an innocent and humble way: "The Sagely Emperor regards people in all directions as his sons. When a son comes to his father why should he be afraid? My family has been in the West for generations. I took the edict to come to Tibet and build the Chaityas for two years." Kubilai Khan wishing to test his skill asked him to repair a bronze statue with complicated arteries and veins. The statue was a model of human body to practice for acupuncture treatment. It was presented by Mongolian rulers to the Song Emperor. It was damaged and had become un-repairable previously.

When Anege saw it, he said that he had not done this kind of repair work but requested for Emperor's permission to try his best. He was successful in restoring it to a better shape. The model of human body was in a way renewed and recreated. The repaired model of human body was more accurately showing the joints of arteries and veins, and the points, which were to be punctured and stimulated to cure a particular inefficiency or disease. As the model looked more expressive and accurate the Emperor admired it. The court artists could not but appreciate and praise Araniko's ability, skill and understanding of the anatomy of human body as God given.

This performance of Araniko (1265) established his credibility and reputation at the Yuan court. There after Kublai Khan always entrusted Araniko with more important Imperial projects. He appointed Araniko as the Supervisor in Chief of Artisans of Yuan Court two years later.

Araniko Builds Bai Ta (White Pagoda, Chaitya or Stupa):

The Emperor was delighted to see Araniko's skill. Pleased with the achievements and all-round success he asked Araniko to build a White Chaitya and a monastery "Da Sheng Sou Wan Shi" for long life and prosperity for the Emperor, in the Capital Beijing in 1271. The White Chaitya, when completed in 1277 was the tallest structure in the Yuan Capital.

An inscription written for Araniko's tombstone says that when the White Chaitya was completed, a mysterious but auspicious column light from the Stupa rose to the sky. The Emperor went to see it and was overjoyed. On the occasion he asked his archers to shoot arrows in four directions .The land covered by the landing arrows was measured 30mu. That piece of land was offered to build monasteries around the Bai Ta. Araniko upon the order of the Emperor started the construction of the monasteries in 1279 and completed in 1287.

In the early period of establishment of new dynasty, Emperor Kublai Khan was inclined to implement the concept of Buddhism to establish peace in the Empire and earn devotion of the Chinese people to the Emperor. Araniko contributed in fulfilling this wish of the Emperor by giving concrete shape, in visible form, to the concept of

Fig. 17 : White Pagoda built by Araniko, Beijing

Buddhism. He constructed Chaityas, Temples, and Monasteries, images of Buddha and deities and divinities of other Chinese religions and other objects of their worship and drew attention of the people to Lord Buddha and his teaching. Thus on the one hand he helped the Emperor to establish peace in the newly established Empire and on the other he provided the people with an object to adhere to and express their devotion and dedication. Therefore Araniko became the most favoured person by the Emperor and highly respected artist and architect in China and nearby Buddhist countries.

According to 'Beijing White Pagoba Temple,' the Temple "Being the biggest and the oldest Tibetan style Buddhist stupa is in existence now in China .The great white Pagoda is now the only well preserved cultural relic of the Great Yuan Capital City of China in Beijing. It has been a great historical monument for the ethnical union of the Han, Mongolian and Tibetan peoples and the unification of this multy-ethnical country. The great White Pagoda is also recognized as a symbol of the wel-established and long standing friendship of the people of China and Nepal." [8]

Araniko at Wu Tai Shan

A-ni-ge (Araniko) the famous Nepali artist and architect was a disciple of Ba-si-ba (Phagpa), the Tantric Buddhist. He knew Wu T'ai Mountain as Manjushree Shrine since his early age. So he revered Manjushree. At the first year of Yuan era (1295), Cheng Zhong had followed his grandfather's order to build Wan-sheng-Hu-Guo Temple for the Empress, and A-ni-ge to supervise the construction works of the Temple. In the same year, the mother of the Emperor came to Wu T'ai Mountain for building this huge project. In two years, the temple was finally completed.

In the third year of Yuan Era (1297) in March of the same year, Emperor Cheng's mother went to Wu T'ai Mountain to worship Manjushree. When she saw the Buddhist Temple and Monastery, which were seen so magnificent and grand, she admired the skill of the architect A-ni-ge and awarded him a gift of ten thousand Liang (1 Liang = 50 Grams) of platinum. In the book "Good virtues of A-ni-ge" written one year before A-ni-ge passed away in 1306 it is said: "It is clear that A-ni-ge has made remarkable contributions by building such Buddhist temples at the Wu T'ai Mountain." A-ni-ge had also constructed a Zhaoti area of mountain and had wished to retire after four years construction works. The Zhaoti place is the

Shifang Zen Temple on Bei Mt. which was the predecessor for Bi San Temple of today (also named Pu Ji Temple). A-ni-ge had lived altogether ten years intermittently at Wu T'ai Mountain. He designed and built the holy Hu Guo Temple and White Pagoda, and also built the Zhao Ti district, (named after Zhao Ti area built by him), on Northern Mountain. He had retired at Wu T'ai Mountain before death. It is obvious to see his devotion to Wu T'ai Mountain. A-ni-ge has increased glory for Buddhism by building the Grand Pagoda and other constructions in Wu-T'ai Mountain. The profound skills of A-ni-ge will remain in the Holy Land of Wu T'ai Mountain to inspire people to deepen their devotion to Buddhism. The grand pagoda will remain as the symbol of Sino-Nepal cultural exchange.

According to Prof. Wang Hung-wei, "Araniko constructed three Stupas, one in Beijing in (1271-79) and two in Wu T'ai Shan in (1301), when Araniko accompanied Phags Pa (Pahaspa) to the holy mountain. In other constructions, nine Buddhist monasteries, two temples and one palace for Taoist deity are important ones. Araniko also made numerous Statues of Buddha, Buddhist and Confucius deities. His craftsmanship also could be seen in making pots, Vajras, bells and other instruments and objects required for rituals and worshipping the deities and divinities."

Fig. 18 : Sarira Pagoda built by Araniko and Temple of Manjushree au Wu Tai Shan

All the Stupa and Chaitya's look similar in structure and are constructed according to the models, methods and processes determined in ancient traditional Treatises and books documented thousands of years ago. The Stupas and Chaityas seen in India, Nepal, Tibet, China and other South and South-East Asian Buddhist countries look similar in construction with some variation according to local environment, climate and views of the local engineers.

After the Stupa and Chaitya's come the statues, images and icons of Buddha and Buddhist deities. They also look alike in facial expressions and different body-postures (or mudras) in all the Buddhist countries. All the divinities are considered to be perpetually young and immortal so the statues are made in the same way ever young and immortal.

As no statue, picture or portrait of Buddha was made in his lifetime, the faces and appearances of statues and picture differ from one another and from one country to another country.[9]

Engineering Technological Marvel

Construction of the stupas in Beijing and Wu Tai Shan by Araniko were the engineering technological marvels of that time in the thirteenth century. The fifty-one meter tall Stupa called as Bai Ta in Beijing was a new height of technological achievement. It could be seen from far and wide. When the countries of the east India, China, Nepal and others were already advanced in art, architecture, science and technology the west was not yet awakened and knowledgeable. The technical skill used by Araniko is yet to be studied and brought to the limelight. The images stupas, chaityas and temples were constructed to dedicate to divinities the names of architect were mentioned in China, but they are not mentioned in Nepal, India and other countries. It was a system prevailing at those ancient times. So in Nepal they are said to be self appeared and like that revered till today.

Fig. 19 : Sarira Pagoda built by Araniko at Wu T'ai Shan

Postal Stamp in Honor of Araniko

As Araniko was grown up in family atmosphere of Nepal agreed to live in the comparatively difficult environment of Tibet and unfamiliar surrounding of China, enlightened the people with the teaching of Buddha through his art and architect, he earned deep respect of Tibetan and Chinese people. Because of his great contribution in awakening the society with the message of Buddha he is remembered with due respect and honor in Nepal, Tibet and China even after seven hundred years till today. Recognizing this devotion of the great artist Araniko the Postal Department of Nepal Government, issued a postal stamp of fifteen paisa denominations with the picture sketched by an artist in his honor belatedly in 1972.

Araniko's Wife goes to China

In 1276, may be perhaps upon the request of Araniko or by his own grace, the Emperor sent Imperial Officers to Nepal to bring Araniko's wife to China. The Emperor also ordered Araniko to change his monk's rob that he used to put-on when Phagpa initiated him to Buddhist faith and join the secular family life.

Araniko's wife Chaitya Lakshmi was with Araniko for about 28 years in China. When Araniko died in 1306, she together with other family members of Araniko, arranged for his last rituals according to the Buddhist religion and Nepali family traditions as instructed by Araniko himself earlier.

Araniko, because of his genius and versatile qualities and undivided loyalty to the Emperor, had been most successful person among the foreigners to be nearest to him. Emperor Kublai Khan having complete trust and confidence in Araniko had bestowed highest Imperial posts, positions, decorations, insignia, wealth and honors to him. Araniko was made Kung (Duke) of Liang state. His successor Emperor also posthumously awarded him the symbolical Title of 'Ming Hui' "the genius". They also maintained all the favors endowed to Araniko by his predecessor and bestowed his own regards to the great artist. The Yuan Emperor in 1306 suspended the proceedings in the Imperial Court to mourn the death of the distinguished favorite, Court Artist Araniko.

Fig. 20 : Ashoka Pagoda built by Araniko at Wu T'ai Shan

Why Nepal-China Relation was not initiated at that time ?

Though Araniko was so near and dear to the Emperor why there was no effort from Araniko or initiative from the Imperial Court to establish formal relation between Nepal and China. In this regard the following reference may give some hint for speculation.

'It is said that Kublai Khan was planning to attack India and Nepal (ca.1286) by sending his armies through Tibet. Shang Tsun, the administrator at Sakya, strongly objected to such a plan. The Yogi, Ugyen Sengge, sent Kublai Khan a long religious poem asking him to desist from waging war against India (the country of enlightenment of Buddha) and Nepal (the country of birth of Buddha). It would seem the Khan was influenced by these protestations; at any rate, the projected war was not undertaken. [10]

Apprentices from Nepal and Other Countries trained by Araniko

Shalu Association mentions that some Nepali apprentices were also trained by Araniko in the workshop established by him in the premises of the Imperial Palace. These Nepalis together with Tibetans, Mongols and Chinese went to Tibet and Mongolia and other areas. Shalu Monastery, which is at Nyangro near Sigatse Tibet, China, has some paintings of Araniko tradition on its shillings and can be seen even today. In the opinion of Shalu Association, those trainees or disciples of Araniko working together with him or in different places afterwards have maintained and expanded the work to continue the Araniko-style and traditions.[11]

Araniko Mentioned in Classical Book

Araniko's name is mentioned in the classical book of arts, called 'Chao Hsiang Liang Tu Ching' on appropriate measures and proportions of different parts of the body of an image. The book is based on the principles of traditional scriptures and scientifically accurate. The Buddhist Society of China had presented a copy of this book to Mahasthavira Acharya Bhikshu Amritananda of Anandakuti Mahavihara of Nepal in 1959 when Mahasthavira had visited China.

Kublai Khan's Patronage of Religious Arts

Kublai Khan's personal patronage of religious arts, however, began long before this temple Bai Ta was completed. Early in his reign he welcomed to his court the Nepali sculptor A-ni-ko, who went on to become the most celebrated professional artist of the period, renowned for his numerous Buddhist and Taoist images in the temples of the two capitals, Ta-Tu and Shang-Tu. He was put in charge of the Bureau for Imperial manufacture in 1278, a year in which many changes took place within this organization. Under his supervision, new offices also were created. It might be recalled that artists like Liu Kuantao and Holi Huosun were also at work at Khubilai's court around this time. This flurry of activity is indicative of the expansive mood of the period immediately following the pacification of the south and Mongol's early appreciation of the role ceremonial art could play in the glorification of the dynasty. A-ni-ko's work was continued and his traditions carried on by his sons and his most notable follower Liu Yuan.[12]

Arniko's Forty Years Activities

Anige's activities continued for more than forty years. He made various objects for the Court including even an Armillary Sphere and instruments for astronomical observation.

In 1291, his major accomplishments were summarized in the epitaph, nine Buddhist temples, three Stupas, two Ancestral Shrines, one Daoist Temple and countless objects used in and out side of the court and images in ceremonial shrines.

It is important to note that Anige also made Confucian and Daoist images. This suggests that he also mastered traditional Chinese artistic styles. In 1274, Khubilai Khan ordered that Anige make images of Confucius and his ten scholar-disciples for a newly completed Confucian school in Shangdu (near the modern city of Dolon in inner Mongolia). In 1295, Anige built a Daoist Shanhuang Miao (Three Emperors Shrine) in Dadu (on the site of modern Beijing). He also modeled images for a new Daoist Temple Chuzhen Wan Shou. On one occasion in 1299, he worked in one hundred and ninety-one sculptures and sixty-four wall paintings in a Daoist Temple Sanqign Dian. He was assisted, it is said, by a master artist Daoist Zhang Songjian as an advisor on "Daoist iconography."

Araniko's Style of Painting and Portraiture

Drastic change in style was perhaps one of arts of the Yuan Dynasty (1260-1368) in court style of portraiture and religious art were initiated by a Nepali artist Anige (1245-1306) who served at the Yuan Court for more than forty years.

Artistically the portraiture shows both continuation of Chinese Imperial portrait tradition and new technique and stylistic principles. The Yuan Imperial portraits are strikingly different from earlier Chinese Imperial portraits not only in costumes but also in style among the Yuan Imperial portraits and portraiture of Khubilai Khan and that of his Empress Cheboer deserve special attention. The two portraits are obviously painted as a pair and the style betrays a hand of a painter trained in Nepali Buddhist art tradition. My investigation will show that Anige was the originator of the Yuan Imperial style and probably the portraitist.

Before our stylistic investigation, it is necessary to examine images of the Imperial couple. First, the Emperor is depicted as an old man with his eyes looking directly at the viewer. His beard and moustache are neatly trimmed. The hair on each side is knitted into a few knots hanging behind the ears. He wears a soft hat with a band at the front and a flared havelock at the back. The Empress takes a nearly frontal pose. Her eyebrows are shaved while two straight artificial eyebrows are painted instead. She wears an imposing red headgear (Gu Gu) decorated with elaborate networks of pearls. Archaeological and documentary evidences and extant Yuan paintings testify the accuracy of the depiction of the Imperial couple.

Artistically the portraits show both continuation of a Chinese Imperial tradition and some new technique and stylistic principles. The basic shapes in the portraits are defined by ink outline and substantiated by the application of colors. This technique had been used in traditional Chinese Imperial portraits. One example of such earlier Imperial portrait is the portrait of Emperor Wu Xiaowen (502-549) of the Liang Dynasty (520-557). A better-known painting in the traditional Chinese style is the scroll of the Thirteen Emperors attributed to Tang Dynasty (618-907). The Yuan Emperors though Mongols always regarded themselves as successors of earlier rulers of China.

The traditional Chinese technique used in the two Yuan portraits such as the definition of shapes by outlines and the brush method of depicting the tapering lines towards the end of the folds of garments are no doubt derived from earlier Imperial portraits in the Yuan Court collections. However the stylistic sources of other features in the portraits cannot be found in traditional Chinese Imperial portraits. These features appear for the first time in Chinese Imperial portraiture marking some major differences between the Pre-Yuan and later Chinese Imperial portraiture.

First and foremost, a nearly frontal pose replaces the traditional three quarter view. One of the earlier traditional Imperial portraits used to be painted in three quarter view. Secondly, the eyes of the figure meet those of observer. In earlier Chinese Imperial portraits, however, an Emperor never cast his eyes on the viewer. There is no exchange of gazes between the subject and viewer so that psychological contact is avoided. Thirdly, the principle of symmetry is strictly observed in the composition. Every facial feature is carefully arranged bilaterally. Even every curve in Kublai's beard is systematically balanced. But in earlier Chinese Imperial portraits symmetry is not a compositional principle. Fourthly, a quality of static crystallization is created by a meticulous treatment of the facial features. It does not overlap with others nor fall naturally. The extremely regular arrangement of detail creates an impression of orderliness that seems obtrusive in its uniformity. Fifthly, as Wen Feng pointed out some lines used in the portraits are more descriptive. For example the lines depicting the hair-do not break nor change thickness until they taper towards the end. While in traditional Chinese portraits the lines for beard or moustaches are usually more calligraphic. If similar lines are used, a thin ink-wash is added to substantiate the beard and moustaches and give them natural look as is seen in Liu Kuantao's "Whiling away The Summer." Sixthly, great attention is paid to the uniformity of the strings of the pearls in Empress portrait. The emphasis on uniformity of the size and shape of jewels is a new feature in Yuan art. It is derived from decorative motif of Nepali Buddhist art introduced to the Yuan Court. A Bodhisattva predominant in Nepal style wears only uniformed jewels as the major decoration. Lastly, the method of describing highlights on jewelry is particularly those on the two large red stones of the pendants hanging both the Empress' ears are painted with three brush strokes in whitish pink forming an irregular ring. Those on the red and green gems suspending before the Empress' bosom are described by irregular brush strokes in lighter colors of the same hues. In contrast with the lightly controlled brushwork elsewhere in the portrait, the brushstrokes are free and spontaneous. This might suggest the hand of an artist trained in Buddhist art whose artistic freedom is usually seen only in non-figurative, non-iconographical elements. This method is different from Chinese technique, whereby highlight is often painted in the center of jewelry in arbitrary colors.

This particular descriptive element in the Empress' portrait, while unprecedented in Chinese paintings had been a living tradition in the Buddhist art of Nepal. Likewise the artistic principles of frontality and symmetry, the crystallization of the figure in formal precision and refinement and elaboration evenness and regularity of strings of pearls are all particular features of Nepali Buddhist paintings of the same period as is shown in a painting of Buddha Ratnasambhava datable around the 14th century on a stylistic basis. The highlights of the jewelry are painted in the same manner a few irregular brush strokes in lighter green are added on green stones and whitish color and the red gems. The stylistic principles seen in Nepal paintings were derived from the late Pala-Sena schools of Indian Art in Bihar and Bengal regions around the 12th century, tended to crystallize Buddhist and Brahmanical images in formal embellishments.

Chinese portraits before the Ming Dynasty show two dominant values on being the aesthetic ideal of the "Yi" often translated as untrammeled which aims at the capturing of the subjects, and the other ideal of the didactic principle, which passes moral judgment on historical personages. The aesthetic ideal of the "Yi" has the embryo on the philosophical Daoism while the didactic principles are derived from the Confucian ethics. In both cases, however, the spirit of the subjects rather than technical perfection had been the major concerns.

In portraits the ideal of the "Yi" is identified with the free spirit and the unrestrained elegance of noble personages. In a portrait of the great Tang poet Li So known as Libo "Walking and Chanting a Poem" by Liang Kai Ao (mid 13th century) whose paintings are called free and untrammeled by the Yuan critic Zhuang Suao in his Huaji Buyi (1298) Li. So is seen sauntering in a leisurely manner with his head and chin held high and mouth open chanting a poem.

The new artistic principles of the Yuan Imperial portraiture established by Anige are also followed in the Ming and Qing Imperial portraits. The portrait of Empress Jen Xiaowen of the Ming Dynasty, for example, shows all the legacies received from the portrait of Empress Cheboer descriptive and accurate lines, shadings on the cheeks in contrast with the flat colors on the other areas, tapering lines for the folds of the garment, a frontalizing pose, symmetry, formal precision and refinement and the emphasis on the regularity richness and highlights of the jewelry. However, the highlights on the jewels in the Ming portrait have developed into a more subtle tonal gradation from light to dark, not unlike Chiaroscuro.

The formal Imperial portraits of the Qing Dynasty have been influenced by new European portrait techniques. However the rigid frontal pose, strict symmetry and interests in formal depiction rather than spiritual portrayal commonly seen in the Qing Imperial portraits are continuation of the artistic principles of the Yuan Imperial portraits formed by Anige towards the end of the 13th Century.[13]

Statue of Araniko Unveiled

Araniko created the history of friendship of Nepal with China. He was instrumental in spreading the teachings of Buddha by making White Pagoda temples, images and icons of deities and divinities, numerous objects of arts required in the rituals of worship and architects in different parts of China. Most of them over seven hundred years old still stand and draw the attention of the people to the message of Buddha.

The Araniko Society built a life size bronze statue of Araniko in Kathmandu and sent it to China in 2001. The society in co-operation with White Pagoda Relics Conservation Bureau erected the statue in 2002 in the premises of the famous Bai Ta, which was constructed by the great artist upon the command of Emperor Kublai Khan.

The statue will remind the visitors to the Bai Ta Park of the artist Araniko who made great contribution for enhancement of Buddhism, and thereby peace and friendship amongst the people around the world.

Liu Yuan

Amongst more than two hundred students of Araniko, Liu Yuan was the best. Liu Yuan joined Araniko in 1270 and continued working together until 1310, even after Araniko's death in 1306. Liu Yuan grasped Araniko's style and traditions in making various types of artistic creations. Liu Yuan was born in Pao-shi of Hebei. He was a Taoist. His teacher was Chi Taolu of Chingtho. Liu Yuan had made many images of deities and divinities of Buddhists and Taoists. Liu Yuan had modeled images of Taoist attendants, four Lokapalas on a portrait of Tang Dynasty officials in court collection. Many of those images and his other creations, it is said, were unfortunately destroyed by fire. Among his works, very few of them remain. The images made by engraving in wood were established in the temples of Pai Yun Quan, Quang chishi, Xiang Shan Shi and Tung Hua Miao. There are not many people who could recognize the works of Liu Yuan now. The images made by Liu Yuan looked lively and impressive. He had made statues of three Emperors. He could produce their personal characteristics elaborately also in the statues.

Fig. 21 : A Pagoda built by Araniko's disciple Liu Yuan at Bei-hai Beijing

People at his time and later highly appreciated and admired his skill. People who had the opportunity to see the statues used to think that Liu Yuan might have studied their character seriously in minutest details and expressed vividly.

The statue of Ershangti made by Liu Yuan had a serious posture. The statues of other officials around the Emperor looked very similar in their most polite pose and postures-as if they were alive and sitting in the Court in the presence of the Emperor. Before making these statues he had not been able to make up his mind, but when he saw a portrait of an official in the palace, he got inspired with its view and decided to make the statues in that artistic models and expressions. When the artists of the Imperial Court saw the statues they highly admired the artist Liu Yuan.

Liu Yuan had made some images of Buddha to be established in Tibet. They bore great artistic value. Liu Yuan had made them on his own style and would not let any body see these before they were completed.

The Emperor was very appreciative of Liu Yuan's works. He had given two times, precious prizes of palace-girls for his marriage. The Emperor was pleased with him and asked to lead teams of court artists. He was also awarded high posts like Chief of the Office of Culture and Arts, Yi Sueshi, Cheng Feng Taifu and Misu Ch'in (officer of the Imperial archives) and other high ranks.

A white pagoda and statues stand at the top of the hillock of Bie-Hai in the Imperial Palace complex. Any one who visits there admires the pagoda, its creator Liu Yuan and Araniko the artist, who inspired Liu Yuan.[14]

Araniko and Liu Yuan

From the fact that they were given biographical entries in Dynastic History, we can be fairly certain that the Court, despite their specialization in craft, did not regard A-ni-ko and Liu Yuan as common artists. Moreover, the appreciation of their works by both the Mongolian and their Chinese officials suggests that sculpture and religious arts enjoyed an elevated status during the Yuan Dynasty.[15]

Note: The spelling of names of persons and places are maintained as the authors in their original works wrote them. They are as follow:

Yuan History and books in Chinese Language: Aanike or Aarnike. (Pronounced as Aaniko also)

Babu Ram Acharya: - Aneka.

Anning Jing: Anige, Arnige. Anigemu and Anigel. (M.A. Thesis)

Maratha Smith Weinder: Aniko (in her dissertation for Ph.D.)

Wang Hungwei: Arniko Some Thoughts on Sino-Nepal Relations, 'Friendship' (A Journal of China Study Center, Kathmandu 2000.

Hai Lan: Arniko's Architectural Legacy and Beijing's White Dogoba-A Link with the PastA symbol of Friendship Souvenirs, Nepal China Cultural Council, Kathmandu 1980 and 1982.

HMG Nepal's Postal Service Department of Philatelic Bureau: - Arniko, First day of Issue, 13-4-72.

End Notes

1. Satyamohan Joshi. *Kalakar Araniko*. Lalitpur: Shajha Prakashan, 2044 B.S., p. 108.
2. Asharam Shakya. *Araniko, The Pride of Nepal*. Lalitpur: Buddha Jayanti Souvenir, Yampi Mahavihar 2002, p. 26.

3. *Ershisi Shi, (Twenty-four History Books of China), Yuan Shi* Part 15 Xin Hua Shu Zhu, Beijing: Xinhua Shu Dian, 1975, pp. 4545-4546.
4. Shakya, p. 26.
5. Anning Jing. *Anige: A Nepali Artist at the Yuan court,* A thesis presented for the degree Master of Arts in the Graduate School of the Ohio State University, U.S.A. (unpublished), 1989. p. 4.
6. Niranjan Bhattarai. *Nepal China Sambandha.* Lalitpur: Sajha Prakashan 2058 B.S., pp. 165-166.
7. Anning Jing, pp. 5-6.
8. Beijing White Pagoba Temple: Administrative Office of Beijing , Fuchengmennei Street171, Beijing, China. 2008
9. *Wu T'ai Shan Yanjiu (Mt Wutai Researches Contents).* A journal published by Wu T''ai Shan Research Committee: First issue of the Journal, 1997, p. 40.
10. W.D.Shkabpa. *Tibet A Political History.* New York: Potala Publications, p. 70.
11. Information received from Shalu Association Shalu Monastery, Nyangro, Sigatse (via Internet).
12. Marsha Smith Weinder. *Aspects of Painting and Patronage at the Mangol Court, 1260-1368.* A thesis prepared for her Ph. D. degree, Berkeley: University of California, 1998, p. 41.
13. Anning Jing, pp. 14-27.
14. Bhattarai, p. 172.
15. Marsha Smith, p. 42.

Some Important Reference Books on Araniko and Acknowledgements

Niranjan Bhattarai. *Chin Ra Tyassita Nepalko Sambandha.* Kathmandu: Royal Nepal Academy, 1961.

Satyamohan Joshi. *Araniko Sambandhi Chiniyan Sal Miti Ankit Bibaranharu.* Souvenir 3. Kathmandu: Nepal China Cultural Council, 1982.

Hai Lan. *Araniko's Architectural Legacy.* Nepal-China Cultural Council Souvenir 3, 1982.

Wang Hung-wei. *Some Thoughts on Nepal China Relations.* Friendship: December Issue, China Study Center, Kathmandu, 2000.

Anning Jing. *Anige (1245-1306) A Nepali Artist at Yuan Court*: A Thesis presented by for the degree, Master of Arts, Graduate School of the Ohio State University, Department of History of Art 1989 (not yet published).

Marsha Smith Weinder. *Aspect of Painting and Patronage at the Mongol Court:* 1260-1368. A Dissertation presented for Ph. D. in California University 1982. (Not yet published)

Paintings of Araniko Style: Salu Association, Salu Monastery, Nyangro, near Sigatse

Wu Tai Shan Yanjiu (Wu Tai Shan Research Containts) 1st Issue 1997 A Magazine, Published by Wu Tai Shan Research Committee Shan-xi China

Baburam Acharya. *Chin Tibbat Ra Nepal.* Kathmandu: Shree Krishna Acharya, 2059 B. S.

Chapter 7

Relations with Ming Dynasty

Direct Contact

There was no direct contact between China and Nepal either during the Sung Dynasty (960-1276 A.D.) or the Yuan Dynasty (1260-1367). Indeed after the long pause in relation with Nepal, the Ming Dynasty (1368-1644), which succeeded the Mongols initiated to establish relations by exchanging Missions with Nepal.

Chinese Missions to Nepal

When Chu Yuan-chang was seventeen, his parents and elder brother died. Left an orphan, Chu became a monk and for several years wandered around for some time and then joined a band of armed peasants who rose against the Yuan government. He was a brave soldier and was loved by his comrades. Later he became the leader of the army called Red Turbans, fought more than ten years and defeated the Yuan army. In 1368, he proclaimed himself Emperor Tai Tsu and founded the Ming Dynasty of China in Nanking.[1]

In the history of Ming Dynasty[2] it is written that Nepal is in the west of Tibet. Nepali king is elected from the Buddhist monks. Ming Tai Tsu sent a well-known monk Chi Quan as his ambassador to Nepal in the 16th Dynastic year of Hungwu, 1384. He was given a letter with Imperial seal and silk products, golden coins and other valuables as gifts to present to Nepali King Madan Singh Ram Vardhan (Ma-Ta-na-luma). According to some scholars his name is Mati Singh as inscribed in the stone plate found in Itumbahal, Kathmandu and now conserved in the library of the Department of Archaeology, Nepal. The monk Chi Quan was well versed in Buddhist scriptures and Sutras and a good conversant in highly impressive style. He was an intelligent person with well- polished manner.

When he came to Nepal, he described in a very impressive way the greatness of Ming Tai Tsu. Hearing the speech of Chi Quan, the Nepali King was delighted and welcomed the distinguished Ambassador, also a Buddhist scholar from China, and responded to the proposal for promoting relations brought by the mission. The Nepali King, in return, sent his mission together with Chinese mission to the Ming Emperor of China. The Nepali mission had carried a letter from the King to the Emperor, a stupa made of gold, many scriptures and books on Buddhism, high breed horses and local products of high quality and value. This mission had arrived in the 20th year Hungwu accordingly in 1388 in China. The Ming Emperor was very happy to receive the Nepali mission. The Emperor gave many gifts made of gold and silver, silks in different colours and Chinese products to present in return to the Nepali King. Nepali King continued in the interval of some years sending missions to China until the death of Emperor Tai Tsu.

Ming Tai Tsu used to send Baku Pou (a letter written in a piece of bamboo or paper). One half of it was to be given to the head of the mission and another piece to be presented to the king to whom the letter used to be addressed. The subject of letter was complete and understandable when the two pieces with silver stamp put together and read. Then the authenticity of the carrier of the letter would be proved. The Emperor sent silk clothes, silver coins, seal of jade, umbrella of red silk, other materials made of silver and gold and silk in different colors as present to the Nepali King.

The second Emperor of Ming Dynasty, Hong Ti, also sent another mission headed again second time by Chi Quan as ambassador to Nepal. In its return in the seventh year of Yung lo, in 1409 the Nepali King also sent a mission to China. The third Emperor of Ming Dynasty Cheng Tsu also sent a mission headed third time by Chi Quan to Nepal. In 1413, Nepal had sent another mission to the Ming Emperor and carried many valuable goods as gift to the Emperor. In the eleventh year of Yung lo 1414, Chinese Emperor sent a mission headed by Yang Shunpao to Nepal on the occasion of the auspicious coronation of King Shakti Singh to extend felicitations, greetings and good wishes to him.

Chinese Emperor in his letter had praised the King, welcomed his ascension to the throne and made suggestion to reign over his kingdom by keeping the people happy and prosperous. He also requested the Nepali King to cooperate in making relations between Nepal and China durable. Besides the letter, a silver seal plated with gold and other precious gifts were also sent.

In 1414 and 1418, other missions were also sent from Nepal. At that time China also sent a mission headed by minister Teng Cheng. The Emperor had sent imperial letter, valuables and silk products to Nepal. Minister Teng Cheng's mission had also brought gifts for the officials of the countries, Hai Tong, Lang Chang, Pile Kunwa, Ushi Chang and Yenan.[3]

Emperor Xuan Zong of Ming Dynasty had sent a mission headed by Hou Hsien at the second year of Xuande 1427 with a letter with imperial seal and many valuable gifts to the Nepali King.

The exchanges of missions had renewed the official relation established in seventh century during the Tang Dynasty between Nepal and China.[4]

After the exchanges of the missions during the Ming Dynasty, there was a pause again in exchanging missions between Nepal and China. It is said between 1384 and 1427, China had sent five missions to Nepal and Nepal had sent seven to China. After the visits of the following two eminent Buddhist scholars other non-official visits also seems to have stopped for some time. Subsequently official and un-official visits were resumed.[5]

Two Eminent Nepali Buddhists in Ming Emperor's Court

During Ming Dynasty, two Nepali Buddhist monks went to Wutai Mountain to preach Dharma. One is Sahaja Shri and another is Shri Sariputra.[6]

Sahaja Shri

Sahaja Shri was born in Kshatriya family. First he studied Theravada and Mahayana, and then he went to the Himalayas to practice meditation for 12 years. Because he revered Manjushree, and was eager to visit Wu Tai Mountain, after traveling for four years in cold and hot seasons, he arrived to Wu Tai Mountain in the second year of Hong Wu era in 1369. He lived in Shou An Zen Temple, visited and paid homage to all temples and preached dharma to enlighten people. He received deep admirations of monks in the whole mountain. The seventh year of Hong Wu era (1374), Emperor Tai Zhu heard his name, invited him to Jiang Mountain. The Master preached Dharma in the capital; Emperor Tai Zhu granted poems to him with a sentence of "Smile talking with wisdom" (talking wisdom with smile). The following year (1381), the 14th year of Hong Wu era, he moved to Jiang Mountain and built the towers in the Xi Lin Buddhist nunnery. He has written a book, "Instruction (instructive?)

Words" in 3 volumes, and another translated book "Qi-jie", which became popular in later years. Sahaja Shri had lived in Wu T'ai Mountain for five years. He practiced Buddhism and preached Dharma to propagate the ideology and cultures of Esotericism (Tantrika or Tantricism).[7]

Shri Sariputra

Shri Sariputra (1335-1426) was the knowledgeable person. He was also called Wu-ming-Ban-di-ta (a revered or respected person without honourific name). He was the eminent monk of Esoteric Vehicle. The Ming Dynasty writer Minghe's book "Bu-su-gao-sheng zhuan" the 25th volume said, he was named Shri Sariputra. It said he was the second son of King Ge-ma. He was very intelligent while a child; and extraordinary and refined when he grew-up.

Though he was born in the Emperor's family, he did not take any interest in his fame, gain, position, power, money or riches. He had no desire for such things at all. Instead, he was devoted to three gems (Triratna) Buddha, Dharma and Sangha and had cordial faith in them. Therefore, when he was a child, he used to approach eminent monks, go to nearby Monasteries often and listen to Buddhist stories told by the teachers there.

As time passed by, the dews of faith on Dharma, nourished his heart. Since his early age he began to think of becoming a monk who could be free from all attachments with worldly things.

When he was 16 years old, he made a decision of choosing his own future resolutely. He asked his father, the emperor, if he could become a monk, determined to become a wheel-turning king. The father saw he was young and handsome, exceptionally gifted with ability to speak eloquently and just could be ridgepole of the imperial family. So the father was unwilling to let him become a monk. But Shri entreated piteously, firm to become a monk. After being dissuaded for several times, he had not been wavered. Then, his father, the emperor remembered that he paid deep respects to Buddha, Dharma and Sangha even when he was young (depicted by "Bu-su-gao-sheng-zhuan" at the 25th volume, named "Biographies of Eminent Monks"). The father thought that this was his son's preordained destiny, so he accepted his son's request, selected and appointed several ministers to send his son to the Monastery, formally acknowledged person gu-na-ma-er-sa-mi as his teacher. Shri Sariputra was tonsured and then received ordination to start his monkhood. Shri concluded his czarevitch (luxurious and self-indulgent) life of easy gaining (by claiming for achievements with easy access), and become an awakened Buddhist monk who held bowls to beg for food then on. Shri began the life of worshipping Buddha and Bodhisattva, his ascetic monastic life accompanied with blue lamps and yellow books.

After Shri became a monk, under the meticulous cultivation of his teacher, he started his studies. He wakened up with the morning bell and slept late after evening drum. He was just like wooden fish in the monastery, devoted his all energies to read Triple-text (Tripitaka), which contains scriptures texts, discipline texts and commentary text. He looked like diamond drill that nails the broken pan to pursue diligently the true essence of world and super mundane conditions. He practiced both Esoteric (Tantrika) and Exoteric Vehicle (Tantrayana), Meditation and studies of sutras also were attended with strict disciplines.

Within a few years time, he learned the characters (Chinese letters) sound and music, language, literature, industrial art, architecture and painting, Yin-yang and li-shu, medicinal and incantation, logic, theoretical knowledge and practices and also knowledge of other subjects in India. He got a good grasp of five vehicles of law of cause and effect. In the five knowledges phonology and philology, logic, Buddhist studies, all technology, techniques and archaeology, medical science and pharmacology are all included.

So Buddhist monks and nuns and laity in Nepal addressed him as "wu-ming ban-di-da" because of his strict discipline and brilliant wisdom. Ban-di-ta (Bandita or Pandita) (like "Revered without naming?") is a kind of academic title, which a country is authorized to grant to knowledgeable-monk. In modern terms, it may be considered equivalent to the Degree of Doctorate awarded for honor.

Thus, Shri became well-learned and eminent monk. After the completion of learning Triple-text and grasping the real meaning of threefold – learning (discipline, meditation and wisdom or Sheel, Samadhi and Prajna in Buddhist terms) he gained the high degree "wu-Ming Bandita" from an authorized country. Then he started to make pilgrimage trip to "Wu-t'ian", paid respects to the holy sites related to the life of Shakyamuni Buddha. Wu-tian is the abbreviation of five regions, the east, the south, the west, the north and the middle in the ancient India. The full name of it is "wu-tian Zhu" or "five India". Buddha Sakyamuni, the founder of Buddhism, has made sermons on Buddhism for 49 years in India. His footprints are spread all over there.

Shri was a devoted Buddhist. He admired Buddha Sakyamuni with all devotion and dedication. Therefore, until his study was completed, he made pilgrimage trips to all over India and Nepal. He visited Lumbini Grove where Buddha was born, Lilaian River where Buddha had taken bath before Enlightenment, the Bodhi Tree where Buddha had gained enlightenment, the Deer Park where Buddha started turning wheel of Dharma, the Gridhrakuta Hill where Buddha had resided for preaching the dharma, the Bamboo Grove, Jeta Grove Monastery, and Sala Trees of Kusinagara where Buddha had achieved Nirvana.

At the same time, he also visited Saptaparna Cave where five hundred Arhats held an assembly and edited Buddha's teachings for posterity and the institution of higher learning in India. He not merely made pilgrimage to the holy places related to Buddha, but visited all around India, propagated Buddhism while on his way, and redeemed many people. Any pagodas and temples he encountered, he bowed and paid great respects. If he saw a broken temple, he would advise the concerned persons of the country to repair. He made a lot good deeds and became the famous monk who was known in India at that time.

According to the 'Wu Tai Shan Research' magazine 1997, "India is the birth-place of Buddhism, China is the second homeland of this faith." But from the Pillars erected by the Indian Emperor Ashoka and historical excavations, conducted by various experts of Buddhist countries including Japan, it is proved that Buddha was born in the Lumbini Garden in present Nepal.

Buddhism came into China during Han dynasty. After Buddhist scriptures were translated and explained through the Northern and Southern Dynasties of two Jin Dynasties, Buddhism has become an integral part of the traditional Chinese culture. From the Tang period Buddhist culture is regarded as one of the components of (three) distinct Chinese characteristics (Taoism, Confucianism and Buddhism). This gorgeous culture, so different and luxuriant, which has the strong prosperous root sprout with luxuriant branch and leaf, is glorious and magnificent. It attracted the foreign Buddhist monks. Since Tang dynasty, many foreign eminent monks eagerly came to China for Dharma. The Ming Dynasty was another piece of unification of China with the social stability and developed economy and prosperous culture matured since Tang Dynasty in China. Chu

Yuan-change, as a founder emperor of the Ming Dynasty, worshiped Buddhism, paid excellent respect to Esotericism.

The eminent monk of Nepal Shri Sariputra climbed snow-covered mountains and passed layers of mountain-ranges similar to spring onions, crossed the Yellow River and covered long distances traveling. Finally, he reached China in the tenth year of Ming Yong Lo. He reached capital in the Ming Dynasty (1414). He met Emperor Ming Chenzhu, who was familiar with Buddhism, in Feng Tian Hall. They had discourses about Buddhism. Shri Sariputra answered questions fluently and got the praises of the Emperor: "Since the sages coming from west, he offers great benefit to redeem people. People will get educated when resided there. Any country which wants to be prosperous; Buddhism must be accepted as national teachings." The events are inscribed on a tablet or the stele – (a carved stone pillar or slab) when the record of rebuilding Yuan Zhao temple made). He had been satisfied to live in Hai Yin temple and with great concentration made researches on Buddhism, cultivated the moral character, nourished the nature secretly, and went to look forward to visit famous temples.

Bodhisattva Manjushree is the Protector God of Nepal. His Shrine in Wu Tai Mountain became the provincial capital at Tang Dynasty. It is facing Gridhrakuta Hill- the Holy Land of World Buddhist Mountain.

Since the first year of Yi Feng in Tang Dynasty (676), Fo Tobo, the Indian eminent monk of Esotericism (Tantra or Tantrik) came to Wu T'ai Mountain with sutras, entered the Diamond Cave and left the magical legendary story of not returning from there. Many domestic and international eminent monks of Esotericism came to Wu T'ai Mountain successively for study, preached dharma and carried on the cultural exchanges of Buddhism. Especially in the beginning of Yuan Dynasty, the teacher of Emperor Hu Bilies, (Kublai khan) Ba Siba, (Phagpa) came to Wu T'ai Mountain for worshipping Manjushree. Tibetan Buddhist teaching came in Wu T'ai Mountain constantly, then, Wu T'ai Mountain became famous Chinese Esoteric (Tantrik) Mountain, which received Imperial Court's attentions of many dynasties, and much reverence of monks. However, eminent monk of Nepal, Shri Sariputra heard early about Wu T'ai Mountain, had been eager for worshiping Wu T'ai Mountain, the pure sacred place for a long time. Then, when he came to the capital, he looked forward to paying homage to Wu T'ai Mountain as soon as possible.

In the 15th year of Yong lo in Ming Dynasty (1415), with order of

Emperor Chen Zhu, Shree Sariputra paid respect to the Clear Cool Mountain or Wu T'ai Mountain. He stayed at Pu Ning Temple, which was built in 1309 year (today the temple is called Yuan Zhao). During his stay in Wu T'ai Mountain, Sariputra visited big Xin Tong Temple, which is famous as White Horse Temple; Su Xing Temple enshrined Bodhisattva Manjushree's images, Xi Tian Temple where Ba Siba (Phagpa) resided once, and Shou Ning Temple of Esotericism. He also paid homage to the images of Buddha's and sacred Bodhisattva Manjushree. Shree visited shrines and scenic spots of five mountain peaks and many holy sites of Bodhisattva Manjushree. Sariputra also watched the dharma activities of temples on Wu T'ai Mountain. He heard and listened to expounding the texts of Buddhism from the eminent monks of Wu T'ai Mountain. Shree has carried forward the Esotericism of India too. Thus Buddhist cultural exchange has been going on.

Later, he returned to the capital of China, paid a formal visit to the Emperor at Wu Ling Hall, and made the report of Wu T'ai Mountain. According to the books "Bu-su-gao-sheng-zhuan", "Da-yi-guo-shi-zhuang" the Emperor "warmly appreciated him, payed homage to sages, and offered a Dharma book to him, Later he got order to stay in Neng Jen Temple.

In the 22nd of Yong Lo year, when Ming Chen Zhong became the new Emperor, Shri Sariputra held the grand ceremony for Emperor's ascendenc to the throne. After the meeting, Ren Zhong ordered him "Settle quiet, protect country and obey the king, faithfully fulfill his (your) duties, his (your) virtues will become much larger". The Emperor gave Shri special award of master of "perfect Enlightenment and entitled to make Ordination".

"He was also granted golden seals, brown sedan-chair, horse, clothes, gold and silver of all kinds beautiful wares at four seasons, treasures at 17.7 kilograms silvers, Agalloch eaglewood, treasure bed, silk cotton-padded mattress, color steamed bun, etc." Shri was treated honorably.

Next year, another Emperor reigned. In June, Xuan Zhong emperor ascended the throne, and Shri also held a grand ceremony. After the meeting, Xuan Zong summoned master and asked him to translate "Buddha's Appearances Sutras." This translated edition when published, became popular with the new generation.

Not only was wu-ming-ban-di-da the Master (Shri), but he also did well at the incantation of Esoteric (Tantrik). When he was in Beijing, he not only preached Esotericism to the emperor in detail, but also taught Esotericism to the disciples. Esotericism is profound mystery dharma taught by Buddha Vairocana. It maintains commonly declared lines of preaching secretly, not declaring to the public. It has praise, laud, dharma, incantation and yoga, etc a whole set of strict rites, which are conveyed through master to apprentice direct and secretly. Certain rituals to gain sudden enlightenment must follow it. Its characteristic is that pay much attention to capability of the disciple, mantra, incantation and meditation. Its main classics are "Maha Vairochana Sutra", "Vajrasikhara Sutra" and "Su-xi-di sutra".

Here in, the master gave different teachings in accordance with their aptitudes and induced step by step to educate the disciples. He never set up a difficult path that people may fear to walk or dare not to advance. Therefore, just in the capital of a country, he had thousands of disciples. The great master in all his life did not desire to have self- importance name and high gains. He showed sound hearer to others, maintained simple appearance, with Buddhism inside. He was so humble when praised by the king he became more disciplined in conducting worldly affairs.

Because the court and the commonality of monks and laymen honoured him, he gained the high reputation in the Ming Dynasty in China. After holding grand ceremony of Xuan Zhong emperor, the master asked to return to Wu T'ai Mountain, Xuan Zong considered, he was getting old and could not stand cold in Wu T'ai Mountain. And life there was far bitter. So Shri was not permitted this time. But he felt time limit for himself. So he called Luo, his disciple, and told him, "I came here from the Western Paradise. Today is time for to return, and I am going soon to leave you and others. You should work hard to protect dharma without nonfeasance." He then handed over his properties received from the Emperor to Duane Chu master and others.

He passed away on the 13th of the first month of the lunar year at the age of 92. He had spent 72 years in monkshood during his life.

When the sad news of master's Nirvana reached the imperial palace, Xuan Zong mourned profoundly, the emperor ordered 24 departments of offices to fast for mourning with burial ceremony with respect, and held a memorial ceremony for cremating the remains had been divided into three parts.

One part enshrined into Buddhist relics towers at Beijing, west Fragrant Hills in the temple named "Zen Jun". The second part was enshrined in a Pagoda, which was built on the Wu T'ai Mountain based on Pu Ming range by imperial envoy eunuch Yang Ying. Now the temple is called "Yuan Zhao Temple". The Shanxi office of Taiyuan also held a memorial ceremony; the remaining relics were enshrined in a Pagoda, which was built in the Taiyuan Temple.

It can be said that to hold a grand memorial ceremony, courteous and generous treatment was acquired. The original Pagoda of Taiyuan was destroyed by the meal fire in 1547. But Beijing Zhen Yun Pagoda and Yuan Zhao Pagoda in Wu T'ai Mountain have been kept intact. They stand towering on the China's land.

The relic pagoda is the typical diamond throne type tower. This kind of pagoda comes from India in which were enshrined main five Buddhas of Vajradhatu with respect. Its characteristic is a big pagoda in center, four corners with four small towers, and carved saddle horses and images of five Buddhas.

This relic pagoda in the Yuan Zhao temple is the oldest diamond throne type of tower. It has been peculiar model, it has square base platform, which has 12.2 meters length, 10.5 meters and width and 23 meters height. There is a very tall and big brick tower up to more than 17 meters, which is in the earthen bowl shape at the middle of the base of tower. Four towers in small brick type are built at each corner platform. This pagoda base seat is double -layers in circle sigmoid, which is tall and big. It is magnificent to decorate well and as stable as Mount Tai.

The body of pagoda is in the urn shape of earthen bowl. It has nine grades of wheels with decorated exquisites, hung with the canopy of the wind-tongued bell on the tip; it is a small tower in earthen bowl type. The small towers in the Four Corners are also of the same type. Pagoda seat has four corners of circle sigmoid throne, five towers are built with bricks, and pagoda is with white color wholly. The pagoda was built in 1434. 39 years earlier than the same Diamond Throne Pagoda Beijing Zhen Ju temple. It is 1.2 meters of height; it is similar to Indian Buddha's relic thrones towers. The seat of tower is lower, other four towers are much lower, but the center tower is especially bigger. The main pagoda is much larger than the four other pagodas. On the contrary, the Zhen Ju temple diamond throne pagoda, a central tower, is very large. The tower seat is very tall and big. The central tower is slightly higher than other four towers.

Thus, Yuan Zhao Temple had the Indian characteristics of diamond throne type tower. It is the sign of Sino-India cultural exchange, and also the symbol of Sino-Nepal friendship. It is still

Fig. 22 : Yuan Zhao Pagoda in Wu T'ai Shan, where relics of Revered Bhikshu Shree Sariputra (1335-1426) of Nepal are enshrined

the earliest and highest relic pagoda in diamond throne type in China. It has important historic significance and realistic meanings.

End Notes

1. *An Outline History of China.* Beijing: Foreign Languages Press, 1958, p. 166.
2. *Ershisi Shi Twentyfour History Books of China, (Ming Shi)*, Part 28 Xin Hua Shu Zhu, Xin hua Shu Dian, Beijing, 1975, pp. 8586-87.
3. Dr. T. R. Ghoble. *China Nepal Relation and India.* Delhi: Deep and Deep Publication, 1991, p. 19.
4. Triratna Manandhar and Tirth Prasad Mishra. *Nepal's Quin Quennial Missions to China.* Kathmandu: Mrs. Purna Devi Manandhar and Mrs. Pushpa Mishra, 1986, p. 6.
5. *Two Eminent Buddhists in Ming Dynasty*, Wu-T'ai Shan Yanjiu: Mt Wu T'ai Researches Contents, a Journal, Published by Wu T'ai Shan Research Committee 1st issue of the Journal: Shan-xi China, 1977, p. 40.
6. Ibid, p. 42.
7. Ibid, p. 43.

Chapter 8

Relations with Ch ing Dynasty

Differences between Nepal and Tibet

During his reign, Raja Pratap Malla had sent an army under the command of his trusted official Bhim Malla in the period of 1645-50 to Tibet. This army crossed Kuti (Nyelamu) and reached Sigatse. There he discussed the problems with the representatives of the Dalai Lama and agreed among other provisions to mint coins with the name and symbol of the Nepali Raja of Kathmandu. Tibet was to pay its remittances in gold and silver.

After some time Ranajeet Malla, the Raja of Bhadgaun and Jaya Prakash Malla, the Raja of Kathmandu, also started sending their coins of silver and got payment in gold. As they found this business lucrative and profitable they seem to have thought of getting more profit from it and mixed more alloy with the silver while minting the new coins. Tibet found it difficult to accept the new alloy-mixed coins in exchange at par with the value of pure silver coins as they used to receive before.[1]

When King Prithvi Narayan Shah created a unified Nepal, he sent a mission to Tibet to convey his wish to maintain good relations between Nepal and Tibet. King Prithvi Narayan Shah also joined the tradition of supplying coins to Tibet minted in Nepal. He wanted to keep his pure silver coins without mixing any alloy into it. He found it difficult to accept alloy-mixed coins sent earlier by the Rajas of Nepal. So he complained against the Tibetan insistence in sending old alloy-mixed coins in exchange of new pure silver coins. This difference developed to an unarguable situation. An agreement was signed in between the Nepali and Tibetan authorities in 1775 to settle the issue. But it could not solve the problem. They thought it was necessary to take a definitive step to settle the dispute. The Nepali army advanced from Kuti (Nyelamu) to Sikhar Jong and from Kerung (Chilong) to Jhunga (Yungya). The Tibetan leadership appealed to the Emperor of China for urgent help. China sent a big army under the command of General Pa Chong together with Governor of Sichuan Au Hui and army Chief Cheng Teh. After their arrival in Tibet they found about an approach by Sankhya Lama to mediate for peace with Nepal by giving 300 silver Dotseds equivalent to Rs. 57600/- as tribute to Nepal annually. Chinese General Pa Chong seems to have thought it to be an easy solution to achieve the objective of peace without fighting.[2]

After the agreement the places occupied by the Nepali Army were evacuated. King Rana Bahadur Shah sent a mission to China with gifts to the Emperor and expressions of goodwill and friendship to China in1789. A music and dance troupe had also accompanied the mission.[3]

As the amount, in the view of Tibetans, was too big to be paid annually the Tibetan administration thought to request Nepal Government to consider and reduce the amount to be paid. They paid the first installment but could not continue sending it in the second year. In the third year also they requested Nepal to reduce the amount and allow Tibet to pay what it could be viable for them. But Nepal insisted on getting the second and third annual amounts as mentioned in the agreement before it could reconsider on their new proposal. Tibet proposed to revise the Kerung agreement what Nepal thought it not acceptable. Both sides stuck to their own positions and did not agree to move from their respective stands, so hostilities broke out between the two neighbors.

War between the Two Neighbors

The Chinese Amban in Tibet reported the encroachment from Nepal to the Emperor and made an urgent submission for armed action stronger than before. Hearing the new developments about the war the former commander of Chinese forces against Nepal General Pa Chong realized his guilt and committed suicide by drowning himself into a river.

The Emperor again ordered to send an army under the former commanders general Ao Hui and Cheng Teh. When informed about the two former commanders were hesitant to advance fast enough as expected, the Emperor sent another batch of armed forces under the command of General Fu Khang-an, accompanied by Generals, Hai Lan-ch'a and Ch'an Chai with more responsibility to fight against the Nepali Army who had already entered into Tibet. The reinforced Chinese army pushed the Nepali Army back and following them entered into the Nepali territory and had fierce fighting in different areas.

Then because of four main reasons – the weather condition was too harsh and unbearable, skirmishes were sudden and fierce, supplies from China via or from Tibet were not regular and dependable, and Communications between the command-quarters and field of action were difficult, the Chinese commanders decided on the one hand to suggest the Nepali side to accept their proposal to sign a Treaty to settle the dispute, and on the other, to request the Chinese Government to allow them to return back home.

Treaty of 1792

But before the Chinese side could get any instruction from home, the Nepali side asserted "The Chinese side has put forward a proposal to sign a Treaty so we agreed to sign the Treaty". The Treaty was singed in 1792 and the Chinese army decided to return. The Nepali side helped them for carrying supplies needed for remaining Chinese army on their way back home to the border. The war was over but the losses on both sides were heavy.[4]

Before the war had started, the Nepali Government, Chinese Commander General Fu Khang-an, the Dalai Lama and the Panchen Lama all had requested the British for their help suitable to fulfill their different kinds of needs and achieve their respective objectives in the event of the ensuing war. But the British offered them all to mediate on their behalf and settle the disputes peacefully. As there was no time to spare for the British approach, the war broke out and the warring sides signed a Treaty and settled the disputes in their own way.[5]

It is mentioned by Li Tieh-sheng in his book, 'Tibet Yesterday and Today', and Francis Tuker in his book 'Gurkha' that the performances of General Fu Khang-an were considered, in the court circle, not satisfactory enough to fulfill the responsibilities in the war with Nepal, the way he was expected to do. Hence he was forced to retire.

After the Treaty, China established a mechanism to mint currencies required for Tibet in Lhasa itself. Thus it solved the root cause of disputes created by import of currencies minted in Nepal. They also drew a borderline between Tibet and Nepal and made arrangements to inspect it by the Chinese Amban annually. China stationed three thousand Chinese and two thousand Mongolian and other soldiers permanently in Tibet and would not allow any incursions from outside into the Tibetan territory.

After signing the agreement Nepal continued to get its interests in Tibet served as usual, enjoy traditional privileges and maintained various other interests mutually beneficial to Nepal and Tibet.

The Nepali Missions were sent to China every five years and the Chinese missions used to come to Nepal on various important occasions. These exchanges of missions were helpful to maintain goodwill of one country to another and enhance friendship between the two neighboring countries. The Quinquennial Missions' visits continued till 1906.[6]

END NOTES

1. Prem Raman Upreti. *Nepal Tibet Relation 1850-1930,* Kathmandu: Nara Publications, 1980, pp. 20-23, 33-46, and 61-87.
2. Triratna Manandhar and Tirtha Mishra. *Nepal's Quinquennial Missions to China.* Kathmandu: Mrs. Purna Devi Manadhar and Pushpa Mishra, pp. 7-8 and 22-47.
3. Niranjan Bhattarai. *Nepal Chin Sambandha,* Lalitpur: Sajha Prakashan 2058 B.S., p. 184
4. Tieh-sheng Li. *Tibet Today and Yesterday.* New York: Bookman Associates, 1960, pp. 73-74.
5. Manandhar and Mishra, pp. 62-72.
6. Gyanamani Nepal. *Nepal Bhot Chin Sambandhaka Kehi Samskritik Paksha.* Kathmandu: Royal Nepal Academy, 2045 B. S., pp. 289-90.

Chapter 9

Nepal s Relations with China during the Republican Period

In 1911, after the Imperial system was abolished and a Republican Government was established in China, the traditional relations between Nepal and China continued. The exchange of visits of pilgrims and special official mission took place on various occasions.

Nepal's Relations with Republic of China

After the establishment of Republican Government in China, there was a period of pause for some time in the development of relation between Nepal and China. There was a sort of feeling of vacuum in both the countries. After the gap of mutual contacts for some time a delegation of three Buddhists visited Nepal in 1929 to study Buddhism, to exchange their experiences with Nepali scholars and to take some Buddhist literature in Sanskrit and Newari languages available in Nepal to China.

As the visit had taken place just before the contemplated visit of government delegation it had contributed to make the atmosphere congenial for the visit of official mission in 1930.

The nationalist government of China dispatched a mission under the leadership of Pa Wenchun, Councilor of the Committee of Mongolian and Tibetan affairs, to renew in a way stalled relations with Nepal government in May 1930. This mission conveyed good will of the Chinese government to Nepal government and also presented honorary titles and gifts to the rulers. The Nepal government appreciated their visit and offered gifts to Chinese leaders and the members of the mission.[1]

In the same way Chinese government with the aim of promoting, bilateral relation sent good will missions in 1932 and 1934. They also conveyed the Chinese government's goodwill to Nepal and expressed the desire of Chinese government to renew contact and traditional relation with Nepal. As it was the tradition, they also brought titles and gifts to the Nepali rulers and carried back gifts presented from Nepal to their leaders and the members of their missions. But the complicated internal situation in China and lack of definitive foreign policy of Nepal were obstacles in the way to precede the two governments to enhance their bilateral relations and mutual cooperation.

When President Chiang-Kaishek visited India in 1942 he met the Nepali ambassador to India, Bahadur Shamsher and talked about the possibility of renewing relation between their two countries. Furthermore, during this visit of the President, the Nepali ambassador presented US$10,000 (equivalent to Nepali Rupees 50 000) to the Chinese Red Cross fund as a friendly gesture from Nepal government to the government of China.[2]

In 1946, a goodwill mission led by Chung Lienshen visited Nepal and presented a letter and gifts from the Chinese Government to the Nepal government and extended goodwill on behalf of the Republic of China[3].

In response to the gesture from the Chinese government Nepal sent in 1947 a mission composed of six members headed by General Krishna Shamsher to convey good- will of Nepal to China, explore the possibility of establishment of diplomatic relations between the two countries and open ways to promote mutual relations further. This mission, like other missions also presented insignia of the Nepali decorations and valuable gifts to the Chinese leaders. The Chinese government appreciated the visit of Nepali mission and assured Chinese friendship to Nepal.

But because of their preoccupation and involvements in internal problems they could not take decisions towards the establishment of diplomatic relations and enhance bilateral relations.[4]

End Notes

1. Vijaya Manandhar. *Nepal China Relations*, Vol. II, pp. 171-2.
2. Asad Husain. *British India's Relations with the Kingdom of Nepal.* London: George Allen and Unwin, 1970, p. 222.
3. Ibid, p.144.
4. Ibid, pp. 121-174.

Chapter 10

Forging New Relationship

Relation between Nepal and China based on Buddhism had started in the beginning when the story of birth of Buddha at Lumbini reached in China in 2 B.C. Since then Chinese scholars started taking keen interest about Buddha and his teaching. From the fifth century A.D. Buddhist scholars of Nepal and China like Buddhabhadra, Fa-Hsien, Pao Yun and others started to visit each other's countries, shared their knowledge and experiences about Buddhist philosophy, its institutionalization and rituals. In the seventh century during the Tang Dynasty, Nepal and China exchanged political missions for the first time, but it could not continue for long. The bilateral relations continued to develop solely on the basis of exchange of knowledge of Buddhist philosophy and its implementation in life till the seventeenth century. Because of differences between these neighbors, a war broke out in the eighteenth century. After the settlement exchanges of political missions were initiated, it continued till the Republican era. After the establishment of the Peoples Republic, political relations between the two countries remained in a pause for a while.

Moves for Renewal of Traditional Relations

The government of the People's Republic was established in China in 1949. After the reassertion of China's authority over Tibet, Premier Chou Enlai, while meeting with Indian ambassador K. M. Panikker, asked him to convey his suggestion to Indian government to have a meeting of the representatives of the governments of India, China and Nepal to discuss and find a peaceful solution of the historically unsettled border problem in the South of the Himalayas between the three countries. In this regard Ambassador Panikkar says in his book *In Two Chinas*, "in regard to Tibet, they were a little uncertain about our attitude. I expressed hope that they would follow the policy of peace in regard to Tibet." In the same meeting he asked, "he had heard that the Nepal government had offered to send troops to help the Tibetans and wondered if it was true? He also asked for India's good offices to China for the establishment of direct diplomatic relations with Nepal."[1]

The reason why the People's Government of China did not contact Nepal Government directly for the establishment of diplomatic relations with them, and instead sought India's good offices for it when Nepal and China had bilateral relations from ages and moreover Nepal's Consulate General was already working in Tibet since long time. The reason which might have led the People's Republic of China, not to contact Nepal directly to establish diplomatic relations instead seeking India's assistance, might be that the provisions of Nepal's treaty with Tibet made in 1856, which had provided extra territorial rights of Nepal over Tibet and an obligation for Nepal to help Tibet in its difficult times.

The cause may also be, it is said, that the new government of China had made a decision to establish diplomatic relations with those countries who agree to abrogate old unequal treaties and agreements and establish relations on the basis of equality and mutual benefit. They were not sure whether the government of Nepal would be prepared to negotiate by peaceful means to establish relations on the new basis. Therefore they might have sought good offices of India, who already had established relations on the basis of new principles, to extend their good offices for establishment of direct diplomatic relations also with Nepal.

On July 4, 1952, on the occasion of the inauguration of the Advisory Assembly, King Tribhuvan said, "In northern boundary our traditional relation with Tibet is maintained as before. We expressed our good wishes to the central People's Government of China. Our concerned officials have good relations with Chinese officials. We have good relations with Tibet. There are friendship and goodwill between the two countries. New situation in Tibet have not made any change in our traditional relations with Tibet." This way King Tribhuvan had expressed goodwill to the Government of the People's Republic and also indicated to have renewed relations with the new Government there.[2]

In 1953, with the objective of promoting relations with the People's Republic of China, the Nepal-China Friendship Association was constituted. In the same year a youth delegation headed by Great Poet Lakshmi Prasad Devkota visited China and expressed

Nepal's friendship and good wishes of the Nepali people to Chinese people.

After the establishment of the People's Republic in China, in the first session of the People's Congress (House of the Representatives of the People) on September 23, 1954 Premier Chou Enlai while presenting the report on the work of Government said that China was prepared to establish diplomatic relations with Nepal on the basis of equality. This gesture had received welcome response from the Government of Nepal.

Nehru and Chou Enlai come closer

At the invitation of Chinese Premier Chou Enlai, Prime Minister Jawaharlal Nehru paid an official visit to China in 1954 and signed an agreement on the basis of Panchashila. He seems to have signed the agreement without claiming inheritance for the rights and privileges established by the British Government over Tibet and normalized relations with the Government of the People's Republic of China. They also discussed and decided to develop their relations further. It seems at that time also Nehru did not express any response to the suggestion about the solution of the border problem as Chou Enlai put it forward through the Indian ambassador K.M. Panikkar to the Indian Government earlier.

After the two neighbors signed an agreement and normalized relation between India and China, contacts were developed between Nepal and China for the establishment of diplomatic relations on the basis five principles of peaceful coexistence Panchashila formulated by Indian Prime minister Nehru and Chinese Premier Chou Enlai.

In 1955 at the Bandung Conference, Premier Chou Enlai met the Nepali delegation and indicated to have diplomatic relations between the People's Republic of China and Nepal. Nepal welcomed the indication and agreed to have diplomatic relation with China on the basis of Panchashila.

According to the former Ambassador Yang Gungshu, while negotiating the Nepali side's suggestion of an amendment in the third clause of the five principles about non-interference to include "non interference of political, economic or any other kind" (or ideological character) was added.[3]

When both the countries agreed in principle to renew their relations, a Chinese delegation led by General Yuan Zhongxian arrived at Katmandu at the end of July 1955 for negotiation and establishment of diplomatic relation between Nepal and China.

A delegation led by Principal Advisor Gunja Man Singh of Nepal and Chinese delegation led by the Chinese Ambassador to India Yuan Zhongxian negotiated and finalized the Agreement to establish diplomatic relations between the two countries. The Agreement was signed and a Joint communique was published on the first of August 1955. On the fifth of August the Chinese ambassador presented his credential to King Mahendra who was wearing the Crown on the occasion of the ceremony while receiving the credential. It had added special significance to the occasion.

New Agreement

Another Agreement between the Kingdom of Nepal and the People's Republic of China to maintain friendly relations and on Trade and Intercourse between Nepal and Tibetan Autonomous Region of China was signed on September 19, 1956.

According to Article three of the Agreement, all Treaties signed in the past between Nepal and China including those between Nepal and Tibet were abrogated. The relations between Nepal and China were reaffirmed as based on the five principles of Panchashila.

After that an official cultural delegation led by Education Minister Balachandra Sharma visited China, expressed the goodwill of Nepal Government to the Chinese Government and the people, exhibited the cultural performances to introduce Nepal to different provinces of China and renewed age old relations so happily subsisting between the two countries. Chairman Mao Zedung met the delegation, welcomed them and also affirmed China's desire to enhance friendship with Nepal. Premier Chou Enlai and other Government leaders also met the delegation and assured them of China's friendship to Nepal.

The delegations were shown places of cultural heritage, historic importance and achievements made in the past with the help of Buddhist scholars who exchanged visits to Nepal and China. They were also shown Stupas made by Araniko, Liu Yuan and other artists and architects. The Ministry of Culture of China in Beijing and officials in other cities also organized receptions and cultural performances in honour of the Nepali delegation and availed them with the opportunity to get acquainted with the Chinese culture.

Exchanges of Visits

Prime Minister Acharya Visits China

On the friendly invitation of Chinese Premier Chou Enlai, Prime Minister Tanka Prasad Acharya made the first ever-official visit of Nepali Prime Minister to China from 26th September to 7th October 1956. On arrival at the Beijing airport he said, "What has produced a deep impression on the people of Asia is the resurgence of China and the awakening of the Chinese people."

"The generations of the past have done their duty to which the precious legacy of friendship which they have bequeathed to us bears silent but eloquent evidence. It is for us of the present generation to start afresh from the point where they left off and consolidate and enhance friendship and cooperation."

In reply to the welcome address by Premier Chou Enlai at the Banquet, the Nepali Prime Minister said, "Nepal feels very happy to be between the two great and most progressive Republics in Asia, China and India. It is indeed gratifying to note that Nepal enjoys the best of friendship and goodwill from her two great neighbors."

In welcoming the Nepali Prime Minister, Premier Chou Enlai in his banquet speech referred to the Agreement to maintain the friendly relations between China and Nepal and on Trade and Intercourse between the Tibetan Region of China and Nepal and said, "Nepal has abrogated the treaties which had rendered the relations between China and Nepal not entirely normal. We appreciate very much this expression of friendship on the part of Nepal. In our relations with Nepal in future, we will strictly adhere to the five principles of peaceful co-existence (Panchashila) initiated by China and India." In the joint communiqué published to mark the occasion of the Nepali Prime Minister's visit to China. Nepal and China reaffirmed the five principles (Panchashila) of peaceful co-existence, initiated by China and India as the fundamental principles guiding their relations.

Chairman Mao had received Prime Minister Acharya and his delegation and had cordial talks with them.[4] Prime Minister Acharya and Premier Chou Enlai in the presence of Chairman Mao signed an "Agreement between China and Nepal on Economic Aid" for Indian Rupee 60 million to assist Nepal's national reconstruction.[5]

Nepal Supports China's Readmission in the UN

Nepal was admitted in the United Nations on December 14, 1955. From the first time it attended the General Assembly session in 1956,

Nepal continuously supported the resolution to restore its legitimate seat for the People's Republic of China in the United Nation, its agencies and other international fora until China regained the seats in the General Assembly and the Security Council in 1971.

Premier Chou visits Nepal

On the friendly invitation of Prime Minister Tanka Prasad Acharya, Chinese Premier Chou Enlai visited Nepal from January 24-29, 1957. Acharya at the Banquet hosted in honor of Chinese Premier expressed warm welcome to the distinguished Premier of China. He said, "India's respect for Nepal's sovereignty and co-operation and assistance are known to all. At the same time China's respect for sovereignty of Nepal and sympathetic co-operation and assistance extended to Nepal by China is not less -known. In fact the sympathy and goodwill, which I could feel during my tour of China and which I could also find out in the policy of your government, has been a source of great satisfaction for Nepal".

In reply, Chou Enlai said, "It is more necessary for our two countries to strengthen our co-operation in inter-national affairs and make greater efforts for the maintenance of world peace together with our great neighbour India and all peace loving forces in the world. We have full sympathy for the efforts made by the government of Nepal and Nepali people to build up their country and are willing to give continued support within our ability."

A joint communiqué issued at the end of Premier Chou's visit on January 29, 1957 said, "In the spirit of the intimate and friendly talks which they had in Peking, the two premiers recalled and affirmed the traditional friendship which has existed since the time immemorial."

The two Premiers expressed interest in the all-round development of their countries and held that world peace was very necessary for the progress and prosperity of China, Nepal and other countries of Asia and the world.

The Premiers reiterated their support for Bandung-principles and expressed satisfaction over the broad support and acceptance by many countries in Asia, Africa and the world of the five principles of peaceful co-existences (Panchashila) jointly initiated by China and India.

King Mahendra had received the distinguished guest from China Premier Chou Enlai and had cordial talks with him. [6]

Proposal for Boundary Agreement

In 1959, Chinese Ambassador Pan Tzu-Li had visited Nepal to propose a boundary agreement to settle the boundary question. He met with Dr Tulsi Giri, the Minister for Development and discussed the proposal with him. The Minister had expressed positive response to the Chinese proposal. This led to the visit of Prime Minister B. P. Koirala to visit China and sign the agreement' on the question of the boundary between the two countries.

Prime Minister Koirala Visits China

The first democratically elected Prime Minister of Nepal Bishweshwar Prasad Koirala, on a friendly invitation of the Chinese Premier, visited China on March 11-21, 1960. During his visit Prime Minister Koirala was received by Mao Zedung, Chairman of the Central Committee of the Communist Party of China, and had substantive and fruitful talks with him. He was also received by the Chairman of the People's Republic, Liu Shaochi and had cordial talks with him. Official talks were held between Prime Ministers Koirala and Chou Enlai.

It may here be useful to quote the following passage mentioned in the book *Diplomacy of Contemporary China* written by Vice Foreign Minister Han Nienlung:

"The Sino Nepali boundary, about 1,400 kilometers in total length and mostly snowy mountains, had never been formally demarcated, but it involved few disputes, and the delineation of the boundary line on the maps of the two countries was quite similar, reflecting basically the traditional customary line and the present line of actual control. This constituted sound basis for the settlement of the boundary question. The talks held between Premier Chou Enlai and Prime Minister Bishweshwar Prasad Koirala had agreed the following three principles for the settlement of the boundary question between China and Nepal:

(1) To affirm the status quo, both sides take traditional customary line and the actual jurisdiction as the basis.

(2) To make specific adjustments in individual disputed areas in accordance with the maps in the following ways: Where the delineation of the boundary line on the maps of the two sides is identical, the boundary line may be fixed with the territory north of the line conclusively belonging to China and the territory south of the line conclusively belonging to Nepal. Where the delineation of

the line on the maps of the two sides is not identical but the state of actual jurisdiction by each side is undisputed, the delineation may be unified through survey according to the terrain features and the actual jurisdiction by each side. And where there are discrepancies in the delineation and the state of actual jurisdiction is disputed, it would be better to settle the question at the present talks or refer it to a joint committee.

(3) It is hoped that disputes may be resolved this time, and an agreement on the boundary question signed. After that, a formal boundary treaty should be signed in order to better promote the friendship between the two countries. Both sides should ensure the maintenance of the status quo and non-aggression pending the signing of the boundary treaty. Even if some disputes are not resolved this time, such mutual assurance should still be made.

These principles proposed by China were approved by the Nepalese side.

The two sides deferred mainly on the question of Mount Qomolangma (or Sagarmatha as called by the Nepali side), which the Nepali side claimed for Nepali territory but, on the map it provided, was on the boundary line. According to Chinese maps published previously, some marked Mount Qomolangma on Chinese territory, while others made it a boundary mountain based on foreign delineation.

As pointed out by Premier Zhou Enlai to Prime Minister Koirala, this world-famous mountain, as the token of a nation's spirit, concerns the national feelings of the Chinese people. What's more, we should pay due regard to the national feelings of the Nepali people.

China agrees to the delineation of the boundary line right through Mount Qomolangma according to Nepal's map so that Mount Qomolangma will be jointly owned by both sides with the northern slop of the mountain belonging conclusively to China and the southern slop of the mountain to Nepal.

When meeting with Nepali Prime Minister Koirala, Chairman Mao Zedong said:

"It would be too hard on our feelings if the whole mountain were turned to you. Likewise it would be too hard on your feelings if the whole mountain were placed under our ownership. Therefore, it would be better to go fifty-fifty, and the mountain could be renamed as Mount Sino-Nepali Friendship."

Through friendly negotiations, the two sides signed the

agreement on boundary question on 21 March 1960. However, the question of Mount Qomolangma remained to be solved.

During His Majesty King Mahendra's visit to China in the autumn of 1961, the two sides finally reached agreement on the question of Mount Qomolangma. The Chinese side accepted the delineation of the boundary line between the two countries as passing through Mount Qomolangma as shown on the map submitted by the Nepali side, according to which the south of the peak was to be incorporated into Nepali territory while the north into Chinese territory."[7]

According to the joint communiqué issued on March 21, 1960, during the talks the two sides held frank and free discussions on matters of common interest, in particular, the question of consolidating and further developing friendly relations between China and Nepal. In order to ensure tranquility on the border of the two countries and bring about the formal delimitation of the boundary between China and Nepal as soon as possible, the Prime Ministers of the two countries signed the "Agreement Between the Governments of the Peoples Republic of China and His Majesty's Government of Nepal on the question of Boundary between the two Countries." Under the guidance of the Five Principles, the two sides moved forward to settle smoothly and through friendly consultations the boundary question and added a new chapter to the annals of friendly relations between the two countries. The Agreement provides for formation of a Joint Boundary Commission consisting of officials of the two countries which will make detailed, the spot, survey of the whole boundary, scientifically delimit it, formally demarcate the existing traditional customary boundary between Nepal and China and prepare a draft of he treaty and report to their respective governments for their final consideration and to sign he Boundary Treaty. Such scientific demarcation of our boundary will further strengthen the cordial relations between the Kingdom of Nepal and the People's Republic of China.

Out of its profound desire to maintain lasting peace and close friendship between the two countries, the Chinese Government proposed that the two countries also conclude a Treaty of Peace and Friendship. Prime Minister Koirala appreciated this proposal of the Chinese Government. The two sides agreed that they would discuss and sign the Treaty of Peace and Friendship between the two countries during Premier Chou Enlai's visit to Nepal.

The Government of China agreed to extend a free grant of Indian Rupees one hundred million to Nepal without any political conditions attached.

To further strengthen the ties and co-operation between the two countries, the two Governments agreed to establish their respective Embassies in Peking and Kathmandu.

The two sides affirmed that the continuous development of friendly co-operation between China and Nepal was not only in the interest of the peoples of the two countries but also in the interest of the solidarity of Asian countries and world peace. [8]

Second Visit of Premier Chou to Nepal

On the friendly invitation of Prime Minister Koirala, Premier Chou Enlai visited Nepal for the second time in April 26-29, 1960.

The Nepali Prime Minister and Chinese Premier led their respective delegations for official talks between the two Governments of the Kingdom of Nepal and People's Republic of China. The talks were held in a friendly and cordial atmosphere. Both sides were satisfied at the out-come on the talks. Chinese Premier while addressing the joint Session of the Mahasabha and Pratinidhi Sabha mentioned that the Chinese Government and people were willing to strengthen further the cooperation with His Majesty's Government of Nepal and Nepali people in continuing to make concerted efforts for safe- guarding world peace and promoting solidarity and friendly cooperation among Asian and African countries. Prime Minister Koirala and Premier Chou on behalf of their respective Governments signed the Treaty of Peace and Friendship between the People's Republic of China and the Kingdom of Nepal.

At the end of Premier Chou's visit to Nepal a joint communiqué was issued and according to it the Chinese Premier and Nepali Prime Minister pointed out with satisfaction that their respective visits to China and Nepal have served to further enhance the mutual understanding and friendship between the Chinese and Nepali peoples. The Treaty of Peace and Friendship and the Agreement between the Governments of the People's Republic of China and His Majesty's Government of Nepal on the question of the boundary between the two countries signed between the two sides during their mutual visits marked the entrance of Sino-Nepali friendly relations into a new phase.[9]

As King Mahendra was on the visit to the United States of America and not in Nepal, Prince Himalaya, the Chairman of the Regency Council, received Premier Chou Enlai and had cordial and friendly talks with him.

King Mahendra and Queen Ratna Visit China

King Mahendra, who took keen interest in developing relations between Nepal and China and in articulating the framework, visited China in September 28 - October 15 1961. It was the first ever visit of a Head of State of Nepal to China on a friendly invitation of the Chinese President. It was a landmark in the history of Nepal-China relationship.

King Mahendra signed the treaty for delineating the boundary between Nepal and China together with President Liu Shaochi. An agreement to construct a road from Kathmandu to Kodari was also signed by respective foreign Ministers Dr. Tulsi Giri and Marshal Chen Yi during the visit. The King had official talks with President Liu Shaochi and Premier Chou Enlai.

Chairman Mao Zedung received the King. The Chairman also paid a return visit on him at the guesthouse. On both occasions talks were held in a cordial and friendly atmosphere. The talks were useful to indicate definitive direction to the friendly relations between the two neighboring countries Nepal and China.

In his welcoming speech at the Banquet hosted in honor of King Mahendra and Queen Ratna, President Liu Shaochi said that under His Majesty's leadership, the Kingdom of Nepal had all along been most friendly towards China and admired the independent policy of peace and neutrality of the Kingdom of Nepal.

In replying to the speech by the Chinese President, the King said that the relation between our two countries have developed since ancient times and expressed hope and belief that the ties of friendship between our two peoples will grow stronger from day by day.[10]

King Mahendra, at a mass rally to welcome the King and Queen and to celebrate the signing of the boundary treaty said: "In the course of the past few days we have had the pleasure and the opportunity to meet your great leaders Chairman Mao-Tse-tung, Chairman Liu Shaochi, Premier Chou Enlai and other leaders. We have been much impressed by their wisdom and statesmanship. I take the liberty of recalling a part of the conversation we had with Chairman Liu Saochi in which he frankly stated that like all big powers the People's Republic of China might have had the tendency to ignore the just and rightful claims and respect the rights and susceptibilities of small neighbors and nations, that China in the past oppressed others and had in turn been severely oppressed by other people and that the present government led by the Communist Party of China have learnt the lesson of history very well and will never take the road of aggression and invasion against the territorial sovereignty and political independence of its neighbors and for that matter any other countries, that China will take meticulous care to avoid the repetition of such blunders. We have taken note of this assurance made by Chairman Liu Shaochi and we deeply appreciate the sentiments, which led to the expression of this statement. And it is at the same time a significant message to the world at large. This shows the wisdom and statesmanlike spirit of your leaders."[11]

According to a joint communiqué issued at the end of the visit of the King and Queen of Nepal to China, in the course of the visits the King and Queen saw many places of interests, both modern and ancient, in Canton, Peking, Xi-an, Sanmen Gorge, Luoyang, Wuhan, Nanking Hang chow and Shanghai. In Peking, the King and Queen took part in celebration of the 12th anniversary of the founding of the People's Republic of China. They were much impressed by the achievements of peaceful construction made by the People's Republic of China in the fields of industries, agricultures, science and cultures.

King Mahendra and Premier Chou Enlai held preliminary talks with a view to exploring the possibilities of further economic co-operation between the two countries. They agreed, according to the communiqué, to the extension of economic co-operation particularly in industries, road buildings and communications.[12]

After completion of their visit of China, the King and Queen also paid a state visit to Mongolia.

King Birendra and Queen Aishwarya visit China

King Birendra paid his first visit to China when he was Crown Prince in 1966. Chairman Mao Zedung had received him and expressed his appreciation and admiration to the brave and independent spirit of the Nepali people.

King Birendra and Queen Aishwarya paid state visit to China at the friendly invitation of President Tung Piwu from December 7-14, 1973.

Premier Chou Enlai received the King and Queen at the airport, hosted an official banquet in their honor. King Birendra held official talks with Premier Chou Enlai.

At the banquet, Premier Chou welcomed the King and Queen and praised the long history and splendid culture of Nepal, admired Nepal's foreign policy of peace and neutrality and nonalignment and opposition to power politics and spheres of influence. The Premier said that the prestige of Nepal has risen steadily. He said the Chinese Government expressed its high appreciation and admiration for the just stand and bold heroism to safeguard sovereignty and national independence of the Nepali people. The Chinese Government and the people will, as always, resolutely support the Government and people of Nepal in defending the independence and state sovereignty.

King Birendra, replying to the speech made by the Chinese Premier, expressed his pleasure to be in the company of our friends of this great land, extended greetings and warm goodwill from the Nepali people. He said, "The atmosphere of complete trust emanating from close co-operation following the establishment of diplomatic ties has further developed these relations to the mutual benefit of both of our countries. In Nepal we cherish the memory of our revered father, the late King Mahandra. Imbued with a sense of realism, it was he, who took personal interest in cultivating friendship with China whose people and government have not only extended cooperation but also understanding of the Nepali urge to maintain its own identity and way of life. On this occasion we affirm our faith in continuation of this policy of good neighbourliness".

Chairman Mao Zedong received the King and Queen and had cordial and friendly conversation with them.

The King and Queen toured Peking, Nanking, Soochow, Canton and Kunming where they visited factories, a people's commune, historical sites and scenic spots.

King Birendra and Premier Chou Enlai held friendly and sincere talks on further developing the friendly relations and co-operation between the two countries on international issues of common interest. Both sides were of the opinion that every nation big or small has an inherent right to exist without committing itself to any power block.

A joint communiqué was issued on this occasion of the visit of the King and Queen to China. According to the communiqué, both sides noted with satisfaction that their visit to the People's Republic of China has made a positive contribution to further enhancing friendly relations and cooperation between China and Nepal and friendship between the two peoples.[13]

King Birendra and Queen Aishwarya Visit Tibet

In 1976, King Birendra and Queen Aishwarya visited Lhasa, the Tibet Autonomous Region of China in 1976. It was the first ever visit by any foreign Head of State to Tibet. On the occasion the people of Tibet who had continuous intercourse with the Nepali people since the time immemorial, were most happy to receive the King and Queen of Nepal who had carried goodwill and friendship of the Nepali people to them. The Tibetan people felt highly honored and were enthusiastic to extend warm and sincere welcome and express friendly sentiments to the distinguished guests from Nepal. The Xinhua commentary on the visit said that people of Tibetan Nationality treasure the friendship between the people of China and Nepal. As it put it, "China-Nepal friendship towers higher than the Himalayas and measures longer than the Sino-Nepali Friendship High Way."

They were also happy to know that the King and Queen flew over the Himalayas and made an aerial -bridge between Nepal and China. After the creation of this trans-Himalayan bridge it has helped to increase exchange of mutual visits, promoted trade and tourism and thereby enhanced friendship and understanding between Chinese and Nepali peoples.

Vice Premier Deng Xiaoping Visits Nepal

After assuming the Vice Premiership, Deng Xiaoping made his first foreign visit to Nepal in January 1978 by the same 'aerial-bridge' built by the King over the Himalayas and was happy to mention it in his speech at the Banquet. He was accorded highest honors and welcome on the occasion.

King Birendra and Queen Aishwarya received the distinguished guest Deng Xiaoping and had a quiet dinner with him. On this occasion a high-level discussion on wide range of subjects was also held between the two sides.

Prime Minister Kirti Nidhi Bista hosted an official banquet in his honor and said that the visit of the distinguished Chinese leader was a symbol of the friendly relations developed since historic times.

Vice Premier Deng Xiaoping in his reply speech expressed his happiness for the opportunity he had to visit Nepal and meet the people of Nepal. The Himalayas have joined our two countries and the highest peak Mt. Qomolangma (Sagarmatha) has become the symbol of friendship between China and Nepal. As Nepal and China both belong to the third world, their friendship and co-operation will continue and enhance without interruption.

At the civic reception the honored guest said that Chinese people and government consider their relation with the Nepali people and Government very important and precious. We will make every effort to further strengthen the friendship between our two countries.[14]

Because of the great successes achieved in getting China modernized and prosperous under the wise guidance of Deng Xiaoping, the Chinese people honor and regard him as the successor of their great leader Mao Zedong who created the New China.

Prime Minister Bista visits China

Prime Minister Kirti Nidhi Bista, after his official visit to China at the invitation of Premier Chou Enlai in 1972, visited China a second time at the invitation of Deputy Premier Deng Xiaoping at the end of September 1978. Deputy Premier Deng in his welcome speech in the Banquet said that China is ready to promote the relations between China and Nepal together with Nepali friends. In reply speech Prime Minister Bista said he feels that the traditional relations between Nepal and China was not only secured but continuously growing under the guidance of wise leaderships of the two countries.[15]

King Birendra pays return visit to China

King Birendar paid his return visit at the invitation of Vice Premier Deng Xiaoping in 1979. The two leaders of Nepal and China reaffirmed their desire to continue further promotion of the reletion between their tow contires.

As the other Chinese Premiers, Premier Zhao Ziyang also had visited Nepal in January 1981.

President Li Xiannian visit Nepal

President Li Xiannian with Madam Lin Jiamei began first ever visit by a Chinese President with the first lady of China, to Nepal on March 20, 1984.

King Birendra and Queen Aishwarya extended warm welcome to President Li and Madam Lin. In the welcome speech at the banquet, the King said, "I am happy to note that our friendship is free from problems. As a close neighbour and friend, Nepal has viewed with interest the way China has roused herself from a critically fragile state that embarked on a journey to modernization by safeguarding her independence. As for Nepal she has set for herself the twin goals of peace and all-round development of the people. Nepal may have been mountain kingdom endowed with the beauty of nature, yet from the point of view of economic reconstruction she has proved to be a difficult and least developed country. Nonetheless our efforts have continued. In this endeavor it is only natural that we seek goodwill and co-operation from friends.

By having shown an understanding to our difficulties, China has extended co-operation to us for which the people of Nepal have always remained grateful.

Indeed, we hold in common similar perceptions and views on many inter-national problems of the day. Let us, therefore, look forward to strengthening our ties still further with a view to mutually contribute to the cause of peace and security throughout the world.

In his reply speech President Li said, "Sino-Nepal relations were characterized precisely by mutual respect, equality, mutual trust and sincere co-operation. We firmly believe that the friendly relations and co-operation between China and Nepal established on the basis of the five principles of peaceful co-existence have great vitality and with careful cultivation of friendship between our two sides the flowers of Sino-Nepal friendship will blossom with great luster. One of the essentials of our foreign policy is to strengthen unity and co-operation with third world countries including Nepal. We are ready to join efforts with all the other peace loving countries and peoples to ease the international tension."[16]

Premier Li Feng visits Nepal

At the invitation of Prime Minister Marich Man Singh Shrestha, Premier Li Feng and Madam Ju Lin paid a friendly visit to Nepal in November 19-21, 1989. Prime Minister Shrestha welcomed the distinguished Chinese guests and hosted a banquet in their honour. He described the process of development of Nepal China relations since historical times. Exchanges of the visits of the leaders of our two countries and opinions among them have helped to consolidate the relations so happily subsisting between the two countries. Replying to the welcome address made by the Nepali Prime Minister, Premier Li Feng said Nepal enjoys a long history and shining civilization and admired the achievements made by the industrious and brave Nepali people. He appreciated Nepal's contributions in establishing new international economic order and in promotion of South Asian Association of Regional Cooperation.

King Birendra and Queen Aishwarya received the Chinese Premier and Madam Ju Lin and had cordial and friendly talks with the distinguished guests.

The respective delegations of the two countries discussed all aspects of economic cooperation between the two countries. In the discussions road construction, joint venture, trade, tourism and long-term loans were included.

At the press conference on November 21, the Premier Li said that Nepal was presently finding itself in certain difficulties. Chinese on its part would try its utmost to provide moral and other supports to Nepal.

He also said, "Our fundamental objective is to increase the defense of the countries concerned and also to ensure their safety. The supply of such equipment is fully justified as it is not directed against other countries."

Turning to another question about Nepal, he said, "China understands the current situation concerning Nepal. We consider it unjustified for a neighboring country of Nepal to impose a blockade against the Kingdom because the direct victims of the blockade are ultimately the Nepali people."

He said, "China expected to see the improvement of relation between Nepal and India. As a big country in south Asia, we hope, India, in handling this issue, will be more magnanimous and generous."[17]

(Because of some differences on policy matters, including the issue of buying some arms by HMG for the Nepal army from China at that time the Indian Government had imposed in 1989 a blockade on trade and other kinds of movements for a certain period of time by closing 13 of the 15 transit-points of trade into Nepal.)

Prime Minister Girija Prasad Koirala visits China

Prime Minister Girija Prasad Koirala paid an official visit to China as a leader of an elected democratic Government of Nepal, in March 16-22, 1992. The Nepali Prime Minister was accorded official welcome by Chinese Premier Li Feng at the Eastern Plaza of the People's Great Hall and had cordial talks with him.

A joint communiqué was issued on the occasion. During the visit Prime Minister Koirala and Premier Li feng held talks in a sincere and friendly atmosphere. Leaders of the two countries reviewed with satisfaction the steady progress of their bilateral relation on the basis of five principles of peaceful coexistence and agreed to further strengthen cooperation between the two countries in economic, trade, cultural, educational and other fields. The Nepali side thanked the Chinese side for their support and assistance it had rendered to Nepal in its economic development. The two sides signed an agreement on economic and technical cooperation. According to it China agreed to provide Nepal with a grant of 50 million Yuan. The two sides also exchanged letters whereby China agreed to construct a cancer hospital in Nepal.

Prime Minister Koirala apprised Premier Li Feng the recent political developments in Nepal culminating in the new constitution and national elections and of the strategy formulated to promote Nepal's economic, social and cultural development within a system of values developed during the political movement. Premier Li Feng briefed Prime Minister Koirala on China's current situation of political stability and economic development and on its policy guidelines for further reform and opening up aimed at accelerating its modernization drive.

The Chinese side stated that Tibet was an inalienable part of China's territory and that it was resolutely opposed to any attempt or action aimed at splitting China or trying to create independence of Tibet. The Nepali side stated that it understood the position of Chinese Government and reiterated that Nepal has always recognized that Tibet is an Autonomous Region of China. It reaffirmed that Nepal had not allowed and would not allow Tibetans in Nepal to be engaged in any anti-China political activities on its soil.

President Yang Shangkun of the People's Republic of China and General Secretary Jiang Zęmin of the Central Committee of the Chinese Communist party separately received Prime Minister Koirala.

Prime Minister Koirala and his entourage also visited development projects and sites of historical interest in Beijing, Xian and Shenzen.

Prime Minister Koirala was interviewed by journalists in Beijing on March 19, 1992. Koirala said that the elected democratic Government of Nepali Congress has remained determined to develop and promote further Nepal's friendly ties with the People's Republic of China. Following the restitution of democracy in Nepal, the country can understand the spirit of such friendship and accept it. Nepal-China friendship also would be further consolidated in good spirit. He said, "I have not come here just in a give and take spirit. I have come to China to extend to it a hand of friendship. I would like to strengthen this pillar of friendship and strengthen it further."[18]

Prime Minister Adhikari visits China

In April 1995 first ever elected Communist Prime Minister Manamohan Adhikari paid an official weeklong visit to China. He was accorded official welcome by Chinese Premier Li Feng at the eastern plaza of the People's Great Hall at Tiananmen Square. He was received by President Jiang Zemin at the Great Hall and had cordial talks.

Prime Minister Adhikari had official talks with Premier Li, first between the two Prime Ministers and then the other members of their respective delegations joined with them. Opening the talk Premier Li said that China and Nepal had cordial relations since hundreds of years. After the establishment of diplomatic relation, relations between our two countries have been based on the five principles of peaceful existence. He referred the visits of King Mahendra and Birendra and Prime Ministers and other distinguished leaders of Nepal and said these visits have consolidated and further strengthened the relations between China and Nepal.

On this occasion Premier Li said that an atmosphere of peace and stability is essential for China, which is advancing towards economic development. China is a developing country; it needs a period of a few of years to achieve the position of a developed country. Small and big all nations are equal. Whatever political system they may adopt, all of them are participants of world community. Premier Li expressed gratitude to the Prime Minister of Nepal for their One China concept, support for Tibetan affairs and China's views on human rights and said that China's economic cooperation is only symbolic. Premier Li said China welcomes close relation between the two bordering countries Nepal and India. The Nepali Prime Minister extended an invitation to Chinese Premier to visit Nepal.

An agreement on economic and technical cooperation between China and Nepal was signed on this occasion. China, according to the agreement, expressed its willingness to provide eighty million Yuan equivalent to forty six hundred million Nepali Rupees to Nepal to be used for different development projects in Nepal. China also agreed to the request of Nepal to establish a Consulate General in Hong Kong after it rejoined China.

During the visit, a meeting of Nepal China Inter-Government Trade and Economic Cooperation had taken place. Besides other subjects the two sides also exchanged opinions about the ways and means to reduce trade imbalance of Nepal in different meetings.[19]

Prime Minister Deuba visits China

Prime Minister Sher Bahadur Deuba made a week long visit of China beginning April 18, 1996. Chinese Premier Li Feng extended official reception with full honor to Prime Minister Deuba at the eastern Plaza of the People's Great Hall at the Tiananmen Square. Prime Minister Deuba was received by President Jiang Zemin and had cordial talks with him. Prime Minister Deuba and Premier Li, two Heads of Government, had friendly talks first and other members of the two respective delegations joined them later in the official talks.

Opening the talks Premier Li expressed his happiness to have this opportunity to welcome Prime Minister Deuba and his delegation from the friendly country Nepal. The Chinese Premier referred the completion of forty years of the establishment of diplomatic relations and said that the relations between China and Nepal are based on the principles of peaceful coexistence. Chinese Premier expressed satisfaction over the steady development of bilateral relations steadily in a friendly manner.

In the talks held between the two sides the Nepali side renewed its opinion about China as a reliable friend, reaffirmed Nepal's views about Tibet to be an in alienable part of China and reassured China of Nepal's determination not to allow any body to wage any act against the interests of China. The Nepali Prime Minister also had expressed Nepal's consideration of Taiwan as province of China before going to visit China.

On the occasion, an economic and technical Agreement was signed. According to the agreement, China offered to provide Nepal with an assistance of 80 million Yuan to be spent on the development projects as decided by the Government of Nepal. Besides this sum, about 2 crores of Rupees was provided by Chinese Government to construct a Chinese Buddhist temple at Lumbini.

According to another agreement, an arrangement was made to consult each other on development of bilateral relations and regional and international issues of mutual interest.

The third agreement was on a Nepal China Non-Governmental Forum, which would make efforts to explore and institutionalize the process and feasibility of joint investment in trade and commercial ventures. This forum, it was hoped, will help to develop trade and economic cooperation. The industrialists, tradesmen, intellectuals and Government representatives of the two countries will participate in the Forum. The Ministry of Foreign Affairs will organize the forum on behalf of Nepal. Nepal Industrial and Commercial Federation will lead the Nepal side and All China National Federation will be the leader of the Chinese side.

During the stay in China, Prime Minister Deuba also visited historical city of Xian and New Economic Zone of Shen Zhen.

A joint Communiqué was also issued at the end of the visit.[20]

President Jiang Zemin visits Nepal

At the invitation of King Birendra and Queen Aishwarya, President of the People's Republic of China Jiang Zemin made an official visit of Nepal from December 4, 1996. The King extended highest honour and welcome and received the President at the VVIP Bay of the Tribhuvan International Airport.

At the National Conference Hall, in the presence of His Majesty, the Mayor of Kathmandu Metropolitan City presented the key of the Kathmandu City and a civic reception was organized in honour of the visiting honourable guest the Chinese President.

The King and Queen hosted an official banquet in honor of President Jiang. King Birendra in his speech at the banquet said that relation between Nepal and China was based on mutual trust and confidence and understanding of aspirations of each other. The traditional friendship of the Peoples of Nepal and China was nurtured with enthusiasm and good neighbourly relations. King Birendra expressed his appreciation to the goodwill and friendly gesture shown by the President and said that he has taken it as the symbol of relations developed since ages, imbued with the friendship and understanding.

In his reply speech at the banquet, the Chinese President said that the relations between China and Nepal was based on mutual goodwill, friendship, trust, cooperation and support and expressed assurances that China is ready to work together with Nepali people for the development of Nepali people and promote friendship with them. He admired the determination of Nepali people to preserve their sovereignty and appreciated the achievements made in economic development and improvement in the standard of the living of the people.

Before the banquet, an official talk was held between King Birendra and President Jiang in most cordial and friendly atmosphere. Prime Minister Deuba called on the President. The President received the Prime Minister and had cordial talks with him.

At the Royal palace, in the presence of the King and the Chinese President an agreement between the Nepali and Chinese governments was signed. According to it China provided about 560 million of Nepali Rupees for the Celebrations of the Ceremony of the 25th anniversary of Ascension to the Throne by King Birendra. This assistance was also used to build an Indoor Sports Complex at Patan.

Earlier in a statement issued on arrival at the airport, the President had explained the objectives of the visit to promote friendship, deep understanding and enhance all-round cooperation between China and Nepal. The objective, he believed, could be achieved by their joint efforts.[21]

King Birendra's 10th Visit to China

On his first leg of the weeklong state visit to China at the invitation of President Jiang Zemin, King Birendra arrived at Boao of Haikou provincial capital of Hainan on February 26, 2001. President Jiang met on Tuesday the 27th at Boao with King Birendra. President Jiang said His Majesty the King's visit to China, the first visit to China by a head of state in the new century, demonstrated the good neighborliness between China and Nepal. He said His Majesty the King's presence at Boao Forum for Asia 'added colour' to the Forum. The King thanked President Jiang for his invitation and said he was glad to attend the Boao Forum. The Forum was opened in Boao, a small town some 160 kilometers South of Haikou, capital of Hainan province.

Talking about the Forum President Jiang said the Forum would focus on Asia and be a place for people interested in Asian development to exchange information and conduct co-operation. The Forum will help to enhance mutual understanding and co-operation among Asian countries and between Asia and other parts of the world.

In honor of the King and Queen a Banquet was hosted on February 29 after they came to Beijing. President Jiang in his welcome address said that China is willing to work with Nepal side for a continuous growth of China-Nepal good neighbourly co-operative relations in the new century. President Jiang made the remark when meeting with King Birendra. It was the tenth visit to China by the King.

Because of availability of convenient means of transport it has become normal for frequent visits between the leaders of neighboring countries. President Jiang said the tenth visit to China by the King fully demonstrate the importance the Nepali side attaches to its relations with China. The King's current visit will be another milestone in the relation between the two countries.

President Jiang had visited Nepal in 1996. The President and the King at that time had agreed that the basic policy for bilateral relations is to establish a "good neighborly partnership for generations."

President Jiang on the occasion said consolidating and developing good neighborly relations with Nepal continuously are also a set policy of China. China has always advocated that all countries regardless of their size and power are members of the international community and therefore should be respected and treated equally.

The King thanked China for its long-term support and assistance. He stressed that Nepal has no dispute with China and the cooperation and exchanges between the two countries are going smoothly.

King Birendra said Nepal hoped to strengthen its relations with China especially in the economic and trade areas. In particular, he said, Nepal hoped to conduct more economic cooperation with China's Tibet Autonomous Region bordering Nepal.

King Birendra receives Premier Zhu.

During his audience with King Birendra, Premier Zhu Rongji told that he believed King Birenda's current visit would further promote the good-neighborly relations of co-operation between the two countries in the new century.

Zhu described the King "a respected and well-known friend of the Chinese people," who has a "deep friendship" with Chinese leaders of three generations and made a great contribution to the growth of Chinese-Nepal relations.

Although China and Nepal are different in many respects, Zhu said, the two countries have maintained healthy and stable growth in bilateral ties. Sino-Nepal relationship can be called a model of friendly coexistence among big and small nations and countries with different social systems, Zhu said. The premier expressed appreciation for the Nepal government's adherence to the One China policy and its support to China on such issues as human rights, Tibet and Taiwan over the years. On economic and trade cooperation, Zhu said such cooperation constituted "an important part" of the bilateral ties, adding that the Chinese side was satisfied with the current development although great potential remained to be tapped. China is ready to explore new ways of cooperation in transportation, contracting projects and trade together with Nepal, he said. China is also willing to continue to provide necessary assistance within its capacity to Nepal's economic construction, Zhu said.

The King said he was glad to visit China again so that he could meet with old friends and make new ones. He spoke highly of the traditional friendship and cooperation between the two countries and expressed thanks to the Chinese government for its support and assistance to Nepal. He told Zhu that the purpose of his visit was to consolidate and enhance friendship with China and to expand economic cooperation between the two countries in the new century. He also spoke highly of China's role in maintaining world stability and peace and promoting economic development.

On the occasion King Birendra extended an invitation to Premier Zhu to visit Nepal at a mutually convenient time. The Premier accepted the invitation with pleasure.

King Birendra receives Vice President Hu

At the reception by the King Birendra, Chinese Vice President Hu Jintao said that China believes the friendship between China and Nepal will further develop in the new century. Hu noted that China and Nepal enjoy traditional friendship, and the bilateral relations have had new development over the past years as leaders of the two countries paid great attention. The relations are now characterized by equal treatment friendship and trust, mutual support and sincere cooperation. Hu said, "China is willing to work with the Nepali side to build a good-neighborly partnership to last for generations between the two countries."

King Birendra said he agreed with Hu's comments on bilateral relations and stressed the Nepali side will always observe a policy of friendship with China. The King also praised the friendly cooperation with China in international and regional issues, and thanked China for its long-term support of Nepal.

The King also received the former Premier and Chairman of the People's Congress Li Feng and had cordial talks with him. The Chairman appraised a brief account on his recent visits to different countries and discussed on the matters of mutual interest.

The King and Queen also visited places of historic importance and developmental- research.[22]

Premier Zhu Visits Nepal

Premier Zhu Rongji visited Nepal in May 14-16, 2001 at the invitation of Prime Minister Girija Prasad Koirala. Prime Minister Koirala received him at the airport and all the high honors were extended to him. A civic reception was organized in his honor and the key of the Kathmandu city was presented.

Prime Minister Koirala hosted a banquet in honor of the distinguished guest. The Prime Minister held official talks with the Chinese Premier in a cordial atmosphere. Both sides reaffirmed the friendship between Nepal and China and make efforts to continue and develop it further. The Chinese Premier extended an invitation to Prime Minister Koirala to visit China at a mutually convenient time.

King Birendra received Chinese Premier and expressed his welcome to Zhu's visit and his belief that the Chinese Premier's visit has achieved constructive results. He said, over the years, China has shown great understanding to Nepal's efforts in defending national sovereignty and safeguarding national dignity and provided Nepal selfless help.

The King asked Zhu to convey the gratitude of the Nepali people to China and the Chinese people and said he is confident that Nepal-China relations will further develop in the new century.

Premier Zhu said he was pleased to have the opportunity to meet King Birendra again on the beautiful land of Nepal. He recalled his acquaintance with King Birendra during the King's successful state visit to China in March, saying that he still has fresh memories of the pleasant talks held with His Majesty the King. He told the King that this was his first time to visit Nepal and he felt the most touching fact is that China-Nepal friendship has a broad basis among the Nepali people. Just as the King has said, there are no outstanding issues between China and Nepal and the only task the two countries are facing is to make bilateral relations grow stronger and faster. The Chinese Premier also told the King that he had had very fruitful talks with Prime Minister Koirala and reached consensus on every issue they discussed. He said China and Nepal also signed six cooperative documents, which he believed, certainly play a positive role in promoting economic and trade relations between the two countries.

Zhu spoke highly of the achievement Nepal has made under the leadership of King Birendra. Zhu said His Majesty the King pays close attention to Nepal-China relations and has visited China ten times, making contribution and development of Nepal-China relations.

The Chinese Premier said he is confident that under the framework of good-neighborly partnership for generations established by Chinese President and the His Majesty the King, China-Nepal friendly cooperation will grow forever.

During the visit, agreements were signed for financial assistance to construct a hospital for civil servants, completion of Syaprubesi-Rasuwa Gadhi Highway. And a memorandum of understanding was also signed for the development of tourism regarding Nepal as an outbound tourist destination to Chinese tourists.

Zhu's visit to Nepal was aimed at broadening contact, developing goodwill and forging new areas of cooperation. In summing up, the visit of the Chinese Premier has been proved successful in further enhancing cordial friendship so happily subsisting between the two countries.[23]

Four Points Proposal to Guide Nepal China Relations

The President put forward four point proposal which include conducting exchanges of visits to various fields, expanding economic cooperation, promoting cooperation between Tibet and Nepal and strenghtheng the coordination, contacts and cooperation in regional and international affairs during the visit of former King Gynandra in 2002. According to Ambassador Wu Congyong, the four point proposal put forward by the President "bears great significance to consolidate and continue our friendship in the next century and will serve as a guideline for bilateral ties."

The trade treaty for trade and intercourse between Nepal and Tibetan Autonomous Region of China was also renewed. The agreement signed on this occasion provides for automatic renewal of the treaty for every ten years. The treaties were signed separately amid a function organized at the Great Hall of the People in the presence of former King Gyanendra and President Jiang.

On the occasion of former King Gyanendra's visit, the Federation of Nepalese Chambers of Commerce and Industry and All China Federation of Industry and Commerce signed an MOU for the promotion of trade and investment including bilateral ties on hydropower, tourism, agriculture, transport, and civil aviation at the Great Hall in the presence of former King Gyanendra. The two federations also have agreed to form a Task Force for making practical recommendations for promotion of economic ties between the two countries.[24]

China Associated to SAARC as Observer

Nepal appreciated the desire of China to be associated as observer to the South Asian Association for Regional Cooperation (SAARC).

Nepal supported the proposal to welcome it as an Observer to the SAARC. This decision is made according to the friendly policy of Nepal to China, which was initiated to support China's admission to the United Nation and its agencies and other international forum. This issue was discussed in the SAARC Foreign Ministers conference before the summit for their recommendation where Nepal extended its support for it.

China's Foreign Minister Li Zhaoxing had put forward five proposals for cooperation with the SAARC at the 14th SAARC Summit opening ceremony: "The Chinese Government supports the objectives and priority areas of SAARC; China respects the position of SAARC countries and principles of equality mutual trust and win-win cooperation, and is ready to carryout exchanges and expand practical cooperation with SAARC to contribute to the cooperation process of SAARC and peace and development in South Asia, China's proposals include discussing with SAARC about establishing a mechanism for poverty alleviation and carrying out comparative study on models of poverty alleviation, exploring with SAARC the possibility of establishing a China SAARC regular meeting mechanism for cooperation on disaster relief and mitigation to share experience and information; China will invite SAARC countries to attend multilateral human resources training programs organized by China, and will consider hosting bilateral training programs for SAARC countries; it will encourage Chinese enterprises to make investment in SAARC countries and develop infrastructure and energy sectors in cooperation with SAARC countries on the basis of equality and mutual benefit; China will also invite a delegation of senior South Asian diplomats to visit China this year and plan to host a seminar on China-SAARC relations." These proposals were appreciated by the summit members and the Heads of state/ Government, and decided to associate China as an observer to SAARC.

The decision was included in the declaration as follows: The fourteenth SAARC summit held in Delhi welcomed the People's Republic of China, Japan, European Union, Republic of Korea, and the United States of America to be associated as Observers to SAARC. The region will benefit from these external linkages and help its economic integration with the international community. The Heads of State or Government also welcomed the Islamic Republic of Iran to be associated as Observer to SAARC.[25] (29th clause of the Delhi Declaration.)

Primeminister Pushpa Kamal Dahal Prachanda Visits China

After Nepal was declared to be a Federal Democratic Republic, the newly elected Prime Minister Pushpa Kamal Dahal Prachanda in his address to the nation proclaimed Nepal's relation with all the friendly countries including neighbouring ones will be based on the Five Principles of Peaceful Co-existence.

At the invitation of Chinese government the Prime minister visited China for four-days visit (24th - 28th August) to participate in the closing ceremony of 29th Olympic games held at Beijing on the 24th of August 2008.

Chinese President Hu Jintao met visiting Nepali Prime Minister Pushpa Kamal Dahal Prachanda here today to exchange views on bilateral relations and the Beijing Olympic Games. Hu welcomed the newly elected prime minister to the Beijing Olympics' closing ceremony and expressed thanks for the support of the Nepali government and people for the Beijing Games. "Prime Minister has come to the Beijing Olympics' closing ceremony within a week after being sworn in. This fully demonstrates the great attention. Nepal attaches to relations with China and its profound friendship with the Chinese people. We highly appreciate that," Hu said.

Prachanda said the Beijing Games had turned over a new leaf in Olympic history and the Nepali people feel proud of the Chinese. China and Nepal are "good neighbours, good friends and good partners", said Hu. "The two countries have established a good neighbourly partnership and enjoyed friendship generation upon generation," he added.

The Chinese government respects the path of development chosen by Nepal and supports the Himalayan country's efforts in safeguarding its sovereignty and territorial integrity, Hu said. He added that the Chinese government was ready to continue to provide every possible help in Nepal's development and promote the long-term development of the Sino-Nepali good neighbourly partnership. The two countries should maintain close communication and co-operation, in a bid to contribute to regional peace, stability and prosperity, the Chinese president said. Prachanda said his country considered China a reliable friend and expected more help from the Chinese side in order to achieve permanent peace and promote economic development in Nepal.

He said Nepal was willing to cement cooperation with China and take bilateral ties to a new high. During the meeting, the Chinese president thanked Nepal for adhering to the one China policy and firmly supporting China on the Tibet issue. [26]

Prime Minister Dahal thanked Hu for his remarks and congratulated the Chinese people on the successful hosting of Beijing Games.

During his meeting with the Chinese premier, Wen Jiabao issues of bilateral relations and the Beijing Olympic Games were disscussed.

Wen said China respected the social system and way of development Nepal had chosen according to its situation. During the meeting, Wen announced US$ 300,000 aid for the Koshi flood victims.

Wen believed it would be possible to realize political stability and economic development through joint efforts of all political parties and under the leadership of Dahal, who was here to attend the Games closing ceremony on Sunday evening.

China and Nepal are good neighbours and China is satisfied with the current development of bilateral relations, Wen said. He noted China would work with Nepal to further reciprocal cooperation in various fields and benefit the peoples of the two countries.

Prime Minister Dahal said the friendship between China and Nepal had endured the test of time. Historic changes were taking place in Nepal's domestic situation. The Nepali government and people were striving for national stability and economic development, and hoped to get support and cooperation from China.

Nepal would, as always, support China's efforts to maintain national sovereignty and territorial integrity, Prime Minister Dahal said.[27]

Prime Minister Pushpa Kamal Dahal Prachanda on Wednesday remarked that his visit to Peoples's Democratic Republic of China, Nepal's northern neighbour remained very successful and added a new dimension to the cordial relations between Nepal and China.

Speaking to the press upon arrival at the Tribhuvan International Airport, PM Prachanda clarified that commitment of the Chinese President Hu Jintao and his counterpart Wen Jiabao for increased cooperation for the economic development of Nepal were achievements of his visit.

"To me and our team the visit has been a very successful one and I think that it has added a new dimension to our friendly relations with China," PM Prachanda stated.

He said that he had a meeting with both the Chinese President Hu and premier Jiabao on the day of the closing ceremony, Aug 25, despite the fact that they were under time pressure for the Olymics ceremony.

"Chinese President's response was quite positive to our mention on the need for increased Chinese cooperation for Nepal in the context of our status of economic development, ongoing processes for taking the peace process to a logical conclusion and drafting a new constitution," he related.

PM Prachanda said that his meeting with his Chinese counterpart was still more extensive. "We told him about the three priorities of the new government, taking the peace process to a logical end, drafting a new constitution in time and meeting people's aspiration for economic development," he said, adding, "Chinese PM assured of extended assistance to our country for achieving these."

PM evaluated that the meeting had been cordial and encouraging. "We invited both of them for their visit to Nepal while they also invited us for an extended next visit to the country."

He commented on the success of the Olympic Game as magnificent and said, "It was an extraordinary combination of the people, leadership and scientific technology."

Saying that he had an opportunity to meet world leaders including British Prime Minister and head of the nations at one spot to apprise about the priorities of the new government in Nepal. He added that the visit had made a good basis for gaining support for peace and development process. [28]

End Notes

1. K.M. Panikkar. *In Two Chinas.* Westport, Connecticut: Hyperion Press, Inc. 1955, p. 105 and p. 171.
2. B.L. Sharma: *Rastrapita Ra Ma.* Kathmandu: Anita Sharma, 2041 B.S., p. 136.
3. Yang Gungshu. A Diplomat's Memoir, Hainan chu pan shi 1995, page 223
4. *Gorakhapatra* 2013-6- 4 B. S.
5. Avtar Singh Bhasin. *Nepal's Relations with India and China,* Delhi: SIBA EXIM Pvt. Ltd, 1994, pp. 564-65.
6. Ibid, pp. 571-73.
7. Han Nienlung: Beijing Diplomacy of Contemporary China, New Horizon Press, 1990, pp. 182-184.
8. Ibid, pp. 575-76.
9. Avtra Singh Bhasin, Ibid, pp. 579-581.
10. Ibid, p. 586.
11. Ibid, pp. 589-90.

12. Ibid, p. 591.
13. Ibid, pp. 624-627.
14. Ibid, p. 648.
15. Ibid, pp. 659-60.
16. Ibid, pp. 675-677.
17. Ibid, pp. 706-708.
18. Ibid, pp. 722-723.
19. *Drishti Weekly*, 2052-1-6 B.S.
20. *Gorakhapatra*, 19 April 1996.
21. *Gorakhapatra*, 5 December1996.
22. *Gorakhapatra*, 27 February 2001.
23. *Gorkhapatra*, 15 May 2001.
24. Chinese Ambassador Wu Congyong, while speaking at the meeting organized by Nepal China Study Center, on the achievements of former King Gyanendra's visit to China, had quoted the statement made by the Chinese President at the meeting with King Gyanendra on the occasion of his visit to China. *Himalayan Times*, 7 August 2002.
25 29th clause of the Delhi Declaration held on the occasion of the 14th SAARC Summit.
26. Himalayan 25th Aug.2008
27. Kathmandu Post 25th Aug.2008
28. Rising Nepal 28th Aug. 2008

Chapter 11

Nepal China Co-operation

Nepal-China Trade and Culture

Nepal and Tibetan Autonomous Region of China are immediate neighbors since writing of history had not yet begun. They used to exchange whatever useful goods they had among nearby border peoples. The Nepali people used to supply grains, vegetables, chili, other edibles and useful goods and commodities produced in Nepal and also goods imported from India. Tibet on its part used to provide salt, wool, dust-gold, sheep, yak, yak-tails, hides and musk. Mutual needs were met with supplies of natural products grown in this or that side. This kind of trade, based on barter system, developed according to the need of times.

In the 7th century, King Srongtsan Gampo opened the passes and peace and security were established there, the exchanges of visits and trade grew significantly. Then Nepali traders started to visit Tibet in large number. And same way Tibetans were coming down to Nepal. Their mutual visits encouraged them to carry goods in large quantities from one side to the other for exchanges under barter system. Trade using currencies began only when Nepal made coins available also to Tibet.

It can be stressed that from the time when the Buddhist books, like Karandabyuha Sutra appeared during the time of King Lha Thothori in Tibet, several intrepid Nepali had also arrived there. These traders, it may be considered, to be the ancestors of business community to start trade, taking Nepali or Indian goods to Tibet and bringing wool, dust gold, Yak tail, musk and hide etc. to Nepal and send them to India and other central Asian countries. After the marriages of King Srongtsan Gampo with Nepali and Chinese princesses the route from Nepal to Tibet and via Tibet to China was opened. Traders from Nepal and India to Tibet could extend their area of trade to China. Same way, Tibetans and also some Chinese could come across the Himalayas for official proposes, trade, for learning Buddhism and also for pilgrimage of holy places in Nepal and in India.

It could safely be presumed that then trade might have developed in a viable and profitable manner. Thereafter Nepal becomes known to be the entrepot (a central point of trade between India, Nepal, Tibet and China). Where the business had developed for the construction of Potala Palace, Jokang, Ramoche, other monasteries and temples and in a way Lhasa city as a whole. The city then looked to be a commercially developed place. And the cause, it could be said, was the emergence of the new land route which facilitated trade between Nepal, China's Autonomous Region of Tibet and a part of mainland China itself.

From the early seventeenth century, the Kings tried to institutionalize the traditional trade between Nepal and Tibet. New agreements were signed to regularize trade and also other aspects of Nepal-Tibet relations developed since historic times. To promote bilateral trade the two sides had agreed to use coins minted for Tibet in Nepal and also to allow Business Houses to be established in Tibet. These decisions used to be interrupted according to the circumstances developed in different times. The trade enormously developed and flourished after the Agreement was signed in 1956 for Trade and intercourse between Nepal and Tibetan Autonomous Region of China.

In 1956, when Nepal and China signed the agreement for trade and intercourse with Tibetan Autonomous Region it renewed traditional system of trade and took steps and decided new ways and means to promote trade between Nepal and Tibet and also through the land route with China itself via the Autonomous Region. This agreement was renewed several times and made up to date. Now it is made automatically renewable for ten years when the period expired.

Trade in Friendship Price

Before moving to usual bilateral trade, it may be useful to understand system of the trade of goods supplied by China under the friendship price. China used to allow Nepal to have a third of assistance in foreign curency. Another one third to buy Chinese products to be sold in Nepal and use the proceeds (money) thus received for the local expenses of construction works or the projects agreed upon between the two countries. The last one third of the assistance was used by Chinese projecect office to buy Chinese machins and equipmenents needed and salaries and other expences for Chinese experts working for the projects in Nepal. According to the practice, Nepali officials used to go to Canton air in China buy goods available there with the one third of the money received in assistence, and bring them to Nepal by sea route and sell them in Nepal to procure Nepali currency for local expenses for the projects to be constructed by the Chinese assistance. There was a "friendship price" system to buy Chinese goods for the projects aided by China, which used to be determined according to the friendship i.e. the need and support of particular country for China. Friendship price were varied in its rates for country to country. Nepal, together with other countries like Pakistan, Egypt and Cambodia enjoyed this privilege for a certain period of late sixties and beginning of the seventies. Other countries in priority to receive goods in friendship price were Vietnam, North Korea, Laos, Albania and other countries.

At this time imports of industrial goods bought under this arrangement mainly came from mainland China. This trade used to be 74 % percent and remaining 26% of trade was conducted with Tibet.

Economic Cooperation and Trade

The People's Republic of China initiated economic assistance to Nepal to consolidate and enhance mutual interests on the basis of non-interference in internal affairs and equality from 1956. By using the sums of economic assistances received in different times from China Nepal has constructed Araniko Highway (114 km), Kathmandu- Pokhara Highway (214 km), Prithivi Highway (176 km), Kathmandu-Bhaktapur Road (13 km), Ring Road (29 km), Gorkha Narayanghat Highway (61 km), and Pokhara Baglung Highway (64 km). Kerung-Syaprubesi Highway (30 km) is under construction. The mountainous country Nepal has been highly benefited with these road constructions. Other road projects are in the pipeline.

In industrial sector, Bhrikuti paper factory, Bansbari leather and shoe factory, Harisiddhi and Bhaktapur brick and tile factories, Hetauda yarn and cotton textile factory, Lumbini Sugar Factory, Gorakh-Kali Rubber Industry, Sunkoshi Hydro Project, warehouses in Kathmandu and Birgunj, Pokhara Water Conservation and Irrigation Project are fulfilling the great necessities of Nepal for moving towards self sufficiency. The National Convention Hall, Nepal International Conference Center, B.P. Memorial Cancer

Hospital, Sports Stadium's indoor and outdoor facilities and other projects necessitated in different times and maintenance of some of the completed projects for certain period of time could be enumerated as important projects constructed under the generous assistance and co-operations of China. The construction of roads and other projects as Nepal's basic infrastructures have helped Nepal to move towards economic development. The products of the industrial projects have helped Nepal to reduce, though in a small proportion, their imports from foreign countries. The National Convention Hall and International Conference Center have helped Nepal to fulfill the timely needs. The B.P. Cancer Hospital is serving the people suffering from cancer. Other projects are expected to continue. On the whole, China's economic assistance, which still continue without interruption, have been very helpful and a significant factor to enhance friendship of Chinese people towards the Nepali people.

China, continuing the tradition of assistance to mark various occasions, is extending about 80 mllion Yuan annually to Nepal as grant assistance for her economic development.

From the time when the first aid agreement was signed in 1956, 77 such agreements for different projects are already signed up by 2005. The total amount of such aid projects has reached 1.5 billion RMB or Yuan.[1]

Besides the unconditional financial assistance, low-interest loans and joint investments in industries, trade and other mutually agreed financial services have been highly beneficial to Nepal.

New links between Nepal and China

After the Kathmandu-Kodari Road was opened, the form and position of Nepal's trade with the mainland and Tibet Autonomous Region have changed tremendously. Commodity composition of Nepal's trade with China consist of a narrow range of items on the export front and a wide range of items on the import front. The structure of exports and imports also differs as between mainland China and Tibet Region. Exports to mainland China mainly consist of handicrafts and Nepali paper products, while those of Tibet Region consist of flour, vegetable, ghee, metal, statues other metal goods and incense etc. In case of imports, the major items imported from mainland China are electrical goods, machinery and parts, cars and other vehicles, thread, chemicals, silk fabric other consumer goods and toys. Major items imported from Tibet Region are raw wool, textile, jean pants, jackets, electric and other goods.

Nepal and China now have various means to link the two countries. The first road was constructed in the form of Araniko Highway to link Kathmandu and Kodari. Kerung-Shyaprubesi Highway is going to be completed soon. Besides regular air flights, bus services are plying between Kathmandu and Lhasa. The Railway from Qinghai to Lhasa, which is already in move is planned to come to Sigatse in a very short time. The railway service from the Station at Sigatse, which will be the nearest point to Nepali border could be extended when the investment becomes economically feasible. Now there is a plan of China to construct a 900 kilometer highway from Lhasa to Kathmandu within three years. These road and air links are expected to facilitate the movements of the peoples as well as trade materials. These movements of peoples and trade materials will without any doubt bring the two countries closer and foster cultural, economic and trade relations further.

To regularize the economic and trade activities, a Trade Agreement was signed between Nepal and China in 1964. Since then, programs are organized to develop economic and trade relations.

The Inter Governmental Ministerial level Economic and Trade Committee

The Inter Governmental Ministerial level Economic and Trade Committee was formed in 1983, with a view to promoting trade and expanding areas of economic co-operation between Nepal and China. The Committee reviews and monitors trade relations within the context of over all economic cooperation and suggest corrective measures, identify projects for mutual benefit, explore areas where long-term arrangements are feasible and undertakes joint studies to promote the economic and trade relation further. The fundamental objective of the committee is to suggest ways and means to accelerate developmental pace with greater emphasis being given to the need for creating employment and income generating activities for the poor and disadvantaged section of the society.

The Committee reviews the increased volume of bilateral trade and expresses the desire to further promote bilateral trade through sea route and over land between Nepal and China. Nepal also wants to promote trade with Tibet and via Tibet to Mainland China. The

Nepali side expresses concern over the widening trade gap between the two countries and requests the Chinese side to increase imports from Nepal. The Nepali side desires to step-up exports to Tibet in view of geographical proximity. The committee also expresses its desire to increase the visits of business people from their two countries, encourage the holding of and participate in trade fairs in each others country and facilitate the establishment of offices by the trading companies in their respective countries so as to promote mutual understanding and increase trade volume. The Nepali side request Chinese side to open more additional entry-exit points along Nepal China border for further promotion of bilateral trade between Nepal and Tibet Autonomous Region.

The Chinese side desire to expedite the issuing of the working visa for the personnel of the contracting corporations. As far as the joint ventures are concerned, both sides desire to expand viable areas for investment aiming at the benefits for both the countries.

The inter-governmental committee is striving for the development of economic co-operation and trade between the two.countries. The committee is moving forward in co-operation with each other to realize the objective.[2]

Tenth Session of Joint Economic and Trade Committee

The tenth session of China-Nepal Joint Economic and Trade Committee was held on July 24, 2007 in Kathmandu. Both sides reviewed the development of bilateral trade, economic and technical assistance, and economic cooperation between the two countries since the 9th Session of the Committee, expressed their initiatives to further strengthen and promote the friendly bilateral cooperation, and finalized the Agreed Minutes as follows:

1. Both sides reviewed the development of bilateral trade since the 9th Session of the Committee, and agreed that there was substantial potential for further expansion of bilateral trade.
2. Both sides noted the trade imbalances and agreed to adopt positive measures to relieve the pressure of trade deficit against Nepal on the basis of expanding the scale of bilateral trade.
3. The Chinese side welcomed the Nepal Government's decision to encourage enterprises to participate in various international fairs including China Import and Export Fair in Guangzhou (canton), and assured that it would extend necessary assistance in this regard.

Economic Cooperation

1. The two sides reviewed with satisfaction the development of economic and technical cooperation since the 9th Session of the Committee, and unanimously agreed that the two countries enjoy great potential and prosperous future in this regard, and would like to make joint efforts to further exploit potentials, extensively discuss new scope and modes of cooperation, and overall and deepen the economic and technical cooperation.
2. The Chinese side agreed to encourage competent Chinese enterprises to cooperate with their Nepali counterparts on the basis of business in the field of potential areas including infrastructure.
3. The Chinese side encouraged enterprises from both sides to solve the problems of Upper Modi Hydropower Project and quicken the process of West Seti Hydropower Project through cordial consultation. The Nepalese side agreed and expressed its willingness to look at this matter.
4. The Chinese side agreed to encourage competent Chinese enterprises to invest in Nepal. The Nepalese side expressed its readiness to provide necessary assistance and facilitation to the relevant Chinese enterprises investing in Nepal.

Nepal-China P. R. Economic Linkage in Brief [3]
Nepal's Trade with Mainland China

Value in '000 Rs.

Description	*2004/05*	*2005/06*	*2006/07*
Nepal's Export to Mainland China	53487	108168	54507
Percentage Share in Total Export	0.1	0.2	0.1
Nepal's Import from Mainland China	8254183	6635507	12514258
Percentage Share in Total Import	5.5	3.8	6.5
Trade Balance	**–8200696**	**-6527339**	**–12459751**

Nepal's Trade with Tibet, Autonomous Region of China P. R.

Description	*2004/05*	*2005/06*	*2006/07*
Nepal's Export to Tibet	1835036	784415	323484
Percentage Share in Total Export	3.1	1.3	0.5
Nepal's Import from Tibet	4604999	5447991	4164358
Percentage Share in Total Import	3.1	3.1	2.2
Trade Balance	**– 2769963**	**– 4663576**	**– 3840874**

Nepal's Trade with China P.R.

(Including Tibet, Autonomous Region of China P.R.)

Description	*2004/05*	*2005/06*	*2006/07*
Nepal's Export to China P.R.	1888523	892583	377991
Percentage Share in Total Export	3.2	1.5	0.6
Nepal's Import from China P.R.	12859182	12083498	16678616
Percentage Share in Total Import	8.6	7.0	8.7
Trade Balance	**– 10970659**	**– 11190915**	**– 16300625**

Nepal's Trade with Hong Kong, Special region of China P. R.

Description	*2004/05*	*2005/06*	*2006/07*
Nepal's Export to Hong Kong	129378	111756	824782
Percentage Share in Total Export	0.2	0.2	1.4
Nepal's Import from Hong Kong	1286427	930930	1029464
Percentage Share in Total Import	0.9	0.5	0.5
Trade Balance	**– 1157049**	**– 819174**	**– 204682**

Nepal's Trade with Macau Autonomous Region of China P. R.

Description	*2004/05*	*2005/06*	*2006/07*
Nepal's Export to Macau	—	19	10
Percentage Share in Total Export	—	0.0	0.0
Nepal's Import from Macau	—	—	10084
Percentage Share in Total Import	—	—	0.0
Trade Balance	**—**	**19**	**– 10074**

Year 2004 2005 2006 2007

US $1 = NRs. As of Mid July 74.45 70.64 74.39 71.0

(Average rate of buying and selling)

Figures for 2006/07 are provisional.

Compiled by Research and Information Division of FNCCI from Trade and Export Promotion Center.

Major Export Items (Excluding Tibet) (Value Wise - recent)	*Major Import Items (Excluding Tibet) (Value Wise - recent)*
1. Raw Hides and Skin	Electrical machinery, sound recorder, television images & parts and accessories there of
2. Articles of Plastics	Machinery and mechanical appliance electrical equipment & parts
3. Paper, Pulp and paper board and articles thereof	Wool, fine or coarse animal hair; woven fabric
4. Original sculptures and statuary in any materials	Iron and steel
5. Hand knotted woolen carpet	Inorganic chemicals; organic or inorganic compounds of precious metals and others
6. Articles of apparel & clothing accessories, not knitted or crocheted	Organic chemicals
7. Articles of silver Jewellery	Optical, photographic, measuring, medical or surgical equipments, parts and accessories thereof
8. Incense Sticks	Plastics and articles thereof
9. Spectacles of lenses of glass	Articles of iron or steel
10. Cotton table linen, sacks, bags and other made ups	Fertilizers

Number of Tourists arrival from China P. R.

2007* 11259 3.8 % of Total Tourist arrival
2006 16800 4.3 % of Total Tourist arrival
2005 21170 5.6 % of Total Tourist arrival
2004 13326 3.5 % of Total Tourist arrival
2003 5677 1.7 % of Total Tourist arrival

* By Air Only /The Figures are of first ten months only.

Compiled by Research and Information Division of FNCCI from different sources.

Number of Joint Ventures with China P. R. as of Baisakh 2064 (Mid May 2007)

Operating	*28*	*Under Construction*	*8*	*Licensed*	*11*	*Approved*	*94*
Hotel/ Restaurants	7	Hotel / Restaurants	4	Readymade Garments & blankets	5	Hotel/ Restaurants	28
Hydropower generation & electric goods & related products	2	Hydropower generation	1	Hydropower generation	1	Hydropower generation & electric goods & products	6
Radio Paging	2	Leather & sports shoes	1	Radio Paging	2	Nursing Home & related products	2
Civil Construction	3	Organic Fertilizer	1	Civil Construction	1	Civil Construction	3
Pashmina goods	3	—		—		Readymade Garment, Pashmina, silk items & Napkins	19
Food items	2	Medical products	1	Dairy products	1	Food items	3
Nursing Home & related services	3	—		—		Software development	12
Others	6	Other	—	Other	1	Others	21

Nepal's Trade with China P.R.
(Including Tibet, Autonomous Region of China P.R.)

Value in '000 Rs.

Description	*2001/02*	*2002/03*	*2003/04*	*2004/05*	*2005/06*
Nepal's Export to China P.R.	1040075	1631050	2348150	1888523	892583
Percentage Share in Total Export	2.2	3.3	4.4	3.2	1.5
Nepal's Import from China P.R.	8744459	9098978	9299902	12859182	12083498
Percentage Share in Total Import	8.1	7.3	6.8	8.6	6.9
Trade Balance	**– 7704384**	**– 7467928**	**– 695175**	**– 10970659**	**– 11190915**

Nepal's Trade With Mainland China

Description	*2001/02*	*2002/03*	*2003/04*	*2004/05*	*2005/06*
Nepal's Export to Mainland China	18723	31403	117497	53487	108168
Percentage Share in Total Export	0.0	0.1	0.2	0.1	0.2
Nepal's import from Mainland China	4315803	4760342	5433815	8254183	6635507
Percentage Share in Total Import	0.4	3.8	4.0	5.5	3.8
Trade Balance	**– 4297080**	**– 4728939**	**– 5316318**	**– 8200696**	**– 6527339**

Nepal's Trade With Tibet, Autonomous Region of China P.R.

Description	*2001/02*	*2002/03*	*2003/04*	*2004/05*	*2005/06*
Nepal's Export to Tibet	1021352	1599647	2230653	1835036	784415
Percentage Share in Total Export	2.2	3.2	4.1	3.1	1.3
Nepal's Import from Tibet	4428656	4338636	3866087	4604999	5447991
Percentage Share in Total Import	4.1	3.5	2.8	3.1	3.1
Trade Balance	**– 3407304**	**– 2738989**	**– 1635434**	**– 2769963**	**– 4663576**

Nepal's Trade with Hong Kong, Special region of China P.R.

Description	*2001/02*	*2002/03*	*2003/04*	*2004/05*	*2005/06*
Nepal's Export to Hong Kong	61344	86692	77024	129378	111756
Percentage Share in Total Export	0.1	0.2	0.1	0.2	0.2
Nepal's Import from Hong Kong	2461194	2276995	1641571	1286427	930930
Percentage Share in Total Import	2.3	1.8	1.2	0.9	0.5
Trade Balance	**– 2399850**	**– 2190303**	**– 1564547**	**– 1157059**	**– 819174**

Total Volume of Nepali Trade (with all Countries)

Description	*2001/02*	*2002/03*	*2003/04*	*2004/05*	*2005/06*
Nepali Total Volume of Export	46944800	49930600	53910700	58705700	61167100
Nepali Total Volume of Import	107389000	124352100	136277100	149473600	175108000

Nepal China Non-Governmental Cooperation Forum

It was with a view to promote trade and economic co-operation between Nepal and China by bringing business communities of the two countries closer that the Nepal-China Non-governmental Co-operation Forum was set up in 1996. Following the establishment of the Forum, exchanges of visits and increase in business activities of business communities of the two countries have increased significantly and there are positive indications of increased trade and investment co-operation between the two countries. In this context it was thought to be timely to organize a study focused on analyzing the present status of trade and investment co-operation, cultural exchanges, identifying the problems and constraints, assessing future potentials and suggesting needful policies, measures and programmes would provide valuable insights for informed decision-making body the government as well as business communities of both the countries.

The study was undertaken under the aegis of Nepal-China Non-governmental Co-operation Forum. The Federation of Nepalese Chambers of Commerce and Industry has already published the Report on Nepal-China Trade, Economic and Cultural Co-operation study on December 20, 1999. In order to establish a Task Force, an MOU was signed between the FNCCI and ACFIC on 14 July 2002 for the promotion of trade and investment including bilateral ties on hydropower, tourism, agriculture, transport, and civil aviation. Under the MOU, the ACFTI and the FNCCI shall continue to cooperate with each other for expanding the activities of the Nepal China Non-Governmental Cooperation Forum (NCNGCF) established as per the agreement between the two Governments in 1996.

Nepal and China signed an air agreement in 1978 in order to facilitate for air services between Kathmandu and Beijing and one point beyond. Another air agreement was signed in 1999 for air services to Tibet for promoting tourism, trade, commerce and cultural exchanges between Nepal and Tibet. A new air agreement is also signed for air services from Kathmandu to Shanghai.[4]

New MoU between Nepal and China

With a view to promoting trade and economic cooperation between the two neighboring countries, Nepal and People's Republic of China signed a Memorandum of Understanding (MoU) in Kathmandu on 30 November 2002. The Federation of Nepalese Chambers of

Commerce and Industry (FNCCI) and China Council for the Promotion of International Trade (CCPIT) signed the MoU in Kathmandu. The Acting President of FNCCI and Vice Chairman of CCPIT signed the MoU on behalf of their respective organizations. According to the MoU, both organizations will exchange information and their publications for the promotion of trade and investment including bilateral ties and joint ventures on hydropower, tourism and other potential areas.

Similarly, the two organizations representing the private sector of Nepal and China will increase contacts and exchange information with regard to trade and technical know-how with the objectives of promoting bilateral trade and investment, especially for the small and medium scale industries. As per the MoU, FNCCI and CCPIT have agreed to organize seminars and workshops, trade fairs and consultancy services for entrepreneurs of both the countries.

China is one of Nepal's major trade partners and the trade between the two countries has been increasing significantly in the last few years. Nepal imported goods worth $85 million, which is about 5.5 percent of the total import in fiscal year 2000-01, whereas export to China was only $35,000 during the same period, according to the FNCCI.

The major export to China includes woolen and leather goods and original sculptures, whereas the major import items to Nepal are wool, silk, electrical accessories and equipments, audio video equipment, machinery and mechanical appliances, organic chemical, mineral fuels, mineral oil products, furniture, motor vehicles and their parts.

There are altogether 14 joint-venture industries at present in Nepal and seven are under construction. The major joint investment includes hotels, restaurant, nursing home, food processing, and hydropower and radio paging.[5]

Memorandum of the 9th Meeting of Nepal-China Non- Governmental Forum

The 9th Meeting of Nepal-China Non-Governmental Cooperation Forum was held on June 12-13, 2007 in Kathmandu, Nepal.

Following the inaugural session, a business session was organized. In the business session speakers from China and Nepal made their presentations on different topics.

Besides that the 9th meeting of the Forum agreed to adopt the following:

1. Both sides expressed satisfaction over the activities of the Forum. The Chinese side expressed their appreciation and gratefulness to the FNCCI and the Government of Nepal for the warm hospitality and excellent arrangements of the meeting.
2. Nepal and China both sides agreed to expand cooperation to promote bilateral trade, tourism and investment.
3. Both sides agreed to enhance cooperation, by providing good opportunities, especially in the sectors such as industry, tourism, hydropower, herbal medicine, agriculture, construction, infrastructure, communication and commercial line, niche products namely handicrafts, herbal products etc. to accelerate the bilateral trade to new heights.
4. It was agreed that the Tenth Forum Meeting will be held in China. Both sides agreed to take a more practical and flexible approach with full preparation to organizing the next Forum Meeting. The time, venue and them for the next Forum meeting shall be finalized through mutual consultation between FNCCI and ACFIC.
5. The FNCCI and ACFIC agreed to promote the "Mini Nepal Pavilion" in Jiuzhaigou.
6. This memorandum is signed on 13th of June 2007 in FNCCI Secretariat, Kathmandu, Nepal.[6]

The latest position of Nepal China Trade

According to the article written by President of Nepal Chamber of Commerce and Industry, Kush Kumar Joshi in TODAY, 2008 titled "trade statistics show that the volume of trade between Nepal and China (including mainland, Tibet, Hong Kong and Macau) was around Rs 18. 9 billion in the year 2006/7. Of this goods worth around Rs. 17.7 billion was imported by Nepal from China and Nepal managed to export goods worth around Rs. 1.2 billion only. Nepal's export dropped dramaticallyby 50%in the year 2005/6.

During the year 2006/7 , Nepal managed to export goods worth around Rs. 0.05 billion to mainland China, whileNepal imported goods worth 12.5 billion from the mainland in the same year.Thus ,the current trade deficit with mainland China is Rs.12.45 billion, which is 75%of total trade deficit with China of Rs.16.5 billion. This clearly shows Nepal's huge trade deficit with the mainland.

Nepal needs concessions from China on duty free and preferential treatment for Nepali goods to Chinese markets, to reduce Nepal;s trade deficit. China has agreed to provide Special Preferential Treatment to Nepali goods, and we expect that this facility will be put into effect very soon.

There is ample oppertunity in Nepal to attract Chinese investment in industries producing goods to be exported to developed countries in the context of being a WTO member enjoying special previlage as an LDC. Development of Secial economic Zones in Nepal, spcially focused to attract Chinese investments is required to safeguard the Chinese investors' confidence. [7]

Cultural Relations

First cultural delegation from Nepal with a cultural troupe visited China in 1956. It introduced Nepali cultural activities to China. The Chinese people of all the provinces of China appreciated the performances of the troupe.

Cultural cooperation between Nepal and China started with the provision of scholarship to Nepali students to study different subjects in China in 1957. Various forms of cultural co-operation that exist between the two countries are: (1) scholarship programs for Nepali students in China and facilities to Chinese students to study different subjects in Nepal; (2) exchanges of sport delegations and assistance for development of sports complexes in Nepal by China; (3) exchanges of visits of cultural troupes of both countries and shows of Chinese acrobatic and other cultural performances in Nepal and Nepali cultural shows in China; (4) visits by academicians, officials, scholars and distinguished personages, journalists and renowned individuals of both of the countries; (5) providing teachers for teaching Chinese language in Nepal; and (6) holding of education exhibitions, book exhibitions, photo exhibitions, trade fairs, and other such activities as may be appropriate for enhancing the understanding between the two countries.

In order to regularize the cultural activities, a Cultural Agreements were signed between Nepal and China. First cultural agreement was signed in 1964 followed by the second in 1999. But cultural exchanges and activities were already begun before these agreements were signed.

Teaching Chinese Language in Nepal

During the tenure of Prime Minister Ranoddip Singh, there was a reference to a Chinese teacher named Dhunkho Chhoo, who was appointed by the Nepal government to teach Chinese language in Nepal and he was given a salary of two hundred and forty rupees per month. It was also reported that during his tenure Prime Minister Bira Shamsher also had appointed a Chinese citizen to teach Chinese language in Nepal.[8]

The School of International Languages was the first institute to initiate teaching foreign languages. It started by teaching French, German, Russian Chinese and Nepali languages at the begenning. Teachers to teach other languages except Chinese were available to start the school in formal way. So Niranjan Bhattarai, the Founder Principal of the school himself had to start the program to teach the Chinese language in the beginning till the Chinese teacher Professor Chang Wei, who was appointed by the Chinese government arrived. The Chinese government provided the travel expenses and salary for him. The teacher lived in the Chinese Embassy premises. The school used to provide a car to take him from the Embassy to the school and back. This arrangement of providing a teacher to the school (now a Campus) continues regularly. The students who have studied Chinese language in the school (Campus) are employed in different business institutions as interpreters and also working as tourist guides to explain the Chinese tourists about the importance of the places renowned as ancient heritage in Kathmandu and other parts of Nepal.

There are now many other institutions run by the government of China or other non-government organizations providing facilities to learn Chinese language to the Nepali students.

Recently under an agreement between the Kathmandu University and the National Office for Teaching Chinese as A Foreign Language has been established inside the premises of Kathmandu University at Balkumari Lalitpur. It is hoped the Confucius Institute will not only provide opportunities for the Nepali students to study the Chinese language in Nepal but also wide open the gate for them to go to China for further studies in Chinese language, literature, culture and also history of Nepal-China relations and other subjects.

In Nepal, non-governmental organizations are also helpful in promoting cultural relation between the two countries.

Exchange programs for academicians and researchers, research and studies on various facets of Nepal-China relation both in Nepal and also in China, organizations of seminars and talk programs on issues of common interest to both the countries with the participation of Nepali used to be organized on local expenses.

The Araniko Society of Nepal and the Dong Fang International Centre for Educational Exchanges and China Scholarship Council, wishing to cooperate on the purpose of promoting educational cooperation and providing services and assistance to Nepali students intending to go to China, signed an MOU to hold a Chinese Education Exhibition in Nepal in April 11-13, 2003 in Kathmandu. Thirty universities of China participated in the exhibition, which provided information regarding the facilities for the Nepali students in their universities. They provided information on the subjects the Nepali students wanted to study, the expenses for the studies, for living expenses in China and other information. About 2,500 students visited the Exhibition, expressed their desire to go to China for their studies and filled necessary forms for admission to some Chinese Universities. Since then the Education Exhibition is being organized every year.

Friendship Associations

The Nepal-China Friendship Association was established in 1953 after the People's Republic of China was established. The Nepali youth, inspired by the emergence of new China, were active in institutionalizing their enthusiasm to promote closer relations with China. Their enthusiasm led them to establish the Nepal-China Friendship Association, the Nepal-China Cultural Council and other such organization with the objective to enhance friendship with China. The Nepal-China Friendship Association is continuing its activities regularly. In China, the Chinese Association of Friendship with Foreign Countries was established to reciprocate the objectives of such friendship organizations in different countries. A China-Nepal Friendship Association also is organized in China recently.

Now there is Nepal China Society, which is engaged in the activities for enhancement of relations with China. The China Study Center is active for promotion of friendship with China since 1999 by publishing books on various aspects of developments in China. The students, who had opportunity to go to China for their studies and were employed in different organizations in Nepal after their return to Nepal, have organized since 1980 an association of alumni named the Araniko Society. The objective of the Society is to promote, enhance and consolidate friendly relations with China by organizing various programs, academic and cultural, by themselves and also if necessary, in co-operation with similar Chinese organizations. They are holding education exhibition every year to facilitate Nepali students to have information about education in different subjects in different Chinese Universities.

In 2002, the Society in co-operation with the White Pagoda Relic Preservation Bureau has established a life size statue of the great Nepali architect Araniko at the premises of the "Bai Ta" Park. A weeklong Nepal festival was also organized on the occasion.

The Araniko Society of Nepal has also installed a bronze image of Manjushree at the central peak of Wu T'ai Shan on the occasion of the 50th anniversary of establishment of diplomatic relation between Nepal and China on the 4th of Bhadra 2062 B.S (2005). in a grand ceremony attended by high-ranking Chinese officials, officials of Araniko Society, distinguished Buddhist Bhikshus and guests.

The Nepal China Executives Council was established with the objectives to promote friendly relations with an emphasis on economic and trade relations in 2003. The Council organizes Trade Fair in Nepal every year inviting many Chinese business companies to facilitate the Nepali business community to have direct contacts with them. It Also helps Nepali business institutions to participates in trade fair in Cina and encurrages and leads many representatives of Nepali institutions engaged in trade and commerce to China to promote mutual contacts and understanding between the business communities of Nepal and China.

End Notes

1. Nepal China Relation. Kathmandu: Institute of Foreign Affairs, 2005, p. 29.
2. Avtar Singh Bhasin. *Nepal's Relations With India And China.* New Delhi: SIBA EXIM PVT. LTD, 1994, pp. 1422-23.
3. Charts, Compiled by Research and Information Division of FNCCI from various publications of Trade Promotion Center and Nepal Rashtra Bank.
4. Nepal-ChinaTrade Relations p23, 2008
5. *Himalayan Times,* 18 July 2002.
6. Report of the 9th Nepal China Nongovernmental Forum, 12-13 June 2007.
7. The latest position of Nepal China Trade.
8. Vijaya Manandhar. *Nepal-China Relations,* Vol. II , New Delhi: Adroit Publisher, 2004, pp. 284-285.

Chapter 12

Conclusion

Nepal-China Relations

Nepal-China relations are very cordial and deep rooted since ages. It is marked by social, religious-cultural, economic and politically close ties. Occasional differences between the two countries are solved by amicable and peaceful means. Thus the friendship between the two nations remains remarkably intact in the history of relations of both the countries.

Contribution of Buddhism in Nepal-China Relation

The relations between Nepal and China were founded on the basis of teachings of Lord Buddha and other aspects of Buddhism developed later and continued till Ming Dynasty. In that period of one and half millennium, development of official or unofficial relation of the two countries had not taken shape in the way as we find them now. The relations, officially established in Tang Dynasty and developed with the support of Buddhist Emperors of the Ming Dynasty, were also short lived.

Of the philosophical ideals founded in the earlier period, Confucian and Taoism had most influential position. They, together with Buddhism, introduced during the Han Dynasty, formed the "Three Doctrines", the main branches of religious and philosophical thoughts in China.

The story of Birth of Buddha reached China in 2 B.C. Since then the Chinese scholars continued taking interest in what Buddha had taught. Buddhism continued then on to be a part of Chinese life and development.

Buddhabhadra of Kapilavastu, Nepal went to China as early as at the beginning of 5th century, to explain the teaching of Lord Buddha. Buddhabhadra and Fa Hsien met in Nanjing, China, and worked together to translate the Buddhist scriptures brought by Fa-

Hsien, from the countries he visited, into Chinese language and consolidated the trend of development of Buddhism in China.

During the Tang Dynasty, Nepali and Chinese Princesses Bhrikuti and Wen Cheng, themselves well versed in Buddhist philosophy, together with their Buddhist scholar-companions Shila Manju and Huo-Shang, respectively, had contributed in introduction and development of Buddhism in Tibet. In this way, they helped Tibet to be developed into a Buddhist kingdom. It was also in the Tang dynasty in 646 exchanges of official delegations took place and official relation between Nepal and China was established.

In the time of Ming Dynasty(1368-1644), the Emperors renewed sending official Missions to Nepal and received Nepali Missions to China. In this period of Ming Dynasty from 1384-1427 China had sent six missions to Nepal had sent seven to China.

During the same period two eminent Nepali Buddhist scholars – Sahaja Shri in 1369 and Shri Sariputra (1335-1421) – visited China and helped the Emperors and Buddhist devotees to enhance understanding of teaching of Buddha and perform rituals of Imperial ceremonies including the coronations.

In the Yuan Dynasty, Araniko the eminent cultural Emissary of Nepal, visited China and contributed in fulfilling the wish of Emperor Kublai Khan to establish Buddhism as the guiding ideal for his Empire by giving concrete shape, in visible form, to the concept of Buddhism. He constructed stupas, temples, and monasteries images of deities and divinities of Buddhist religion and drew attention of the people to Lord Buddha and his teaching. Thus on the one hand he helped the Emperor to establish peace in the empire and on the other provided the people with an object to adhere to and express their devotion and dedication. In this way the genius artist from Nepal visited Tibet and China with the help of Phagpa, the Imperial Preceptor, and became an effective instrumental to spread and consolidate Buddhism in the vast area from Tibet to China.

Being the biggest and oldest Tibetan style Buddhist Stupa in existence now in China, the Great White Pagoda constructed by Araniko is now the only well-preserved cultural relic of the Great Yuan Capital City in Beijing. It has been a great historical monument for the ethnical union of the Han, Mongolian and Tibetan peoples and the unification of the well-established and long standing friendship of China and Nepal.[1]

During the Ming Dynasty (1368-1644), the Emperors renewed sending official Missions to Nepal and received Nepali Missions to

China. In the same period two eminent Nepali Buddhist scholars – Sahajashri and Shri Sariputra – visited China and helped the Emperors and Buddhist devotees to enhance understanding of teaching of Buddha and perform rituals of Imperial ceremonies including the coronations. There was an interruption in exchange of visits for some time.

For a short period of Ch'ing dynasty Nepali Kings used to mint coins for Tibet also. The coins used to be made of silver and Tibetans used to pay for it in gold. But some rulers thought it to be profitable to mix more alloy with the silver. After some time an issue about the rate of exchange for pure silver coins and the coins mixed with alloy arose. It created differences between Nepal and Tibet to an insoluble extent. Then upon the request of Tibet Chinese government sent an army to fight against Nepal. When both the warring sides found it difficult to continue the war an agreement was reached in 1792 to stop the war. China decided to mint coins for Tibet also to solve the problem of coinage forever. Then Nepal and China decided to exchange political missions and normalize relations between them. The Nepali side sent Quinquennial missions every five years and the Chinese missions used to come to Nepal on various important occasions. These exchanges of missions were helpful to maintain goodwill of one country to another and promote friendship between the two countries.

In 1911, after the Imperial system was abolished and Republican Government was established in China, the traditional relations between Nepal and China continued. The exchange of visits of Buddhists and special official mission took place on various occasions.

The Republican government of China dispatched a mission under the leadership of Pa Wenchun, Councilor of the Committee of Mongolian and Tibetan affairs, to renew in an ay stalled relations with Nepal government in May 1930.

In 1946, a goodwill mission led by Chung Lienshen visited Nepal and presented a letter and gifts from the Chinese Government to the Nepal government and extended goodwill on behalf of the Republic of China. [2]

In response to the gesture from the Chinese government Nepal sent in 1947 a mission composed of six members headed by General Krishna Shamsher to convey good- will of Nepal to China, explore the possibility of establishment of diplomatic relations between the two countries and open ways to promote mutual relations further.

Renewal of Relations

After the People's Republic was established, exchanges of visits of Buddhist delegations have continued. A Chinese Buddhist delegation led by the President of Chinese Buddhist Association Chao Puchu visited Nepal to take part in its program in the 4th International Buddhist Conference of the World Fellowship of Buddhists hosted by the Dharmodaya Sabha of Nepal in 1956. Dr. Ambedkar, a prominent constitutionalist of India, who was a member of the oppressed class according to Hindu religion and converted himself to the Buddhist religion, also had come to participate in the Conference. The Chinese delegation visited Lumbini and Kapilavastu and paid respect to the places of Pilgrimage related to life of Buddha in Nepal. They at that time pledged to extend Chinese assistance for the development of Lumbini and near by areas where Buddha had spent parts of his life when he was young and returning after his enlightenment. The Chinese delegation after that left for India to participate in celebrations of the 2500th Anniversary of birth of Buddha.[3]

A Nepali delegation of Dharmodaya Sabha led by Mahasthavira Bhikshu Amritanand visited China in 1959. They visited the Bai T'a Shi constructed by Araniko and other Buddhist institutions in Beijing and other parts of China. The Buddhist Association had presented to Bhikshu Amritananda a copy of the book 'Chao Xiaing Liang Tu Ching' (on proportions and measures to make images of deities and divinities), in which Arniko's name and works are appreciatively mentioned.

A second Nepali delegation visited China in 1964 on the occasion of the inauguration of the newly constructed temple for enshrinement of the Tooth Relic of Lord Buddha.[4]

The Buddhists of Nepal and China have continued to visit their respective countries and benefited by exchanging opinions on Buddhist philosophy, coordinating their activities in maintaining and enhancement of learning Buddhism and applying it in their lives. The tenets of Buddhism were the foundation of Nepal-China relations since ancient times and continue in better shape and size till now.

The Government of the People's Republic has donated twenty million Rupees to construct a Chinese temple at Lumbini. It is active in disseminating Buddha's teaching to the people who visit Lumbini from different countries. The temple also has a book on two thousand years of development of Buddhism in China. Chinese Bhikshus of the temple explain the historical events of development of Buddhism in China. Thus Buddhism is still playing important part to promote peaceful relations between Nepal and China.

Development of China in other spheres

China is a continuous society and self developed civilization with its own social, cultural, spiritual and scientific characteristics. This tradition continues from the appearance of Beijing man to this day when China has put a manned- vehicle in the orbit and got it landed at an intended place and time. Thus China has proved its capability to move with time from stone age to space age.

Enhencment of Relations

After the emergence of the People's Republic, the objectives of enhencment of relations appeared in a new form and both the Governments of Nepal and China arranged their activities as demanded by the time.

Establishment of diplomatic relations between Nepal and the People's Republic of China in 1955 on the basis of Panchashila, five Principles of Peaceful Coexistence, propounded by Indian Prime Minister Jawaharlal Nehru and Chinese Premier Chou Enlai, followed by the Bandung-spirit which was very much influential agenda in the world in order to promote beneficial relations among the big and small countries the relations between these two ancient countries have developed by every passing day.

The Agreement signed in 1956 on Trade and Intercourse between Nepal and the Tibetan Autonomous Region of China, besides making provisions for mutual benefits, has abrogated the treaties, which had become obsolete and already unsuitable for new situation and given impetus to move forward on the basis of equality and mutual understanding. The Treaty of Peace and Friendship signed by Prime Ministers B. P. Koirala and Chou Enlai has consolidated age-old friendship and peace between the two countries. The boundary Treaty signed by King Mahendra and President Liu Shaochi in 1961 has settled for ever the border problems. The Treaty has helped to establish a border delineated by most up-to-date scientific methods and allowed both the sides to enjoy a peaceful border permanently.

The frequency of visits of Heads of State/Government of the two countries to each others' countries and exchanges of opinions between them on the issues concerning relations between the two countries and other matters of mutual interest, have been a sort of regular phenomenon. Kings Mahendra and Birendra and Presidents Li Xiannian and Jiang Zemin, Premier Chou Enlai, Deputy Premier Deng Xiaoping, premiers Li Feng and Zhu Rongji from China and Prime Ministers Tanka Prasad Acharya, Bishweshwar Prasad Koirala, Kirti Nidhi Bishta, Girija Prasad Koirala, Mana Mohan Adhikari and Sher Bahadur Deuba from Nepal have regularly exchanged their visits. Besides high officials of other Government and non-government organizations and distinguished persons have made their mutual visits to each other's countries in regular manner.

Recent visit of Pushpa Kamal Dahal Prachanda, newly elced Prime minister after Nepal became a Federal Democratic Republic, has made great contributions to renew and update the relation to suit the revolutionary changes recently taken place in Nepal. Prime Minister Dahal has also invited Prsident Hu Jintao and Premier Wen Jiabao of China to visit Nepal so that the leaders of the two countries could continue exchanges of opinions for consolidation and enhancement of bilateral relations further.

These visits and exchanges of opinions between them on such occasions have helped to promote understanding between the two countries and contributed to enhance trust and confidence among the leading personages.

The policy of peaceful coexistence and non-alignment of Nepal is appreciated by China. The treaties and agreements signed in the period of over fifty years period after the establishment of diplomatic relation have facilitated peaceful cooperation between the two neighbors. China extends economic assistance to Nepal for its development works and supports Nepal Government on issues of common interest in international affairs.

Nepal also had helped to get People's Republic of China readmitted at the United Nations and its agencies and different international forum when the People's Republic was in need of such assistance and the cooperation continues further. Nepal has supported China to get associated to SAARC as Observer.

Chinese Government treats governments formed by different parties in Nepal equally without any discrimination and continues cooperations for development in the interest of Nepal. China does not interfere in enternal affairs of Nepal so receives great regards equally from every government.

Nepal has maintained its pledge for its one China policy and is determined not to let any one to wage hostile acts from its territory against any of its two neighbors India China. It suppressed the rebels who had entered Nepali territory from Tibet and waging sporadic hostilities against China in 1974. Nepal is also cooperating with India to suppress terrorist in border area of the two countries. Thus Nepal has made all possible efforts to keep the borders in South and North and the surrounding areas peaceful. The Government and people are conscious and alert to maintain this peaceful situation.

Nepal regards China to be a reliable friend. China admires and appreciates the non-aligned foreign policy of Nepal and respects it as a good neighbor. There is very good understanding between the two countries, and there exists no problem. Whenever a problem crops up, the two countries consult each other and find mutually satisfactory solutions immediately. Both Nepal and China are committed to the peaceful means of solving the issues.

Nepal and China maintain these commitments and scrupulously observe and fulfill the Treaty obligations. They are meticulously nurturing their mutual relationship and therefore further development of their friendship is considered to remain beneficial for both the neighbors as at present and also in the future.

End Notes

1. Beijing White Pagoda Temple Administrative Office: A Brief Picture Biography of Arniger, 2008
2. Vijay Kumar Manandhar. *Nepal China Relations.* Vol. II, Delhi: Adroit Publishers, 2004, p. 172.
3. *Report of International Buddhist Conference*: Kathmandu: Dharmodaya Sabha, 1956.
4. *The Buddha's Tooth Relic Pagoda.* Beijing: Buddhist Association of China, 1966.

Appendix 1

Chronological Table of Chinese Dynasties

Hsia	21st–16th century B.C.
Shang	16th–11th century B.C.
Western Chou	11th century – 771 B.C.
Eastern Chou	770–221 B.C.
Spring and Autumn Period	770–475 B.C.
Warring States Period	45–221 B.C.
Chin	221–206 B.C.
Western Han	206 B.C.– A.D. 24
Eastern Han	25–220
Three Kingdoms	220–280
Wei	220–265
Shu	221–263
Wu	222–280
Western Tsin	265–316
Eastern Tsin	317–420
Southern and Northern Dynasties	420–589
Sung	420–49
Chi	479–502
Liang	502–557
Chen	557–589
Northern Dynasties	386–581
Northern Wei	386–534
Eastern Wei	534–550
Western Wei	535–557
Northern Chi	550–577
Northern Chou	557–581
Sui	581–618
Tang	618–907
Five Dynasties	907–960

Later Liang	907–923
Later Tang	923–936
Later Tsin	936–947
Later Han	947–950
Later Chou	951–960
Northern Sung	960–1127
Southern Sung	1127–1279
Yuan (Mongol)	1279–1368
Ming	1368–1644
Ching (Manchu)	1644–1911

Appendix 2

Establishment of Diplomatic Relation

Join Communiqué on the Establishment of Diplomatic Relations, Kathmandu, August 1, 1955.

The negotiations conducted in Kathmandu from July 27th 1955 between the Delegation of the Government of the People's Republic of China and the Delegation of the Government of the Kingdom of Nepal for the establishment of diplomatic relations between the two countries have now been concluded successfully. The negotiations were carried on in a very cordial and friendly atmosphere and it has been agreed as follows:

The two Governments desirous of establishing friendly relations between the two countries have agreed to establish normal diplomatic relations and to exchange ambassadors between the People's Republic of China and the Kingdom of Nepal. The two Governments have further agreed that the following five principles, namely:

One Mutual respect for each other's territorial integrity and sovereignty,

Two Non-aggressions,

Three Non-interference in each other's internal affairs for any reason of economic, political or ideological character

Four Equality and mutual benefit;

Five Peaceful Co-existence.

Should form the basic principles to guide the relations between the two countries.

The two Governments believe that the establishment of diplomatic relations will also promote further development in the cultural and economic fields between the two countries.[1]

1. Bhasin p. 553.

Appendix 3

Trade and Intercourse with China s Autonomous Region of Tibet

Agreement between Nepal and China to maintain friendly relations and on trade and intercourse between Nepal and the Tibetan region of China,

Kathmandu, September 20, 1956.

(RATIFIED ON JANUARY 17, 1958)

The Government of the People's Republic of China and the Government of the Kingdom of Nepal,

Being desirous of further developing the friendly relations between the two countries as good neighbors on the basis of the long-standing friendship between the two peoples,

Reaffirm that the five principles of Panchshila

One Mutual respect for each other's territorial integrity and sovereignty;

Two Non-aggression;

Three Non-interference in each other's internal affairs for any reason of an economic, political or ideological character;

Four Equality and mutual benefit; and

Five Peaceful co-existence;

should be the fundamental principles guiding the relations between the two countries.

The two parties have resolved to conclude the present agreement in accordance with the above-mentioned principles and have for this purpose appointed as their respective plenipotentiaries:

The Government of the People's Republic of China,

His Excellency Pan Tzu-li,

Ambassador Extraordinary and Plenipotentiary of the People's Republic of China to the Kingdom of Nepal;

The Government of the Kingdom of Nepal,

His Excellency Chuda Prasad Sharma,
Minister for Foreign Affairs of the Kingdom of Nepal,
Who, having examined each other's credentials and finding them in good and due form, Have agreed upon the following:

Article One

The high contracting parties declare that peace and friendship shall be maintained between the People's Republic of China and the Kingdom of Nepal.

Article Two

The high contracting parties hereby reaffirm their decision to mutually exchange diplomatic representatives on ambassadorial level.

Article Three

All treaties and documents which existed in the past between China and Nepal including those between the Tibet Region of China and Nepal are hereby abrogated.

Article Four

In order to maintain and develop the traditional contacts between the peoples of the Tibet Region of China and Nepal, the High Contracting parties agree that the nationals of both parties may trade, travel and make pilgrimage in those places in each other's territory as agreed upon by both parties, and the two parties agree to safeguard the proper interests of the nationals of the other party in its territory in accordance with the laws of the country of residence, and for this purpose the High Contracting parties agree to do as follows:

Paragraph one - The High Contracting parties mutually agree to establish trade agencies:

One The Chinese Government agrees that the Government of Nepal may establish trade agencies at Shighatse, Kyerong and Nyalam;

Two The Government of Nepal agrees that the Chinese Government may establish an equal number of trade agencies in Nepal, the specific locations of which will be discussed and determined at a later date by both parties;

Three The trade agencies of both parties shall be accorded the same status and same treatment. The trade agents of both parties shall enjoy freedom from arrest while exercising their functions, and shall enjoy in respect of themselves, their wives and their children who are dependent on them for livelihood freedom from search.

The trade agencies of both parties shall enjoy the privileges and immunities for couriers, mailbags and communications in code.

Paragraph Two - The High Contracting parties agree that traders of both countries may trade at the following places:

One The Chinese Government agrees to specify (1) Lhasa, (2) Shigatse, (3) Gyantse and (4) Yatung as markets for trade;

Two The Government of Nepal agrees that when with the development of Chinese trade in Nepal, it becomes necessary to specify markets for trade in Nepal, the Government of Nepal will specify and equal number of markets for trade in Nepal;

Three Traders of both countries known to be customarily and specially engaged in border trade between the Tibet Region of China and Nepal may continue trade at the traditional markets for such trade.

Paragraph Three - The High Contracting parties agree that pilgrimage by religious believers of either country to the other may continue according to religious custom. Personal baggage and articles used for pilgrimage carried by the pilgrims of either party shall be exempted from taxation by the other party.

Paragraph four - For traveling across the border between the Tibet Region of China and Nepal, the High Contracting parties agree that the nationals of both countries shall use the customary routes.

Paragraph five - For traveling across the border by the nationals of the two countries, the High Contracting parties agree to adopt the following provisions:

One Diplomatic personnel and officials of the two countries and nationals of the two countries except those provided by subparagraphs two, three and four, who travel across the border between the Tibet region of China and Nepal, shall hold passports issued by their respective countries and visaed (visa stamped) by the other party. Nationals of two countries who enter the Tibet Region of China or Nepal through a third country shall also hold passports issued by their respective countries and visaed by the other party.

Two Traders of the two countries know to be customarily and specifically engaged in trade between the Tibet Region of China and Nepal, their wives and children dependent on them for livelihood and their attendants, not covered by sub-paragraph three of this paragraph, who enter into the Tibet Region of China or Nepal as the case may be for the purposes of trade, shall hold passports issued by their respective countries and visaed by the other party or certificates issued by their respective governments or by organs authorized by their respective governments.

Three Inhabitants of the border districts of the two countries who cross the border to carry on petty trade, to visit friends or relatives, or for seasonal changes of residence, may do so as they have customarily done heretofore and need not hold passports, visas or other documents of certification.

Four Pilgrims of either party who travel across the border between the Tibet Region of China and Nepal for the purposes of pilgrimage and need not hold passports, visas or other documents of certification, but shall register at the border check posts or the first encountered authorized government office of the other party, and obtain permits for pilgrimage there from.

Five Notwithstanding the provisions of the foregoing sub-paragraphs of this paragraph, either Government may refuse entry to any particular person.

Six Nationals of either country who enter the territory of the other party in accordance with the foregoing sub-paragraphs of this paragraph may stay within the territory only after complying with the procedures specified by the other party.

Article Five

This Agreement shall be ratified. It shall come into effect after mutual notice of ratifications, and remain in force for eight (8) years. Extension of the present Agreement may be negotiated by the two parties if either party requests for it six (6) months prior to the expiry of the Agreement and the request is agreed to by the other party.

Done in Kathmandu on the 20th day of September 1956, in duplicate in the Chinese, Nepali and English languages, all texts being equally authentic.

Sd/-	Sd/-
CHUDA PRASAD SHARMA	PAN TZU-LI
Plenipotentiary of the Government of the Kingdom of Nepal.	Plenipotentiary of the Government of the People's Republic of China.

Appendix 4

Sino-Nepali Treaty of Peace and Friendship, Kathmandu, April 28, 1960.

The Chairman of the People's Republic of China and His Majesty the King of Nepal, desiring to maintain and further develop peace and friendship between the People's Republic of China and the Kingdom of Nepal,

Convinced that the strengthening of good-neighbourly relations and friendly co-operation between the People's Republic of China and the Kingdom of Nepal is in accordance with the fundamental interests of the peoples of the two countries and conducive to the consolidation of peace in Asia and the world,

Have decided for this purpose to conclude the present Treaty in accordance with the Five Principles of Peaceful Co-existence jointly affirmed by the two countries, and have appointed as their respective Plenipotentiaries:

The Chairman of the People's Republic of China:

Premier Chou En-lai of the State Council,

His Majesty the King of Nepal:

Prime Minister Bishweshwar Prasad Koirala.

The above-mentioned plenipotentiaries,

Having examined each other's credentials and found them in good and due form,

Have agreed upon the following:

Article I

The Contracting Parties recognize and respect the independence, sovereignty and territorial integrity of each other.

Article II

The Contracting Parties will maintain and develop peaceful and friendly relations between the People's Republic of China and the Kingdom of Nepal. They undertake to settle all disputes between them by mean of peaceful negotiation.

Article III

The Contracting Parties agree to develop and further strengthen the economic and cultural ties between the two countries in a spirit of friendship and co-operation, in accordance with the principles of equality and mutual benefit and of non-interference in each other's internal affairs.

Article IV

Any difference or dispute arising out of the interpretation or application of the present treaty shall be settled by negotiation through normal diplomatic channel.

Article V

This present Treaty is subject to ratification and the instruments of ratification will be exchanged in Peking as soon as possible.

The present Treaty will come into force immediately on the exchange of the instruments of ratification and will remain in force for a period of ten years.

Unless either of the Contracting Parties gives to the other notice in writing to terminate the Treaty at least one year before the expiration of this period, it will remain in force without any specified time limit, subject to the right of either of the Contracting Parties to terminate it by giving to the other in writing a year's notice of its intention to do so.

Done in duplicate in Kathmandu on the twenty-eighth day of April 1960, in the Chinese, Nepali and English languages, all texts being equally authentic.

Plenipotentiary of the People's Republic of China	Plenipotentiary of the Kingdom of Nepal
Sd/- CHOU EN-LAI	Sd/- B.P. KOIRALA

Appendix 5

Sino-Nepal Boundary Agreement, Peking, March 21, 1960.

The Government of the People's Republic of China and His Majesty's Government of Nepal have noted with satisfaction

That the two countries have always respected the existing traditional customary boundary line and lived in amity.

With a view to bringing about the formal settlement of some existing discrepancies in the boundary line between the two countries and

The Scientific delineation and formal demarcation of the whole boundary line, and

To consolidating and further developing friendly relations between the two countries,

The two Governments have decided to conclude the present Agreement under the guidance of the Five Principles of Peaceful Co-existence and

Have agreed upon the following:

Article I

The Contracting Parties have agreed that the entire boundary between the two countries shall be scientifically delineated and formally demarcated through friendly consultations, on the basis of the existing traditional customary line.

Article II

In order to determine the specific alignment of the boundary line and to enable the fixing of the boundary between the two countries in legal form, the Contracting Parties have decided to set up a Joint Committee composed of an equal number of delegates from each side and enjoin the Committee, in accordance with the provisions of Article III of the present Agreement, to discuss and solve the concrete problems concerning the Sino- Nepali boundary, conduct survey of the boundary, erect boundary markers, and draft a Sino- Nepali Boundary Treaty. The Joint Committee will hold its meetings in the capitals or other places of China and Nepal.

Article III

Having studied the delineation of the boundary line between the two countries as shown on the maps mutually exchanged (for the map submitted by the Chinese side, see attached Map 1; for the map submitted by the Nepali side, see attached Map 2)....[1] and the information furnished by each side about its actual jurisdiction over the area bordering on the other country, the Contracting Parties deem that, except for discrepancies in certain sections, their understanding of the traditional customary line is basically the same. The Contracting Parties have decided to determine concretely the boundary between the two countries in the following ways in accordance with three different cases:

1. Section where the delineation of the boundary line between the two countries on the maps of the two sides is identical:
   In these sections the boundary line shall be fixed according to the identical delineation on the maps of the two sides. The Joint Committee will send out joint survey teams composed of an equal number of persons from each side to conduct survey on the spot and erect boundary markers.

   After the boundary line in these sections is fixed in accordance with the provisions of the above paragraph, the territory north of the line will conclusively belong to China, while the territory south of the line will conclusively belong to Nepal, and neither Contracting Party will any longer lay claim to certain areas within the territory of the other Party.
2. Sections where the delineation of the boundary line between the two countries on the maps of the two sides is not identical, whereas the state of actual jurisdiction by each side is undisputed:

   The Joint Committee will send out joint survey teams composed of an equal number of persons from each side to conduct surveys on the spot, determine the boundary line and erect boundary markers in these sections, in accordance with concrete terrain features (watersheds, valleys, passes etc.) and the actual jurisdiction by each side.

3. Sections where the delineation of the boundary line between the two countries on the maps of the two sides is not identical and the two sides differ in their understanding of the state of actual jurisdiction:

   The Joint Committee will send out joint teams composed of an equal number of persons from each side to ascertain on the spot the state of actual jurisdiction in these sections, make adjustments in accordance with the principles of equality, mutual benefit, friendship and mutual accommodation, determine the boundary line and erect boundary markers in these sections.

Article IV

The Contracting Parties have decided that, in order to ensure tranquility and friendliness on the border, each side will no longer dispatch armed personnel to patrol the area on its side within twenty kilometers of the border, but only maintain its administrative personnel and civil police there.

Article V

The present Agreement is subject to ratification and the instruments of ratification shall be exchanged in Kathmandu as soon as possible.

The present Agreement will come into force immediately on the exchange of the instruments of ratification and will automatically cease to be in force when the Sino-Nepali boundary treaty to be signed by the two Governments comes into force.

Done in duplicate in Peking on the twenty-first day of March 1960, in the Chinese, Nepali and English language, all texts being equally authentic.

Sd/-	Sd/-
CHOU EN-LAI	B.P. KOIRALA
Plenipotentiary of the	Plenipotentiary of
People's Republic of China	His Majesty's Government of Nepal

Appendix 6

Boundary Treaty, Peking, October 5, 1961

The Chairman of the People's Republic of China and His Majesty the King of Nepal

Being of the agreed opinion that formal settlement of the question of the boundary between China and Nepal is of fundamental interest to the peoples of the two countries;

Noting with satisfaction that the friendly relations of long standing between the two countries have undergone further development since the establishment of diplomatic relations between the two countries, and

That the two parties have, in accordance with the Five Principles of Peaceful Co-existence and in a spirit of fairness, reasonableness, mutual understanding and mutual accommodation,

Smoothly achieved and overall settlement of the boundary question between the two countries through friendly consultations;

Firmly believing that the formal delimitation of the entire boundary between the two countries and its consolidation as a boundary of peace and friendship not only constitute a milestone in the further development of the friendly relations between China and Nepal, but also are a contribution towards strengthening peace in Asia and the world;

Have resolved for this purpose to conclude the present Treaty on the basis of the Agreement between the Government of the People's Republic of China and His Majesty's Government of Nepal.

On the Question of the Boundary between the two countries of March 21, 1960 and Have agreed upon the following:

Article I

The Contracting Parties, basing themselves on the traditional customary boundary line and having jointly conducted necessary on the spot investigations and surveys and made certain adjustments in accordance with the principles of equality, mutual benefit, friendship and mutual accommodation, hereby agree on the following alignment of the entire boundary line from west to east, Chinese territory being north of the line and Nepali territory south thereof:

1. The Chinese-Nepali boundary line starts from the point where the watershed between the Kali River and the Tinkar River meets the watershed between the tributaries of the Mapchu (Karnali) River on the one hand and the Tinkar River on the other hand, thence it runs southeastwards along the watershed between the tributaries of the Mapchu (Karnali) River on the one hand and the Tinkar River and the Seti River on the other hand, passing through Niumachisa (Lipudhura) snowy mountain ridge and Tinkarlipu (Lipudhura) Pass to Pehlin (Urai) Pass.
2. From Pehlin (Urai) Pass, the boundary line runs along the mountain ridge southeastwards for about 500 meters, then northeastwards to Height 5655 meters, thence continues to run along the mountain ridge northwestwards to Tojang (Tharodhunga Tuppa), then northeastwards passing through Height 5580.6 meters to Chimala Pass, thence it runs generally northwestwards,, passing through Chimala to Lungmochiehkuo (Numoche Tuppa); thence the boundary line runs generally eastwards, passing through paimowotunkuo (Kitko Tuppa) and then runs along chokartung (Kitko) mountain spur down to the Chilungpa (Yadangre) stream, then it follows the Chilungpa (Yadangre) stream northwards to its junction with the Mapchu (Karnali) River, then it follows the Mapchu Karnali River generally eastwards to Yusa (Hilsa). At Yusa (Hilsa) the boundary line departs from the Mapchu (Karnali) River and runs northeastwards along the mountain spur up to Chialosa (Takule), then along the mountain ridge, passing through Kumalatse (Kumalapche), Kangpaochekuo (Ghanbochheko) and Mainipaimikuo (Manepamango) to Kangkuona (Kangarje) then northwards passing through Kangchupeng (Kandumbu) and Height 6550 meters to Nalakankar.
3. From Nalakankar, the boundary line runs generally

northeastwards along the watershed between the tributaries flowing into the Manasarowar Lake and the tributaries of the Humla Karnali River passing through Nalakankar Pass to Latsela (Lapche) Pass; thence it runs generally southeastwards along the watershed between the tributaries flowing into the Manasaroar Lake and the tributaries of the Machuan River on the one hand and the tributaries of the Humla Karnali River, the Mugu Karnali River and the Panjang Khola on the other hand, passing through Changla mountain, Namja Pass, Khung (Thau) Pass and Marem Pass to Pindu Pass, then it continues to run southeastwards along the watershed between the tributaries of the Machuan River on the one hand and the tributaries of the Barbung River and the Kali Gandaki River on the other hand gradually turning northeastwards to Height 6214.1 meters.

4. From Height 6214.1 meters, the boundary line runs northeastwards along the mountain spur, passing through Height 5025 meters and crossing the Angarchubo (Angarchhu) stream to Height 5029 meters; thence it runs generally eastwards along Tuchu (Thukchu) mountain spur passing through Height 4730 meters and Bungla (Panglham) to the foot of Tingli Bhodho spur at its northwestern end, then turn northeastwards and runs along the southern bank of the Roumachushui (Rhamarchhushu) seasonal stream to the foot of Tingli Bhodho spur at its northeastern end; thence turns southeastwards, crosses the junction of two seasonal streams flowing northwards, and runs to the junction of three seasonal streams flowing northwards, and then up the eastern stream of the above three seasonal streams to Height 4697.9 meters, then turns southwestwards crossing a seasonal stream to Height 4605.8 meters; thence it runs generally southeastwards passing through Pengpengla (Phumphula) and then along Chukomaburi (Chhukomapoj) mountain ridge, passing through Height 4676.6 meters and Height 4754.9 meters to Height 4796.6 meters, thence along the mountain ridge northeastwards passing through Hsiabala, then generally eastwards passing through Height 5044.1 meters to Chaklo.
5. From Chaklo, the boundary line runs generally southwards along the watershed between the tributaries of the Yalu

Tsangpo River and the tributaries of the Kali Gandaki river, passing through Height 6724 meters to Lugula Pass, thence it runs generally eastwards along Lugula snowy Mountain and the watershed between the tributaries of the Yalu Tsangpo River and the tributaries of the Marshiyangdi River to Gya (Gyala) Pass.

6. From Gya (Gyala) Pass, the boundary line runs along the mountain ridge eastwards to Height 5782 meters, then southeastwards to Lajing Pass, then it runs along Lajing mountain ridge, passing through Height 5442 meters and Lachong (Lajung) pass to height 5236 meters, then turns southwestwards to Sangmudo snowy mountain; thence generally southeastwards and continues to run along Lajing mountain ridge, passing through Height 6139 meters to height 5494 meters, and then in a straight line crosses the Dougar (Tom) River to Height 5724 meter; thence the boundary line runs generally northeastwards along the snowy mountain ridge, passing through Height 6010 meters, Height 5360 meters and Height 5672 meter to Thaple Pass.
7. From Thaple pass, the boundary line runs generally northeastwards along the snowy mountain ridge, passing through Tsariyangkang snowy mountain to Khojan; thence it continues to run generally southwards along the snowy mountain ridge, passing through Mailatsaching pass, pashuo snowy mountain and Langpo snowy mountain to Yangrenkangri (Yangra) snowy mountain.
8. From Yangrenkangri (Yangra) snowy mountain, the boundary line runs along the mountain ridge southwards to Tsalasungkuo and then generally eastwards and then northeastwards along a dry stream bed and passes through Jirapo (Kerabas) to reach the Sangching (Sanjen) River, then follows that river southeastwards, passes through its junction with the Changchieh (Bhryange) River and continues to follow the Sangching (Sanjen) River to a point where a small mountain spur south of Genjungma (Pangshung) pasture ground and north of Chhaharey pasture ground meets with the Sangching (Sanjen) River; then it runs along the above small mountain spur eastwards and then southeastwards to Height 4656.4 meters, then runs eastwards to the back top; thence it runs

along a mountain spur to the junction of the Bhurlung River and the Tanghsiaka (Khesadhang) stream, then runs eastwards along the Bhurlung River to its junction with the Kyerong River; thence follows the Kyerong River southwards and then eastwards to its junction with the Tungling Tsangpo (Lende) River; then runs northeastwards up the Tungling Tsangpo (Lende) River, passing through Rasua Bridge to the junction of the Tungling Tsangpo (Lende) River and the Guobashiachu (Jambu) stream; thence turns eastwards up the Guobashiachu (Jambu) stream, passing through the junction of the Chusumdo Tsangpo River and the Phuriphu Tsangpo River, both the tributaries of the upper Guobashiachu (Jambu) stream to reach the boundary marker point at Chusumdo.

9. From the boundary marker point at Chusumdo, the boundary line runs generally southeastwards along the ridge of Tsogakangri (Seto Pokhari) snowy mountain, Langtang snowy mountain, Dorley mountain and Gulinchin (Phurbo Chyachu) mountain to Chakesumu (Kharaney) mountain; thence runs down to reach the Changnibachu (Kharaney) River and then follows that river southwards to its junction with the Bhochu (Bhote Kosi) River; then follows the Bhochu (Bhote Kosi River southwards, passing through Dalaima (Bhaise) Bridge to the junction of the Bhochu (Bhote Kosi) River and the Junchu (Jum) River; thence eastwards up the Junchu (Jum) River to its source at Tsaje Mountain (Jum Khola Ko Sir Ko Tuppa); thence the boundary line runs generally northwards along the mountain ridge to Chomo Parmari (Height 6208.8 Meters).
10. From Chomo Pamari (Height 6208.8 meters), the boundary line runs generally northwards along the mountain ridge to Height 5914.8 meters, then generally northeastwards along Shonodemo Kangri (Sudemo) snowy mountain passing through Height 5148 meters, and then crosses two tributaries of the Shondemo Chu (Shongdemo) Stream, passing through Shondemo (Sudemo) which lies between the above two tributaries to Gyanbayan, then it runs along Gyanbayan mountain spur downwards, crosses the Pinbhu Tsangpo River (the western tributary of the Lapche River), and then along the mountain spur up to Height 5370.5 meters at Sebobori (Korlang Pari Ko Tippa); thence the boundary line turns

southeastwards along the mountain spur downwards, crosses the Lapche Khung Tsangpo River (the eastern tributary of the Lapche River), then it runs along Bidin Kangri (Piding) snowy mountain to Height 5397.2 meters; thence the boundary line turns westwards along the mountain ridge to height 5444.2 meters at Kobobori (Raling), then generally southwards along Rasumkungpo (Rishinggumbo) mountain ridge to Niehlu (Niehle) Bridge.

11. From Niehlu (Niule) Bridge, the boundary line runs generally eastwards to Chejenma (Gauri Shankar), and then eastwards along the mountain ridge and then northwards along the watershed between the Rongshar River and the Rongbuk River on the one hand and the tributaries of the Duydhkosi River on the other hand to Nangpa pass, and then runs generally southeastwards along the mountain (Gnire Langur), Mount Jolmo Lungma (Sagar Matha) and Lhotse, to Makalu mountain; then runs southeastwards and then eastwards along the mountain ridge to Popti Pass.
12. From Popti pass, the boundary line runs along the mountain ridge eastwards passing through Tsagala (Kepu Dada) to Kharala (Khade Dada), and then generally northeastwards passing through Lanapo (Lhanakpu) and Chebum (Chhipung) to the source of the Sunchunchu (Shumjung) River; then it follows the Sunchunchu (Shumjung) River to its junction with the track leading from Kimathangka to Chentang, then it runs along the track to the bridge on the Karma Tsangpo (Kama) River; thence it runs generally southeastwards along the Karma Tsangpo (Kama) River passing through its junction with the Pengchu (Arun) River, and along the Pengchu (Arun) River to its junction with the Nadang River, then continues to follow the Pengchu (Arun) River westwards to its junction with the Tsokangchingpo (Chhokang) River; thence the boundary line departs from the pengchu (Arun) River and runs generally eastwards along a mountain spur passing through Angde and Dalai (Tale) pass to Dalaila (Tale), and then runs along the mountain ridge passing through Jungkan (Dukan), Kaijungkan (Khachunkha), Renlangbu (Relinbu) and Sulula to reach Ragla (Rakha) pass.
13. From Ragla (Rakha) pass, the boundary line runs generally

eastwards along the watershed between the tributaries of the Nadang River and the tributaries of the Yaru River on the one hand and the tributaries of the Tamur River on the other hand, passing through Ombola (Ombak) pass, Theputala (Tiptala) pass, Yangmakhangla (Kangla) pass and Chabukla to the terminal point where the watershed between the Khar River and the Chabuk River meets the watershed between the Khar River and the Lhonak River.

The entire boundary line between the two countries as described in the present Article is shown on the 1:500,000 maps of the entire boundary attached to the present Treaty; the location of the temporary boundary markers erected by both sides and the detailed alignment of certain sections of the boundary are shown on the 1:50,000 maps of those section attached to the present Treaty.

Article II

The Contracting Parties have agreed that wherever the boundary follows a river, the midstream line shall be the boundary. In case a boundary river changes its course, the original line of the boundary shall remain unchanged in the absence of other agreements between the two parties.

Article III

After the signing of the present Treaty, the Chinese-Nepali Joint Boundary Committee constituted in pursuance of the Agreement of March 21, 1960 between the two parties on the question of the boundary between the two countries shall set up permanent boundary markers as necessary on the boundary line between the two countries, and then draft a protocol setting forth in detail the alignment of the entire boundary line and the location of the permanent boundary markers, with detailed maps attached thereto showing the boundary line and the location of the permanent boundary markers. The above-mentioned protocol, upon being signed by the Governments of the two countries, shall become an annex to the present Treaty and the detailed maps shall replace the maps now attached to the present Treaty.

Upon the singing of the above-mentioned protocol, the tasks of the Chinese-Nepali Joint Boundary Committee shall be terminated, and the Agreement of March 21, 1960 between the two parties on the question of the boundary between the two countries shall cease to be in force.

Article IV

The Contracting parties have agreed that any dispute concerning the boundary, which may arise after the formal delimitation of the boundary between the two countries shall be settled by the two parties through friendly consultations.

Article V

The present Treaty shall come into force on the day of the signing of the Treaty.

Done in duplicate in Peking on October 5,1961 in the Chinese, Nepali and English languages, all three texts being equally authentic.

Sd/-	Sd/-
LIU SHAO-CHI	MAHENDRA BIR BIKRAM SHAH DEVA
Chairman of the People's Republic of China	His Majesty the King of Nepal

Appendix 7

Trade Agreement, Kathmandu, May 19, 1964.

His Majesty's Government of Nepal and the Government of the People's Republic of China (hereinafter referred to as the contracting parties)

For the purpose of further developing the friendship between the two countries and strengthening the economic and trade relations between the two countries,

Especially the traditional trade relations between Nepal and the Tibet Region of China,

Have on the basis of equality and mutual benefit, agreed as follows:

Article I

The two Contracting parties shall take all appropriate measures to develop the trade between their two countries, and agree to promote the exchange of goods between them.

Article II

The trade between the two countries may be conducted through the state trading organizations in Nepal and China, as well as through other importers and exporters of the two countries.

Article III

The exchange of goods between the two countries shall be conducted in accordance with their respective laws, regulations and procedures regarding import and export and foreign exchange regulations in force from time to time in the two countries.

Article IV

The trade between the two countries shall be based, as for as possible, on the principle of equilibrium between the total values of imports and exports.

The two Contracting parties shall, through periodical consultations, determine what goods one country can make available to the other; and they shall mutually accord to each other as favorable treatment as possible in respect of the issuance of import and export licenses for such goods.

Article V

The two Contracting parties shall grant to each other the most-favored nation treatment in all matters relating to customs duties and other taxes, fees and charges of any kind to be levied on exportation and importation of commodities, and to the rules, formalities and charges of customs management. These provisions, however, shall not apply to:

1. Advantages resulting from any customs union or other agreement on customs-free trade to which either Contracting Party is or may become, in the future, a party; and,
2. Advantages accorded by multilateral economic agreements relating to international commerce.

Article VI

Payment in connection with the importation and exportation of commodities and goods as well as other payments between the two countries shall be made in convertible pounds Sterling or any other mutually agreed currency.

Article VII

Border inhabitants of the two countries may, within an area of 30 kilometers from the border, carry on the petty traditional trade on barter basis, which shall not be subjected to the limitations of the above- mentioned provisions.

Article VIII

Nothing in this Agreement shall be construed to derogate from any obligations of either of the contracting parties under any international convention or agreement entered into before or after the conclusion of this Agreement.

Article IX

Any dispute arising out of the implementation of this Agreement shall be settled through peaceful and friendly consultations between the Contracting parties.

Article X

This Agreement replaces the paragraph II of article IV of the Agreement to Maintain Friendly Relations between the Kingdom of Nepal and the People's Republic of China and on Trade and Intercourse between Nepal and the Tibet Region of China concluded between the two Contracting parties on September 20, 1956.

This Agreement shall come into force on and from the date of signing and its validity is for two years. If neither party notifies the other in writing to terminate this Agreement at least six months before its expiration, the validity shall be automatically extended for another two years.

After the expiration of this Agreement, all obligations arising there from shall be carried out in accordance with the provisions of this Agreement.

The present Agreement is concluded in Kathmandu on 19th May 1964.

Done in duplicate in the Nepali, Chinese and English languages, all the three texts being equally authentic. In case there should arise any difference in interpretation between the Nepali and the Chinese texts, the English text shall be taken as final.

Sd/-
Plenipotentiary of
His Majesty's Government
of Nepal

Sd/-
Plenipotentiary of the
Government of the People's
Republic of China

Note 1. The above-mentioned texts of treaties and agreements between Nepal and China are quoted from the relevant chapters of the book Nepal's relations with India and China written by Avtar Singh Bhasin.

Appendix 8

Life of Buddha

Lumbini when Buddha was born

At the time of the Buddha's birth at Lumbini there were several states around the small republic of Kapilavastu. The Uposatha Wagga of the Anguttara Nikaya mentions as many as sixteen states which existed in the region about that time or a little later, viz., Anga, Magadha, Kashi, Kosala, Vrijji, Malla, Chedi, Vatsa, Kuru, Panchala, Matsya, Surasena, Ashmaka, Awanti, Gandhara and Kamboja. Some of them were republics and others monarchies. But here, we refer only to those states which were in the immediate vicinity of Kapilavastu and which were directly concerned with the life-story of Buddha.[1]

Closely related by matrimonial alliance with the Shakya rulers of Kapilavastu were the Koliya chiefs. Koliya is also known as Devadaha. According to the Dharmpada Arthakatha, the Rohini River flowed between their territories, demarcating their frontiers. Rohini River begins from the Churiya Range, and runs through the district of Kapilavastu, Nepal and flows into the Rapti River at Gorakhpur, India. On one occasion, the peoples of Kapilavastu and Koliya also called Devadaha, quarreled over the question of sharing the water of this river for irrigation and imminent conflict could be averted only through the direct intervention of Buddha himself. The Malla republics of Pawa and Kushinagar lay to the south of Kapilavastu, while further south, extended the mighty kingdom of Magadha. The territory of Kosala, another strong monarchical state stretched to the west. To the north of Kapilavastu there might have existed a number of independent states or petty principalities. In the valley of Kathmandu, as the historical annals speak, a strong Kirat sovereign ruled. To quote the Vamshawali (annals) according to D. Wright, one Kirat King, Jitedasti by name, was ruling over the valley during the lifetime of Buddha.

The republic of Kapilavastu was situated at the foot of the Churiya Hills, the foot- hills of the Himalayas. It was surrounded by large and small states as described above. King Shuddhodana was ruling over it. Then the chiefs of small republics also held the title of 'Raja' or King. Shuddhodana, the chief of the republic of Kapilavastu, was one such 'Raja'. He had two queens, Maya Devi and Prajapati Gautami. They were the daughters of Anjana, chief of another republic, Devadaha. The distance from Kapilavastu to Devadaha, as stated in the commentary of the Majjhima Nikaya, was five yojanas (nearly thirty five miles). According to the Jataka Arthakatha Nidan, the pleasant woods known as the Lumbinivana, which was to be hallowed by the birth of Lord Buddha, lay between Kapilavastu and Devadaha. It was a pleasure grove that the residents of both the states could come and enjoy. According to the Arthakatha, the royal families of both the Shakya and Koliya states used the lake of Devadaha as a holy bathing place. Several Buddhist texts such as Deeggha Nikaya Arthakatha, Samyukta Nikaya etc. mention the common access of both states to the grove of Lumbini.

The Jataka Katha Nidana and Lalitavistara speak elaborately of which family, at what place and in what country Buddha would be born. It also mentions how in the future he would descend from one of the heavens and enter into the womb of Queen Maya Devi to be born in human form in order to deliver the humanity from its sufferings.

Queen Maya Devi was in the tenth month of her pregnancy, when she expressed her desire to go to her parental palace in Devadaha. King Shuddhodana, ever willing to fulfill her wishes, arranged for her departure with all possible alacrity. When everything was ready, she set out for Devadaha with all attention.

The royal entourage had to pass through the Lumbinivana, a grove thickly wooded with Sal trees (Shorea Robusta). It was the Full Moon day of the month of Vaishakha, i.e., the month of May in the year 563 B.C. It is said that the day was Friday. The Sal trees were in full bloom. The beauty of the grove was singularly charming on that occasion. The two famous Chinese Buddhist travellers Fa Hsien and Hsuan Tsang, who visited Lumbini in the 4th and the 7th century respectively, have immortalized the Lumbini grove by mentioning it in their Travel Accounts. The beauty and sanctity of Lumbini is beyond description as it was the place, which the future Buddha selected for his birth. [2]

The scenic beauty of the arbour induced Queen Maya Devi to

stop her journey "to alight from her palanquin and enjoy the sight around. She began to stroll about, leisurely taking one step after another. Thus while she was standing spellbound at the natural grandeur around, she began to feel the pain of labor. She quickly raised her right hand and caught hold of the drooping branch of a Sal tree and the babe, the future Buddha, was born.

This great epoch is thus described in the Jatakakatha Nidan, "...The Great Prophet was born, not in the usual way ... he was born standing upright. As soon as he was born he looked towards the east, south, west, upward and downward and all the ten directions... Then he looked towards the north and took seven steps... at every step he walked, one lotus flower appeared on the ground".

Glimpses of events of life of Buddha in Kapilavastu

Name giving Ceremony

On the fifth day of birth the ceremony of name giving took place. A hundred and eight Brahmins were invited to the festival at the palace, and eight of these were interpreters of bodily marks. The eighth, a young man known from his clan as Koudanna, prophesied his Buddhahood as a certainty. The Brahmins also told the king that his son would leave the world after seeing the four signs, an old man, a sick man, a corpse, and an ascetic. Accordingly, guards were stationed at the four quarters to prevent these four from coming to the sight of his son.

This is the account of the Nidana-Katha, which omits to mention the name bestowed, but later on uses the name Siddhartha, which, in the Lalita-vistara is Siddhartha, 'he whose aim is accomplished'.[3]

Luxurious Life

About the life of the Bodhisatta (before enlightenment, Siddhartha Gautama is mentioned as Bodhisatta.) we have only one incident mentioned in the Canon, that is, Buddha's account of his luxurious life as Prince:

Buddha said, "I was delicate, O monks, extremely delicate, excessively delicate. In my father's dwelling, lotus-pools had been made, in one blue lotus, in another red, in the third white, all for my sake. I used no sandalwood that was not of Benares. My dress was of Benares cloth, my tunic, my under-robe, cloak and all night and day and all the time a white parasol was held over me so that I should not be touched by cold or heat, by dust or weeds or dew.

I had three palaces, one for the cold season, one for the hot, and one for the season of rains. Through the four rainy months, in the palace for the rainy season, entertained by female minstrels I did not come down from the palace."

When the three palaces were ready, the King thought that as his son was grown up, he would raise the royal parasol over him and see the glory of his kingdom. He sent letters to the Shakyas saying, "my son is grown up, and I intend to establish him in the kingdom. Let all send the girls that have grown up in their houses, to this house." On hearing the message, they said, "the young man is merely fair and fit to look upon, but he knows no art. He will not be able to support a wife. We will not send our daughters." When the king heard this, he went to his son and said, "What art should the Bodhisatta show, my son?" "I must string the bow requiring the strength of a thousand men, so let it be brought." The king had it brought and gave it to him. The Great Being sitting on a couch had the bow brought to him, and wrapping the string round his toe he drew it with his toe and strung the bow. Taking a stick in his left hand he drew it with his right and struck the string. The whole city was roused. People asked what the sound was, and said it thundered. But others said, "Do you not know that it is not thundering, but that prince Angirasa has strung the bow requiring the strength of a thousand men. He is striking the string, and that is the sound of the blow." By so much the minds of the Shakyas were decided. The Great Being asked what else he was to do. (Twelve marvelous feats with the bow are then described.) And this was not all, but on that day the Great Being conforming to the custom of the world displayed all his art. Then the Shakya kings each arrayed his daughter and sent them. They were forty thousand dancing girls. So the Great Being dwelt in his three palaces like a god.[4]

The Renunciation

At the age of twenty-nine, after a life spent in worldly enjoyments, Siddhartha Gautama was startled out of his ease at the first sight of old age, sickness, and death. Fleeing secretly at night from his home he became an ascetic (One of these occurs in the continuation of the above quoted description of the luxurious life in the three palaces).

He said, "Then, O monks, did I, endowed with such majesty and such excessive delicacy, think thus, "an ignorant, ordinary person, who is himself subject to old age, not beyond the sphere of old age, on seeing an old man is troubled, ashamed, and disgusted, extending the thought to himself. I too am subject to old age, not beyond the sphere of old age, and should I, who am subject to old age, not beyond the sphere of old age, on seeing an old man be troubled, ashamed, and disgusted. This seemed to me not fitting. As I thus reflected on it, all the elation in youth utterly disappeared."

The same is then repeated of sickness and death, and "the elation in life utterly disappeared." Here we have the first mention of the signs that according to the legend awakened in Gautama's mind the problems of existence, his first sight of an old man, a sick man, and a corpse, to which is added the fourth sign of an ascetic.

Another canonical passage, the Sutta of the Noble Search (Majjhi 163), also put into Buddha's mouth, describes his conversion in still more general terms:

"Thus, O monks, before my enlightenment, while yet a Bodhisatta and not fully enlightened, being myself subject to birth I sought out the nature of birth, being subject to old age I sought out the nature of old age, of sickness, of death, of sorrow, of impurity. Then I thought, "what if I being myself subject to birth were to seek out the nature of birth and having seen the wretchedness of the nature of birth, were to seek out the unborn, the supreme peace of Nirvana." (Repeated similarly of old age, sickness, death, sorrow, and impurity.)"

According to the Jataka commentary, Shuddhodana on the name-giving day, after hearing from the eight Brahmins the prophecy that his son, if he saw the four signs, would leave the world, set guards to ward them off from the sight of his son. But while the Bodhisatta was living in luxury in his three palaces, the gods decided that it was time to rouse him.

"Now one day the Bodhisatta wishing to go to the park summoned his charioteer, and told him to harness the chariot. He obeyed and adorning the great splendid chariot with all its adornments, yoked the four state horses white as lotus-petals, and informed the Bodhisatta. The Bodhisatta ascended the chariot, which was like a vehicle of the gods, and went towards the park. The gods thought, "the time for prince Siddhartha to attain enlightenment is at hand: we will show him a previous sign." So they made a god appear, worn out with old age, with broken teeth, gray hair, bent, with broken-down body, a stick in his hand, and trembling. It was the Bodhisatta and the charioteer (only) who saw him. The Bodhisatta asked his charioteer, as in the Mahapadana-sutta, "What man is this? Even his hair is not like that of others," and on hearing his reply said, "Woe to birth, when the old age of one that is born shall be known." With agitated heart he thereupon returned and ascended his palace. The king asked why his son had returned so quickly. "O king, he has seen an old man, and on seeing an old man he will leave the world." "By this you are ruining me. Get together dancing girls for my son. If he enjoys luxury, he will have no thought of leaving the world." And so saying he increased the guards, and set them in all directions to the distance of half a league."

At length the day of the Great Renunciation arrived. He set out for the park as before, and saw a man who had abandoned the world. The charioteer inspired by the gods explained, and praised the virtues of renunciation. That day the Bodhisatta, taking pleasure in the thought of abandoning the world, went on to the park. After bathing, he sat on the royal rock of state to be robed, and his attendants stood round about him.[5]

Birth of the son

When he was returning from the park to the city, his father sent him a message that "the Princess Yashodhara had given birth to a son". The Bodhisatta on hearing it said, "Rahula is born, a bond is born," and his father therefore gave the order, "Let Prince Rahula be his name."[6]

Leaving the Palace

"He awoke to find his female musicians sleeping round him in disgusting attitudes. Then filled with loathing for his worldly life he made his decision, and ordered his charioteer Channa to saddle his horse Kanthaka.

The Bodhisatta having sent Channa thought, "Now I will look at my son," and rising from where he had been sitting cross-legged, he went to the abode of the mother of Rahula, and opened the door of the chamber. Just then a lamp of scented oil was burning. On the bed strewn with heaps of Jessamine and other flowers the mother of Rahula was sleeping with her hand on her son's head. The Bodhisatta, standing with his foot on the threshold looked, and thought, "If I move aside the queen's hand and take my son, the queen will awake and this will be an obstacle to my going."[7]

He left the city on his horse Kanthaka with the charioteer clinging to the tail.

It was on the full-moon day of the month Uttarasadha (June-July) that the Bodhisatta departed.

This account as a whole is not found in the Scriptures, but the story in its main outlines is told of Vipassin Buddha in the Mahapadana-sutta.[8]

The Bodhisatta then meditates in the seraglio (walled palace), makes his resolution at midnight, and summons his charioteer Chandaka, who tries in vain to persuade him to seek enjoyment first. He goes beyond the Shakyas, the Kodyas (Koliyas), and the Mallas, and at daybreak reaches the town Anuvaineya of the Maineyas, six leagues away. There he gives his ornaments and the horse to Chandaka. The Bodhisatta cuts off his hair and changes his robes for yellow ones. (Kashaya, which were sent by one of the gods of the Pure Abode).[9]

The seraglio and the king awake, and seeing a god bringing the Bodhisatta's royal robes, and Chandaka following with the horse and the ornaments, thinks that the Bodhisatta has been killed for the sake of his precious robes, but Chandaka tells them that it is impossible to bring back the Bodhisatta until he has attained complete enlightenment.

Austerities and Enlightenment:

"Now before my enlightenment, while yet a Bodhisatta and not yet fully enlightened (Buddha), I thought, oppressive is the life in a house, a place of dust. In the free air is abandonment of the world. Not easy is it for him who dwells in a house to practice a completely full, completely pure, and perfectly religious life. What if I remove my hair and beard, and putting on yellow robes go forth from a house to a houseless life.

Now at another time, while yet a boy, a black-haired lad in the prime of youth, in the first stage of life, while my unwilling mother and father wept with tear-stained faces. I cut off my hair and beard, and putting on yellow robes went forth from a house to houseless life."

The Mahasaccaka-sutta (Majjh. i 240 ff.) after describing the going forth as given above, continues:

"Then striving after the good, and searching for the supreme state of peace, I gradually made my way to the Magadhas, and went to Uruvela, the army-township. There I saw a delightful spot with a pleasant grove, a river flowing delightfully with clear water and good fords, and round about, a place for seeking alms. This surely is a fit place for striving of a high-born one. Then I sat down there, a fit place is this for striving."

(After going through the process of austerities...) "Then I thought, it is not easy to gain that happy state while my body is so very lean. What if I now take solid food, rice and sour milk? Now at that time five monks were attending me, thinking, when the ascetic Gautama gains the Doctrine, he will tell it to us." But when I took solid food, rice and sour milk, then the five monks left me in disgust, saying, "The ascetic Gautama lives in abundance, he has given up striving, and has turned to a life of abundance."

"Now having taken solid food and gained strength, without sensual desires, without evil ideas I attained and abode in the first trance of joy and pleasure, arising from seclusion and combined with reasoning and investigation. Nevertheless, such pleasant feeling as arose did not overpower my mind. With the ceasing of reasoning and investigation I attained and abode in the second trance of joy and pleasure arising from concentration, with internal serenity and fixing of the mind on one point without reasoning and investigation. With equanimity towards joy and sorrow I remained mindful and conscious, and experienced bodily pleasure, what the noble ones describe as 'dwelling with equanimity, mindful, and happily', and attained and abode in the third trance. Abandoning pleasure and abandoning pain, even before the disappearance of elation and depression, I attained and abode in the fourth trance, which is without pain and pleasure, and with purity of mindfulness and equanimity.

Thus with mind concentrated, purified, cleansed, spotless, with the defilements gone, supple, dexterous, firm, and impassable, I directed my mind to the knowledge of the reminiscences of my former existences. I remembered many former existences, such as, one birth, two births, three, four, five, ten, twenty, thirty, forty, fifty, a hundred, a thousand, a hundred thousand births; many cycles of dissolution of the universe, many cycles of its evolution, many of its dissolution and evolution there. I was of such and such a name, clan, color, livelihood, such pleasure and pain did I suffer, and such was the end of my life. Passing away thence I was born elsewhere. There too I was of such and such a name, clan, color, livelihood such pleasure and pain did I suffer, and such was the end of my life. Passing away thence I was reborn here. Thus do I remember my many former existences with their special modes and detail. This was the first knowledge that I gained in the first watch of the night. Ignorance was dispelled, knowledge arose, darkness was dispelled, and light arose. So is it with him who abides vigilant, strenuous and resolute.

Thus with mind concentrated, purified, cleansed, spotless, with the defilements gone, supple, dexterous, firm and impassable, I directed my mind to the passing away and rebirth of beings. With divine, purified, superhuman vision I saw beings passing away and being reborn, low and high, of good and bad color, in happy or miserable existences according to their karma. Those beings who lead evil lives in deed, word, or thought, who speak evil of the noble ones, of false views, who acquire karma through their false views, at the dissolution of the body after death are reborn in a state of misery and suffering in hell. But those beings who lead good lives in deed, word, and thought, who speak no evil of the noble ones, of right views, who acquire karma through their right views, at the dissolution of the body after death are reborn in a happy state in the world of heaven . . . This was the second knowledge that I gained in the second watch of the night . . .

Thus with mind concentrated, purified, cleansed, spotless, with the defilements gone, supple, dexterous, firm, and impassible, I directed my mind to the knowledge of the destruction of the asavas (defilement and intoxicating liquid like wine or other substance). I duly realized (the truth) 'this is pain.' I duly realized (the truth) 'this is the destruction of pain.' and I duly realized (the truth) 'this is the way that leads to the destruction of pain.' I duly realized 'these are the asavas' 'this is the cause of the asavas' . . . 'this is the way that leads to the destruction of the asavas.' As I thus knew and thus perceived, my mind was emancipated from the asava of sensual desire, from the asava of desire for existence, and from the asava of ignorance. And in me emancipated arose the knowledge of my emancipation. I realized that destroyed is rebirth, the religious life has been led, and done is what was to be done. There is naught (for me) beyond this world. This was the third knowledge that I gained in the last watch of the night. Ignorance was dispelled, knowledge arose, darkness was dispelled, and light arose. So is it with him who abides vigilant, strenuous, and resolute."[10]

Four Noble Truths:

1) "Now this, monks, is the noble truth of pain, birth is painful, old age is painful, sickness is painful, death is painful, sorrow, lamentation, dejection, and despair are painful. Contact with unpleasant things is painful, not getting what one wishes is painful. In short, the five groups of grasping skandha, factors that make up an individual, are painful."

2) "Now this, monks, is the noble truth of the cause of pain: the craving, which tends to rebirth, combined with pleasure and lust, finding pleasure here and there; namely, the craving for passion, the craving for existence, the craving for non-existence."
3) "Now this, monks, is the noble truth of the cessation of pain the cessation without a reminder of craving, the abandonment, forsaking, release, and non-attachment."
4) "Now this, monks, is the noble truth of the way that leads to the cessation of pain: this is the noble Eightfold Way, namely, right views, right intention, right speech, right action, right livelihood, right effort, right mindfulness, and right concentration."

Sermon at Saranath[11]

The Eightfold Path:

"These two extremes, monks, are not to be practiced by one who has gone forth from the world. What are the two? That conjoined with the passions and luxury, low, vulgar, common, ignoble, and useless; and that conjoined with self-torture, painful, ignoble, and useless. Avoiding these two extremes, the Tathagata has gained the enlightenment of the Middle Path, which produces insight and knowledge, and tends to calmness to higher knowledge, enlightenment, Nirvana."

The Sermon at Sarnath

"And what monks, is the Middle Path, of which the Tathagata has gained enlightenment, which produces insight and knowledge, and tends to calm, to higher knowledge, enlightenment, Nirvana? This is the noble Eightfold Path namely, right view, right intention, right speech, right action, right livelihood, right effort, right mindfulness, and right concentration. This, monks, is the Middle Path of which the Tathagata has gained enlightenment which produces insight and knowledge, and tends to calm, to higher knowledge, enlightenment, Nirvana."

The Sermon at Sarnath[12]

Nirvana

"Nirvana is where the thinking-mind with all its discriminations, attachment, aversions and egoism is forever put away; Nirvana is where logical measures, as they are seen to be inert, are no longer seized upon; Nirvana is where even the notion of truth is treated with indifference because of its causing bewilderment; Nirvana is where, getting rid of the four propositions, there is insight into the abode of reality. Nirvana is where the twofold passions have subsided and the twofold hindrances are cleared away and the twofold egolessness is patiently accepted; Nirvana is where, by the attainment of the "turning-about" in the deepest seat of consciousness, self-realization of Nobel Wisdom is fully entered into, that is the Nirvana of the Tathagatas."

Surangama Sutta

"A middle path, O Bhikkhus, avoiding the two extremes, has been discovered by the Tathagata a path which opens the eyes, and bestows understanding, which leads to peace of mind, to the higher wisdom, to full enlightenment, to Nirvana."

The Sermon at Saranath[13]

Great Apostle of Peace passes away

One fine night in 483 B.C. Lord Buddha was lying down at full length at the foot of two Sal trees in Kushinara, surrounded by innumerable monks and nuns. It was the Vaisakh Full Moon night and the moon was shedding its delightful luster all around. The blossoms of Sal trees were in full bloom, adding grandeur to the atmosphere by their snowy color and pleasant perfume. The Lord had by this time served his fellow beings for full forty-five years and reached the mature age of eighty. In anticipation of his end he had come to Kushinara having made a long journey and having fully instructed his followers in the essence of his teachings.

Thus lying by the right side and with his end approaching nearer every moment, the great philanthropist said as his teachings.

"... I am breathing my last shortly. Let my corpse be burned... no, no, Ananda, don't wail, Ananda, don't weep... I've already told you before... from every one and every thing dear one will be separated... What we love or like do not exist for ever... whoever comes into being perishes... Nothing to the contrary is possible.

"Be a lamp unto yourself, be a refuge unto yourself, seek not refuge outside."

"Hold fast to the lamp of truth, take refuge in truth alone, seek no external refuge...

"Impermanent are all conditioned things. Be diligent and work out your salvation."

With these words the great Apostle of Peace, the great Benefactor of the human race, passed away. This is what we find recorded in the Mahaparinirvana Sutra. But by the time the great Master attained Nirvana, his gospel had already become a mighty force. Whosoever had listened to his message was highly impressed. It gave them light and life, peace and happiness. Thus, by means of the invincible weapon of universal love and brotherhood, the Lord had conquered the domain of human hearts.

Hence, in no time after the memorable event described above, that is to say, immediately after Buddha had expired, Lumbini and other places associated with the important incidents of his life came to be hallowed.[14]

End Notes

1. Bhuban Lal Pradhan. *Lumbini, Kapilavastu Devadaha:* Kathmandu: Research Center for Nepal and Asian Studies, Tribhuvan University, 1978. p. 14.
2. Ibid, pp. 15-16.
3. Edward J. Thomas: *The Life of Buddha.* Delhi: Vanarasidass Publications Private Limited, 1997, p. 43.
4. Ibid, pp. 47-48.
5. Ibid, pp. 51-52.
6. Ibid, p. 53.
7. Ibid, p. 54.
8. Ibid, p. 55.
9. Ibid, p. 57.
10. Ibid, pp. 62-68.
11. Harishchandra Lal Singh: *Modern Interpretation of Buddhism:* Shirish Singh, Lalitpur, Nepal, 1994, p. 29.
12. Ibid, p. 34.
13. Ibid, p. 47.
14. Bhuban Lal Pradhan, p. 19.

A. Buddhism in Nepal

Buddhism Dawns in Nepal

The very conception "Buddhism in Nepal" is a natural reminder of the well-known fact. Lord Buddha, the founder of Buddhism, was born at the Lumbini Grove. He was associated with his native land Kapilavastu for twenty-nine years of his early life. It was during this period when he noticed the grim realities of life on earth that induced him to muse upon the root causes of the pangs of human life and think on their remedy. Both Lumbini and Kapilavastu are situated in the southwestern lowland plains of the present day kingdom of Nepal.

Even after his Enlightenment Lord Buddha repeatedly came to Kapilavastu and preached his doctrines. His first visit to Kapilavastu took place in the very year of his Enlightenment, i.e. 528 B.C. Here he stayed in Ni (ya) grodharam and gave many sermons and explained several sutras. It was on this occasion that he told his father King Shudhodan, stepmother Queen Prajapati and his wife Princess Yashodhara the story of Bisantara Jataka, Chadakinnara Jataka and many other Jataka (Birth) stories. The next day his young brother prince Nanda was ordained, and a week after his own seven year old son Prince Rahul was ordained. On the eighth day the Mahadhamma apla Jataka was explained. On his way back from here to Rajagriha, Ananda, Devadatta, Bhaggu, Anirudha and Kimbilla took ordination. Lord Buddha came to Kapilavastu several times again as stated in Buddhist texts.

Kapilavastu is the present day Tilaurakot of Nepal. We can assume that the above-mentioned first visit of the Lord to Kapilavastu introduced Buddhism into Nepal for the first time. On several other occasions too, Lord Buddha came to Kapilavastu .He came here when his father King Shuddhodan of Kapilavastu and King of Koliyas of Devadaha were about to fight each other, over the question sharing the water of the river Rohini; and when king Widuddhava of Kosala arrived here with his forces, intending to raid it.

Each time the Lord came to his native land Kapilavastu he stayed in either Ni (ya) grodharam or Mahawana and gave a series of discourses (Exposition of the Doctrine) on the Attadanda Sutra, the Phandana Jakata, the Wattak Jataka and other Jakata stories. In fact, the answers, the Lord gave during his stays in Kapilavastu, to the question raised by Mahanam Shakya, his own elder cousin, covered many aspects of his doctrines. A lot of stanzas incorporated in the Dhammapada, too, are connected with the discourses the Lord gave here on these occasions.

Thus the Lord had preached a significant portion of his teachings in Kapilavastu.

As far as the matter of entry of Buddhism into the valley of Kathmandu is concerned the information available from Buddhist texts and the history of Nepal is as follows.

While Lord Buddha was preaching his Doctrines in Magadha, Kosala, Vaisali and so on, Kirata kings were ruling over the valley of Nepal, present Kathmandu. An offshoot of Kiratas known as Nepars were then thriving in the valley. By the sixth and the fifth century B.C. the valley had been open to traders coming from the plains below. There were inter-regional cultural and commercial connection between India and Nepal. One of the Buddhist texts, the Moolasarwastiwad Vinaya Sutra, written in the seventh century A.D. by Jina Mitra, contains the following accounts of the arrival of Bhikshus into the valley in company with a group of traders after a tedious trekking of layers of mountains.

Firstly, when Lord Buddha was residing at Sravasti some Buddhist monks happened to join a band of merchants who were coming to Nepal. The merchant said, " Holy ones, in Nepal the ground is nothing but rocks, and it is as humpy as the back of a camel, Surely you are not going to enjoy your journey."

When the Bhikshus arrived at the valley they began to complain of the bitter cold and wanted to go back as early as possible with the help of the merchants. The monks managed to go back to Sravasti.

Secondly, some time after the massacre of the Shakyas many of the latter, particularly those of the house and family of Bhikshu Ananda, the famous disciple of the Lord, came to Nepal. They, too, suffered from the effects of the cold climate. Ananda was requested by his family members through the merchants to visit them and see their well - being. Ananda accordingly came with the merchants to Nepal but also suffered bitterly from frost- bite.

On his return to Sravasti the other disciples were grieved to find Ananda with his limbs disfigured owing to frostbite.

"The kingdom of Nepal" Ananda said, "is next to the Himalayan Mountains and because of the cold wind and snow my feet and hands have been reduced to this state".

"How are the Bhikshus who have gone to stay in Nepal going on?" asked the other Bhikshus.

Ananda replied, "They wear shoes."

"But why don't you wear them?"

"The Buddha has not yet given permission for their use."

Thereupon the Bhikshus approached the Lord, when he said, "In cold and snowy places the use of shoes is permitted."

Another statement in the Moolsarwastiwad Vinaya Sutra shows how the Indian merchants came to Nepal for importing wool and orpiments (yellow die) in large quantities and filled their carts with them before leaving for India.

Thus in the sixth century B.C. we find that the Bhikhsus used to come to Nepal freely from India and go from Nepal to India. The Shakyas had twice migrated into the valley. Nepal then was a kingdom. Its climate was cold and snowy and the passage was very inconvenient. The Bhikshus in Nepal had to use their shoes for climatic reasons during the very lifetime of Buddha. The rules of the Vinaya (Monastic Discipline) were to be modified when time and circumstances demanded such modification.

There were free export and import trades between Nepal and India, and Indian merchants used to come every now and then for the exchange of their country's products.

The above account is a clear indication that the Shakyas from Kapilavastu continued emigrating into and settled down in the valley when Lord Buddha was still living and preaching his doctrines in the Indian plains. When the yellow-robed Bhikshus, arrived for the first time, it was presumably the first occasion the inhabitants of the valley saw Buddhist monks in their Valley.

The Buddhist Shakyas who had come to settle in the valley consisted of both monks and the laity. The monks observed disciplinary rules of the Monastic order undisturbed while the laymen and women found themselves safe and free to follow their religion and intermingle with the local people.

The Shakya Buddhists had come here not as preachers but as

mere refugees whether they were monks or laymen. Yet the inhabitants of the valley might have been impressed with the Buddhist monks and their fraternal and humanitarian ideals. Most probably some of them may have been converted into Buddhism as laymen or even- as monks. At any rate, that was the earliest occasion that Buddhism dawned into the valley.

Even after these earlier migrations, Shakyas and other Buddhists continued flowing into the valley from southern plains for long.

Ashoka mission to Nepal

Emperor Asoka, the renowned propagator of Buddhism had made a pilgrimage to Lumbini and Kapilavastu and also sent a religious mission to the borderlands in the Himalayan region.

Immediately after the Nirvana of the lord in 483 B.C. Lumbini, his birthplace along with Bodhagaya, Isipatan and Kusinara, the places associated with the important incident of his life, came to be hallowed. There was a continuous flow of devoted people to Lumbini.

Of them the most remarkable is the visit of Emperor Asoka who in 245 B.C., i.e. 238 years after Lord Buddha's Nirvana, came to Lumbini accompanied by Bhikshu Upagupta as his preceptor, and paid homage to it. Lumbini was the first place he visited in course of his pilgrimage to the four sacred places connected with the Lord and his Life. According to Diwyawadan, the Emperor bestowed one hundred thousand gold coins on the local people. He erected a stone pillar, marking the birthplace of the Lord. From Lumbini the Emperor proceeded towards Kapilavastu, where too he built several Stupas and installed stone pillars at various places. Two of them still remain at the Kapilvastu district in Nepal.

I) The Lumbini Pillar: This pillar, stands at Lumbini, bearing Asoka's imperial inscription. Though its top is now missing the inscription is intact and interpreted to mean the following:

"When king, beloved of gods, had been anointed twenty years, he came himself and worshipped here where Buddha Shakyamuni was born. He caused a stone-horse (a horse carved in stone) to be made and put on a stone pillar in order to show that the Blessed One was born here. He made the village of Lumbini free of taxes and paying only eighth part."

II) The Gotihawa Pillar: There still stands at Gotihawa, a part of a stone pillar built by emperor Asoka during his historic Pilgrimage to Kapilavastu. According to Carlyle, the inscription on it was partially visible until 1904, though very faint. The upper portion is now missing but the lower one still stands intact.

III) The Niglihawa Pillar: Near a large tank, known as Niglisagar at Niglihawa, there must have stood an Ashoka stone pillar for centuries though it now lies on the ground broken. Of the two broken pieces the upper one lies on the ground on the edge of the tank. The shorter piece bears an Ashoka inscription, which reads as follows:

"His majesty King Priyadassina in the 14th year of his reign, enlarged for the second time, the Stupa of the Buddha Kanakamuni, and in the twentieth year of his reign, having come in person, did reverence and set up a stone pillar." Or

"King Piyadassi, after he had been consecrated king fourteen years increased the Stupa of Buddha Kanakamuni to the double and having been consecrated twenty years came himself and worshipped it."

The upper piece, too, contains an inscription of Ripu Malla, a Buddhist king of West Nepal around 1312 A.D. This pillar was built by Emperor Asoka in memory of Kanakamuni Buddha. His imperial inscription on it attests this.

Emperor Asoka made pilgrimage to Lumbini, Kapilavastu and Devadaha, situated in the low land Plains southwest of the Kathmandu valley and erected a pillar and stupas there. Therefore, it may be possible, if more Ashoka monuments are further discovered in Parasi Bhiknathori and other parts of Nepali terrain plains.

Moreover, according to the Mahavamsha (The Great Chronicle) of Ceylon, at the close of his reign (around 230B.C.) Emperor Asoka sent a missionary team for the dissemination of Buddhism in the Himalayan region. The team consisted of five Sthawiras (senior monks) and was led by Sthawira Madhyama (Majjhima in Pali). Each of the senior Bhikshus toured a separate place. One of them, Sthawira Kashyapa Gotra is said to have converted one hundred thousand people to Buddhism. Kashyapa appears to have visited the valley.

One of the inscriptions in a stupa, near Sanchi discovered by Cunningham around 1914, mentions Kashyapa as the teacher of the whole Himawat region (the Himalayan Border land). In Patan, the second city in the valley, there still exist four Stupas at its four corners, traditionally called "Asoka Stupas." Babu Ram Acharya, the late veteran historian of Nepal, is of the opinion that these stupas had been built by the new disciples of Sthawira Kashyapa or by their descendants. He writes:

"The Majjhima team sent by Emperor Asoka towards the

Himalayas for preaching Buddhism at the close of his reign arrived here just before or immediately after his dethronement (around 228-7 B.C.). The Nepars (the aboriginal inhabitants of the valley) showed high regards for this religion. But with the ancestors of the present-day Magars, Murmis, Sherpas and Thamis (offshoots of the Kirat Tribe who then lived in immediate vicinity of the valley) in the hillside it was not so popular because teachings of Buddha were not so easy to practice. The Nepars could understand them, but found them very hard to follow in everyday life. They however practiced them as far as they could. The Kirat kings first accepted this religion. Had the kings themselves not taken initiatives it could not have so quickly spread. The next generation of the new Nepar proselytes became Buddhists and consequently five Stupas were built in the then capital city, the present day Patan. These Stupas still exist in the form of Mounds and are wrongly accredited to Asoka.

The Kiratas had inhabited the Himalayan regions from earlier than Buddha's times and the Nepars who inhabited the valley during the Ashoka age, were one of the offshoots of the same Kirat tribe. The Sthawiras of the Ashoka mission seemed to have converted these different branches of the Kiratas in the Himalayas including the Nepars of the valley".

The full name of Sthawira Kashyapa is Kashyapa Gotra as given in the Ceylonese chronicle. Even today there are people who are surnamed Kashypa Gotra abound in Kathmandu valley. It was then customary for the disciples to surname themselves after their family priest. In this respect it is worth remembering that the Shakyas, the members of the family of Lord Buddha, were called Gautama after their ancestors' family priest Kapila Gautama. This living fact, in addition to the aforesaid Sanchi inscription, attests to the view that Sthawira Kashyapa Gotra might have come into the valley. At any rate the propagation of Buddhism under the Ashoka Mission is a historical fact and there is, every likelihood that the valley people came into direct contact with Sthawira Kashyapa Gotra.

Most probably the stupas at Patan came to be called Ashoka stupas because they contained underground Buddha relics sent by Emperor Asoka through any one of these Sthawiras.

The chronicles of Nepal may not be in the shape of their present day expectation as a full-fledged history but they are the source of valuable and generally reliable materials. Some of them were referred to by Daniel Wright, while narrating the story of Emperor Asoka's visit to the Kathmandu valley. According to his reference, during the reign of the fourteenth Kirati king of Nepal Sthunko, Emperor Asoka came to the valley. He was accompanied by one of his queens, Tishyarakshita, daughter Princess Charumati, Bhikshu Upagupta and a large retinue and visited important places related to Buddhism. He gave princess Charumati in marriage to prince Devapala of Asokapattan (now known as Patan) in whose name the town now called Devapatan nearly two miles east of Kathmandu was founded. Asoka made Devapala ruler of Devapatan. When they came of old age, Charumati built a monastery, now known as the Charumati Vihara (also locally called Chabahil) and stayed in it. Here she died as a nun. This monastery is now in ruins. But, there at Chabahil stands a stupa originally of Ashoka design, markedly modified after repeated restoration several times. Devapala also built a monastery but he did not live long to complete it. An attempt has been made to identify it with the stupa at Dhamnathura two miles northeast of Kathmandu.

Emperor Asoka set up four stupas in honor of Lord Buddha in the four directions of the city of Patan, the second city in the valley, also known as Lalitpur or Asokapattan.

It is said that Asoka had built one more stupa and a monastery in the central part of the city. There is another Stupa said to belong to Asoka at Kirtipur three miles west of Patan. Many more Stupas, which are called Asoka Stupas are believed to have been built by him or built after the particular design attributed to him are to be found within Kathmandu,

The architectural construction of the Stupas at the four corners of Patan is still in- tact and evidences their antique structure. They were probably made later with the development of Mahayani and Vajrayani influences. Similarly the remnants of Chabahil Monastery, which still exists, were supposed to be that of the monastery founded by princess Charumati.

While in repairing the Stupa recently, workers have found some bricks with inscription of Charumati in Brahmi script and other ancient relics. These findings indicate that the Stupa was built 2300 years ago. The officials are investigating the authenticity of the relics.

But the story of Asoka's visits to the valley of Kathmandu is not authenticated by historical facts. No other chronicle of Nepal, except that mentioned by D. Wright as stated above, makes a mention of Asoka's visit to the valley.

Once more according to the chronicle of D. Wright's reference to the present day Hindu Divinity lord Pashupatinath was regarded as a Buddhist deity during the reign of Bhaskar Varma an ancient king of Nepal, and revered as Trailokya Washankara Lokeshwara. It was then in the care of Buddhists King Bhaskara Varma, ever entrusted religious functions of this deity to the Buddhist priests of the Chabahil Monastery. He had the rules and ceremonies engraved in a copper plate and deposited with the Buddhist monks of the Charumati Monastery. The Charumati Monastery, whether established by Princess Charumati or not, was certainly an important Hinayani (Therawadi) Monastery all through ancient times.

Every year on the eighth day of the bright lunar half of the Nepali month of Kartik (October–November), the Idol of Lord Pashupatinath is crowned with a headdress containing the figure of Buddha and worshipped as a Buddhist deity Trailokya Washankara Lokoshwara. This tradition still continues.

Lokeshwaras are Buddhist divinities as conceived by Vajrayani Buddhists of Nepal. Trailakoya Washankara is one of the 12 Lokeshwaras to whom the 12 Nepali months are attributed.[1]

End Note

1. Bhuban Lal Pradhan: *Buddhism in Nepal*: Unpublished book, Babarmahal Kathmandu. pp. 1-6 and -12

B. Buddhism in Tibet

Introduction and Development of Buddhism in Tibet

Nepal and Tibet lived with a common border prior to the commencement of written history. These two close neighbors helped each other with whatever means available in those early days. Nepali side used to export grain, edibles, local products and consumer goods produced in Nepal and also goods imported to Nepal from nearby Indian states to Tibet.

People in Tibet provided salt, wool and dust-gold together with local products, goats, and hide and yak tail. The trade was based on barter system until the Nepali coins were minted for and supplied to Tibet. Due to lack of peace and tranquility before unification, the exchanges of visits were limited to the border area. It was not possible then to reach deep into inner Tibet.

But information about the developments did reach to both sides of the border. It can be presumed that the local social systems together with the new emergence of political and religious thoughts might have spread out and reached to the core of Tibetan elites and concerned population.

The information about the birth of the Buddha, his enlightenment and preaching might have reached there earlier even before the recorded event of the fall of Buddhist sutras, Karandabyuha Sutra, Karma Shataka, Chintamani Dharani and Golden Chaitya from the heaven in the time of the reign of King Lha Tho tho-ri in the second century 173 A.D. as mentioned by W. D. Shakabpa. M. Winternitz's opinion, that the metrical Karandabyuha Sutra was in existence even prior to the 4th century, supports this.

At that time there was no one who could read and translate those sutras and books because they were written in Sanskrit language. So the king called it 'Nyengpo Sangwa' (the sacred) as a secret, it remained for many years, and was revered. After Buddhism was introduced during the reign of Lha Tho tho-ri, the Tibetans honored the King as an incarnation of Samantabhadra Bodhisttwa.[1]

Western scholars like Luciano Petech have written that these Buddhist scriptures belonged to a much later period. However, it is difficult to be certain about these dates, particularly the Karandabyuha Sutra that occupies an extremely important place in Nepali Buddhism. Dr. A. H. Franke writes that a few years after the descent of the Buddhist books, in the time of King Lha Tho tho-ri, several strangers arrived in Tibet.

This gives us a hint of some activities of the Buddhists in Nepal. The Karandabyuha Sutra vividly describes the visit of a group of Nepali merchants, headed by Simha Sarthvaha to Tibet for the business of jewels and gold. If we give credit to this account of the visit of Nepali merchants we can say that there were merchants who used to travel to Tibet in the earlier centuries of the Christian era. Local Nepali tradition gives much credit to this legend.

It is said that Pandit Buddhirakshita and translator Li-These had brought these books, which king Lha Tho tho-ri received, to Tibet. Since the Tibetan king could not read and understand the meaning of the books, the pandits returned.[2]

Regarding the possibility of the introduction of Buddhism in Tibet, Rockhill writes, "It is remarkable that the Karandabyuha Sutra, which does not appear to have been especially venerated in India or China, was one of the favorite books of Nepal and an object of great veneration in the country. This is one of the reasons, which has led me to suggest Buddhism first came to Tibet from Nepal.[3]

Gos Lotshamva mentions Buddhirakshita and the name of Nepali interpreter Li-These were the earliest missionaries of Buddhism in Tibet from Nepal. David Snellgrove and Hugh Richardson have similar views on this. They write, "It is quite possible that Tibetans were aware of the existence of Buddhism even earlier times, for there is a traditional belief that, in the reign of Srongtsen Gampo's (Srong-bsan-Sgam-po) fourth predecessor, certain religious books fell from the heaven on the roof of the palace, but no one could understand them. May be, some intrepid Buddhist monks from Nepal found their way to Tibet in the company of trading companions, only to find that the new books they brought with them were quite incomprehensible in this strange country."[4]

Min Bahadur Shakya says, "Although we can not take these legends as historic facts at their face value, they definitely give us clues to support the assertion that Nepal had an early trade relationship with Tibet and that Buddhism was introduced into Tibet from Nepal."[5]

It is quite probable that whatever the process of sending from Nepal and receiving in Tibet, Buddhist sutras or information regarding the developments of Buddhist thinking in India, Nepal and China might have started reaching there even before and continued after the Karandabyuha and other Buddhist sutras and Chaityas had reached there in the time of Lha Tho tho-ri. There cannot be a complete void or vacuum in the period in between the reign of Lha Tho tho-ri and Srongtsan Gampo. Therefore, it can safely be said that in the centuries in between the reigns of the two kings Lha Tho-tho-ri and Srongtsan Gampo the information about Buddhism and other information useful for the development of social-life might have continued reaching to Tibet in varied forms. This continuation might have helped Tibetans to know some thing about the development of Buddhism in nearby neighboring countries, like Nepal, India and China.

These developments might have inspired the ambitious and energetic new king Srongtsan Gampo (Srong-btsan-Sgam-po) to be inclined towards Buddhism, which was anew and up-to-date conception prevalent at that time in the region. The new king might have considered that it could create a new system in place of Bonpa tradition or Religion, which was considered insufficient to develop a new social system and uphold the unification of the country.

Srongtsan Gampo, the first patron of learning and civilization succeeded in unifying the country and establish peace and security in Tibet. It seems it was not unnatural for him, if he might have thought that it was not possible to depend on the Bonpa ideals and the social system based on scattered and fractious ethnic principalities to build a unified, consolidated, and strong nation. So, it appears, he decided to replace Bonpa-system with Buddhism and a developed social system and institutions based on its principles, prevalent at that time in Nepal, India and China. Therefore, he might have been inclined to marry the two princesses well versed on Buddhism from Nepal and China.

After appropriate arrangements were made, the Prime Minister Mgar Tontsan visited Nepal and then China and brought the two princesses successively for marriage with the Tibetan king. The Nepali princess Bhrikuti brought the images of Akshovya Vajra and Maitreya and carved a sandal wood image of Tara and many Buddhist Sutras. A Buddhist scholar Shila Manju, other officials and maids to help her in Tibet were included in her entourage. She also carried essential materials that she thought might, be necessary for her, during her living in Tibet.

The Chinese Princess Wen Cheng also brought with her the images of Jovo Shakya Muni and other deities and many books on Buddhism. Buddhist Scholar Huo Shang, other officials and maids to assist her in Tibet accompanied her. She also brought many goods that she thought might be essential for her in Tibet. [6]

The elite groups from Nepal and China who went to Tibet with their princesses took with them their knowledge of Buddhism, inventions in industrial and agricultural sectors, and developments of cultures and civilizations in their respective countries. Thus the plan of the king Srongtsan Gampo to make Tibet a unified and developed state devoted to Buddhist principles and dedicated to the preaching of Lord Buddha was helped to be materialized. Avalokiteshvara was revered as the principal deity of Tibet. The King was then proclaimed and revered as an incarnation of Avalokiteshvara, as in other Buddhist countries. Every Tibetan obeyed him as their divine ruler. The two princesses Bhrikuti and Wen Cheng were regarded to be his divine consorts and later regarded as the Harita Tara and the Shweta Tara respectively. The system of divine knowledge promoted by the king at that time thirteen hundred and fifty years ago continues to enlighten the Tibetan people.[7]

King Srongtsan Gampo sent Thonmi Sambhota together with twenty-five other scholars to neighboring countries to study Sanskrit, Buddhist sutras and other books and also to find a suitable script for Tibetan language. Thonmi Sambhota came to Nepal, stayed here for some time for acclimatization and preparation then left for India and visited Nalanda and other academic institutions to study and find a suitable script for Tibetan language.

When he returned, it is said; that the first Sutra he translated was Karandabyuha Sutra, a favorite book in Nepal, and which was believed to have fallen earlier from heaven in Tibet. Then, he translated other scripts and scriptures, which, it is said, are still extant in the well-known Tibetan book Tan-gyuer, the famous classic.

But according to sources quoted by Min Bahadur Shakya, this text of Karandabyuha Sutra preserved in Kanjuer, was translated by Jina Mitra, Danashila and Ye-She-sde, who belonged to the ninth century. It is possible that this translation was new and a second one.

Thonmi Sambhota also translated many other Buddhist Sutras

and books. These translations allowed the king and people to read them and understand Buddhism in their own language. There is no doubt that these translation works helped the people in general and also the king to understand the new concept, the king had introduced into Tibet and wanted the Tibetan people to understand and apply them in their daily life and social activities. This is how Buddhism was introduced, implemented and applied to build a new Buddhist state in the roof the world.

After Srongtsan Gampo's death in 650 A.D. one of his successors Trisong Detsen became the king in 755 and reigned till 797. Like his predecessors, he was also an ardent devotee of Buddha and Buddhism and wanted to continue spreading Buddhism in Tibet.[8]

King Trisong Detsen sent his minister Ba Salnang to Nepal to invite the Indian Buddhist scholar Santarakshita (Shantirakshita, as it is written by Tsepen W.D.Shakabpa) to come to Tibet and teach the doctrine of Buddhism. Santarakshita accepted the invitation, came to Nepal, stayed for some time for acclimatization and preparation and went on to Tibet. The King welcomed him when he arrived in Tibet.

It is said that the Bonpas were very resentful and created oppositions to his scheme of establishing Buddhism in place of traditional Bonpas. Sensing that the people were not yet ready to accept the new religion, Santarakshita returned to Nepal. Before departing, however, he suggested to the Tibetan king that he should invite the great Indian Tantric Master, Padmasambhava to visit Tibet.

Minister Ba Shalnang was again sent to invite the Master Padmasambhava. He on the invitation of Tibetan King came to Nepal enroute to Tibet and stayed in Nepal for about five years 743-747 for acclimatization, and necessary preparations. Shantarakshita, invited by the Tibetan King a second time, also came here enroute to Tibet. During this period the two great scholars discussed the requirements of Tibet among themselves, with Nepali Buddhists and also with Tibetan Buddhists, who visited Nepal during that period. Then Padmasambhava went to Tibet. The King welcomed him. The Master with his full Tantric formulae and rituals was able to overcome the resentment of the Bonpas.

The king was reform minded and sought counsel from Padmasambhava, on how to reduce the great disparity between the rich and poor. Padmasambhava advised the king that he could not forcibly close the gap between the rich and poor. "Our condition in this life is entirely dependent upon the action of our previous life and nothing can be done to alter the scheme of things".

King Trisong Detsen requested Santarakshita to build a monastery in the model of the Odantapuri, which was laid out in the design of Buddhist universe. (It is said that there was a city called Odantapuri in the time of Pala Dynasty in Bihara, now called as Bihar Sharif area of India, with academic facilities as in Nalanda and Bikramashila.) The Monastery commonly called as Samye was completed after twelve years work in Drakmar. A school for the study of Sanskrit was established at Samye and a large number of Buddhist texts from India and Nepal were brought and translated into the Tibetan language. Atisha, a celebrated Indian Pandit who visited Samye in the 11th century wrote that he had never seen such an extensive and thorough system of translation of Buddhist texts, even in India.

King Trisong Detsan called for a debate, which was held in 792-94 to find which of the two systems of Buddhism 'Instantaneous' or 'Slow' (Mahayana or Heenayana?) was appropriate for Tibet. Many scholars from Nepal, India and China participated in it. The Chinese monk Huo Shang, defended the 'Instantaneous System" and Kamalashila the 'Slow System'. At the end of the debate, Kamalashila's opinion in favor of 'Slow System' prevailed. The king issued a proclamation establishing the new religion of orthodox faith for Tibet. The main features of that proclamation were that the three jewels (the Buddha, the Dharma and the Sangha) were never to be abandoned; the various Buddhist temples were to be maintained. The amount given to support the temples was to be continued, and future generations of the royal family were to uphold the provisions of the proclamation. The document prepared by the King was sworn by the prince, chief ministers, the ministers of the interior and the exterior and the generals. Thirteen copies were made and distributed for preservation.[9]

The following is said to be one of the lyrics sung by the king at the festival:

Gold, silver, copper, lead, and iron
Are the five metals found in this land of mine;
Mustard, barley, peas, beans, and wheat
Are the five grains we are accustomed to eat.
Neither heat nor cold does the climate bring
To the country of which I am the king.

With great toil have I gathered this treasure
And I am happy to spend without measure
In spreading the faith of the Buddha,
Gleaned from the land of India.

It was inTho-tho-ri Nyantsen's reign
That The Secret first here came;
Translated in Songtsen Gampo's time,
It has become established in mine.

The temple prayer flags are so fine
The sun complains it dare not shine,
The birds object that they cannot fly
As the flags on the temple are jammed too high.
This temple, not built by human hand,
Has grown by itself from our sacred land.

Evolution and Development of Buddhism

"In the early seventh century, during the reign of the Tibetan King Srongtsan Gampo, Thonmi Sambhota and many other Tibetan students were deputed to India to learn the literature of the Dharma. Having learned Sanskrit grammar and literature thoroughly from Pandit Lha Rigba Sengge and other scholars of Kashmir, these students returned to Tibet. Thonmi Sambhota invented the Tibetan script based on the Nagari and Sharda scripts of the northern and central India respectively. They translated many books into Tibetan.

In the eighth century, during the reign of the Tibetan King Trisong Detsan, many great Indian scholars, such as Acharya Shantarakshita, Padmasambhava, Bimala Mitra, and Kamalashila, were invited to Tibet. Many Tibetan students such as Ishes Wangbo and Vairochana studied Sanskrit and translated numerous books on Mahayana and Vajrayana into Tibetan language. Seven Tibetans became Bhikshus.

In the ninth century, Tibetan King Tri-Ralpachen also invited many scholars, such as Jina Mena, Surendra, Ratna Bodhi, and Bhodi Dhana Shila, who revived the old translations and rewrote them into a more standardized Tibetan language. During the reign of the cruel king Lang Darma, Buddhism declined to low ebb, surviving only in remote Tibetan villages. But many great men, including notably Lachen Gonpa Rapsal, raised it again from its very foundations. Many Tibetan scholars, such as Rinchen Zangpo, Gyaltsen Sengge, and Tsultrim Gyalwa of Nagtso, came to India.

Having completed their studies at Nalanda and Vikramashila viharas, they invited many unrivaled Indian scholars, such as the great Swami Dipamkarajnana, Sakya Shri of Kashmir, and Mritijnana, to Tibet. In course of time they translated all the teachings of the Buddha and the works of the Indian scholars into Tibetan. Thus the sun of the Dharma began to shine in the land of Tibet.

In those days it was not so easy to travel from Tibet to India as it is today. One had to measure the long, hazardous route from Tibet to India via Nepal on foot, step by step. One had to face the dangers of wild animals and oppressive summer heat to such an extent that out of a hundred students only three or four could survive and return to their homes. It is because of their gallant efforts and sacrifices that we received the teachings of the Blessed one in our country, and they even spread to the adjacent countries.

In one of the Sutras Lord Buddha had predicted that after 2500 years of His Parinirvana the Dharma would flourish in 'the country of red-faced people'; In the past, some of the Tibetan scholars had held that this prediction was meant for Tibet. I feel that our lives would be entirely aimless if the Dharma, which was brought to our land by great scholars at such immense cost, were allowed to decay. For my part, I shall make every effort within my power to keep the Dharma alive."[10]

—Dalai Lama

Growth of Buddhism in Tibet

By the eleventh century Buddhism had already became very popular, in Tibet and its rulers were inviting reputed Buddhist savants from India. Through Nepal lie the mountain trails to be followed by Tibetan scholars in their quest for knowledge, and by Indian Buddhist scholars who wanted to journey to Tibet. In Nepal Tibetan scholars used to make a prolonged stay in order to get them accustomed to the hot and humid climate before descending into the plains of India. Here in Nepal, Tibetans learned the rudiments of Sanskrit Grammar, and this enabled them to continue their studies at the great centers of Buddhist learning - Nalanda, Odantapuri and Vikramashila. On their way to and back from Tibet these scholars often met each other in the Kathmandu valley. Thus this valley became a meeting place of Nepali, Indian and Tibetan scholars.

Moreover, towards the close of the twelfth century the political scene in the northern plains of India was rapidly changing. By this time even the northeastern plains were forced to bear the brunt of foreign invasion.

From the eleventh to the close of the fourteenth century Nepal remained a prominent center of Buddhist learning. During this period numerous Nepali scholars went abroad dedicating themselves to the spread of the Buddhist faith. Of course, even before this period Nepali monks had gone far and wide to disseminate Buddhism. As an example Buddhabhadra, a monk from Kapilavastu, who went to China in 409, A.D. taught his faith there at different places finally stayed in Nanking and assisted Fa Hsien in his tremendous task of translating and editing volumes of Buddhist texts, he had brought from India, into Chinese and continued the hard work even after the death of Fa Hsien in 420.

With the growing interest in Buddhism the Tibetans felt the necessity of translating the Tripitakas and other Buddhist texts into Tibetan languege. This was a gigantic task requiring a tremendous intellectual effort. But the devoted Nepali and Indian Buddhist scholars and their Tibetan colleagues did accomplish this remarkable and unique task- the creation of a philosophic language with a good stock of literary idiom, which made possible the Buddhist scriptures to be rendered into Tibetan. In this regard the names of Nepali scholars such as Shantibhadra, Jnanakirti and Lakshmikar are worth mentioning. Ratnakirti, Vairochana, Kanakshree, Vageeshwarakirti and several others went to India and served in the Vikramashila Monastery as teachers. Other scholars Dus Kor-pa, Tham Chun-pa, and others went to Tibet and preached Buddhism there.

Renowned Tibetan scholars such as Ra Lochawa and Ra Champa came to Nepal and studied from Nepali scholars like Mahakaruna, Atulyadas and others. Many learned Nepali scholars named Atulya, Diwakarachandra, and others went to India and became disciples of Adwayavajra, the veteran teacher of Vajrayani Tantrism. Samanta Shree and Koyashree were renowned scholars of Kalachakrayana (a Vehicle of Time wheel) and He' vajratantra. At the invitation of Tibetan disciples, Vibhootichandra went to Tibet and taught them on Yogic practices. Besides being an efficient Tantrician, he was also a master in image making. Raweendra, another renowned iconologist, too, went to Tibet and repaired many images there.

Of the artists and artisans who went abroad during this period, Araniko, who went leading a team of sculptors, artists, architects and builders to Shakya, Tibet built Golden Chaitya and Monasteries and contributed to the development and consolidation of Buddhism there. (See also the sixth Chapter of this book on Araniko).

During the twelfth and thirteenth century a number of scholars from Kashmir came to Nepal. They remained in Nepal for a long period and some of them went to Tibet. Of the Nepali scholars who extended co-operation to them, Buddhashree was the most eminent. He had been a Sthawira (senior Bhikshu) in Vikramashila Monastery and after coming back to Nepal, he was engaged in teaching Tantras and the Prajnaparamita. He went to Tibet with the Kashmiri scholar in 1119 A.D.

Similarly, many Indian scholars also came to Nepal and studied different aspects of Buddhism. Some of them, Vanaratna for example, even settled down in Nepal. He became a disciple of a learned Nepali, Sheelasagar. Many Tibetan scholars, who had come to Nepal, learned from him. He went to Tibet several times. He died around 1168 A.D. in the Kathmandu valley at an advanced age of over 85 years.

These Nepali scholars either taught their students at home or were engaged in studying and teaching works at different monasteries. The Bahals and Bahis (monasteries) were great centers of learning. Various books were written or copied in good handwriting here in Nepal. Pictures or portraits were drawn and tapestries made. These Bahals and Bahis, besides being centers of Buddhist lore and arts, were also well known for astronomy, medicine, mathematics and other sciences.

The Vajrayani priests were also renowned for their Tantric miracles. Some of them whose Tantric feats have become almost legendary are Amarsingha, Wakvajra, Lalitvajra, Lilavajra, Manjuvajra, Surathvajra, Hasavajra, Shaswatvajra, Bandhudatta, Samantaharsha and Sudhakara. Many anecdotes are still told about their feats. Their Tantric lore, however, seems at present to have been lost. These Tantric priests even worked as physicians, treating their disciples and patients from nearby communities in medical as well as Tantric ways.

Some of the well-known Monasteries of that period were the following as is referred to in the Blue Annals of Tibet.

The Lohan (stone) Vihara (monastery) seemed to have been well renowned in the eleventh century. Two copies of the Prajnaparamita, one dated 1008 A.D. and the other dated 1015 A.D. were recovered from there.

The Yampi Maha Vihara of Patan was built at the end of the eleventh century by Sunayashree Mishra, a Nepali scholar of the

Kapilavastu District, who settled down at Patan after his return from Tibet. Only a monk or at least a celibate Vajracharya can be the priest in this Vihara. It is said that Sunayashree Mishra himself had started this tradition.

But according to the Souvenir published by the Yampi Vihar on the Occasion of 2546th Buddha Jayanti in May 2003, the Yampi Maha Vihara was established in the first Century A.D. by Sunayashree Mishra. Asharam Shakya, a senior official of the Vihara, says that according to the Vihar-sources Sunayashree Mishra and his two other brothers Dharmashree Mishra and Jinashree Mishra of Kapilavastu came to Nepal Valley after completion of their studies in Banaras, India. When the three Mishra brothers arrived at the Valley they found the Lalitavana covered with dense forest and surrounded by three rivers Nakkhu, Balkhu and Bagmati. They were enchanted with the beauty and peaceful atmosphere in the area and decided to establish the Yampi Maha Vihara there.

So it seems correct to say that it was not the scholar Sunayashree Mishra who built the Yampi Vihara after coming back from Tibet to Nepal in the 11th Century as stated by Bhuban Lal Pradhan. But it may be another person with the same name who might have come back to Nepal after visiting Tibet and renovated the Yampi Maha Vihara in the eleventh Century.

It may not be out of context to mention here there was another Tantric scholar Sunyashree with his family name 'Mitra' (not Mishra) who visited Tibet in the time of the Fifth Dalai Lama. About his Tantric feat, it is mentioned in traditional stories that, once when he was drinking tea with the Dalai Lama, he threw his tea through the window. When the Dalai Lama, surprised by his manner, asked him the reason for his abrupt action, the scholar replied that as he saw his Monastery (Yampi vihara) in Nepal was catching by fire so he had to throw tea to quell the fire. The Dalai Lama was impressed with the scholar's act of the Tantric feat." Tradition maintains it", says Asharam Shakya.

From a work dated 1045 A.D. it is learnt that King Gunakamadeva, the founder of modern Kathmandu, had built a Vihara known as Padmachakra Mahavihara.

Padmabhumi Vihara seemed to have been exclusively associated with Tibetan Buddhists. Scholars from Tibet used to stay here. They were often engaged in translating Sanskrit works into the Tibetan language.

Some of the renowned Viharas were Dharmachakra Mahavihara,

Naka Vihara, Yo Khachhe Vihara, Karanda Vihara, Kirtipunya Vihara, Vikramshila Mahavihara and Shri vatsa Vihara. To the day, most of them are still in operational condition while the where-abouts of others are unknown.

During this period, hundreds of Nepali scholars, both monks and laymen, went to Tibet, China, Mongolia and also to India. Evidently, it is their devotion to Buddhist Doctrines, love of learning and culture, fraternal feelings for other people and philanthropic spirit of Buddhism that inspired them to go far and wide from their homeland and dedicate their lives to enlightening fellow beings. Their dedication to the noble cause is indeed highly impressive. The examples furnished by them have in fact proved that Nepalis were advanced as scholars and missionaries and had in the past made great contributions to the spread of humanitarian and cosmopolitan teachings of Lord Buddha.[11]

Tibetan Buddhism or Lamaism

According to L. Austine Waddell "...but judging at the close association of the name Padmasambhava with Lamaist sorceries, and special creeds of old unreformed section of the Lama's Nin-ma-pa who profess and are acknowledged to his immediate followers, and whose older scriptures date back within two centuries of the Guru's time, it is evident that his teaching was of that extreme Tantric and magical type of Mahayana Buddhism which was then prevalent in his native country Udayana and Kashmir. And to this highly impure form of Buddhism already covered by so many foreign accretions and saturated with so much demonology, was added a portion of the ritual and most of the demons and indigenous Bonpa religion, and each of the demons was assigned its proper place in the Lamaist Pantheion".

Primitive Lamaism may therefore be defined as a priestly mixture of Sivaite mysticism, magic, and Indo -Tibetan demonology overlaid by a thin varnish of Mahayana Buddhism. And to the present day Lamaism still retains this character".[12]

Lamaism in Practice

The evolution of Mahayana or Tantric Vajrayana school of Buddhism took quite a different turn in the northern region of Nepal. The northern border region of Nepal, forming layers of Himalayan Mountains, runs more than six hundred miles along the Tibetan border and as such the local inhabitants were in close touch with the

Tibetans. In Tibet Buddhism replaced the Bonn religion to a marked degree. The traditional nature worship, however, continued even after the introduction of Buddhism. The mutual influence between Vajrayana and nature worship gave rise to Lamaism in the eighth century. The most influential sect of Tibetan Lamaism the Yellow sect was founded in the fourteenth century. By the thirteenth and fourteenth centuries the cult of saints had also risen. Innumerable male and female deities and demons (evil spirits) and fiendesses (wicked) at different levels had been conceived, some of whom are ferocious and formidable as seen in the Devil Dances.

Mahayana and Tantric variant teachers Vasubandhu, Padmasambhawa, Shantarakshita, Deepankarshreejnana and others, having crossed high mountain passes in the north of Nepal, had gone to Tibet. But the historical evidence of whether or how far they tried to convert the inhabitants there to their respective faiths is not available. At any rate, the modification of Buddhist Doctrines in Tibet eventually resulted in the establishment of Lamaism, which turned out, in several ways, different not only from the pristine Buddhism but also from the Mahayana or Tantric Vajrayana which prevailed in Nepal. And both Doctrines and Monastic Organizations underwent certain changes.

In the sixth century A.D. Nepal was already a thriving Buddhist country. King Srongtsan Gampo (617-650 A.D.) of Tibet married a Nepali princess and a Chinese Princess, who were Mahayani Buddhists. They extended active cooperation and encouraged him to promote Buddhism. It greatly helped him to introduce, enhance and get Buddhism well established in Tibet. This way Buddhist civilization dawned upon Tibet. After two centuries a king, called Lang Darma an adherent of native nature worship, created disruption to the progress. But the devotion of the rulers and people restored Buddhist faith all the more firmly. It was about this time that Padmasambhava and others were called in. Then Buddhism gained popularity rapidly after the long and severe struggles for power, in course of which the Lamaist order became a hierarchy and acquired temporal power.

In 1419 A.D. the Dalai Lama came out to be as both the Spiritual and Temporal final authority. He came to be regarded as the Infallible, Head of Monastery, representative of Adibuddha on earth and the Buddhist Pope-King. When the Dalai Lama died, he was believed to have incarnated in a male baby who happened to be born just about the time he died. In the meantime, Tibetan Buddhist scriptures were being written one after another.

The Lamas of Tibet belong to different sects - Gelukpa, Nyingmapa, Shakya-pa, Kargyupa and so on. These Lamas are found in large numbers not only in hillsides but also in the capital and elsewhere. These Lama Buddhists, whether monks or the laity, with their red or yellow robes of gorgeous dresses, prayer wheels, bells, rosaries, and hand-drums are always striking to the eye.

Lamaism has, indeed, with its rosary of 108 beads, prayer wheels, prayer flags, holy water, unique religious service with peculiar musical instruments and choirs, mystic rites, monastic hierarchy, cult of saints, odd images and tapestries, incarnates, devil (traditionally regarded as evil-spirits) dances and so on, evolved a singular type of Buddhism.

The decoration and equipment of a Lama monastery and the religious services conducted in it, too, have their own peculiarities. The scene in a monastery on a festive day is most impressive. The chief Lama intones the Buddhist scriptures and the monks chant in response, some times accompanied by sounds of large trumpets and the ringing of bells. Incense is burnt before the altars on which repose gold and silver images of Buddha and holy Lamas. Twinkling lights burning before distant shrines add to the religious atmosphere of these temples.

Prayer wheels are constantly being turned both by the monks and laymen. Even while walking along the way the Lamas repeat the mystic Buddhist prayer " Om Mani Padme Hum". They are also fond of fluttering high flags on which the prayers are written on long strips of silk or cloth and fastened to lofty flagpoles in the breeze. The sacred words "Om Mani Padme Hum " which means the jewel is in the lotus or prayers to the one who is on the lotus (i.e. the self-creative force is in the cosmos) are believed to have mystic charm of wonder working. Whenever the flags are blown by the wind, and the holy six syllables are turned towards heaven, it counts as if a prayer was uttered. The prayer, which brings down blessings not only upon the pious devotee at whose expense it was put up, but also upon the whole locality. In every Lama village or on one's residence the prayer flag- staff meets the eye.

The Lamas also play unique instruments including long trumpets, some of which are up to 15ft long and can be heard miles away. Then there are cymbals, usually made of bronze. There are also huge temple drums supported on a wooden stand. On some occasions Devil Dancers put on wonderful brocade dresses and wear fantastic masks.

These monasteries, besides being temples to enshrine Images of Buddha and Buddhist Deities are the repositories of historical relics and other valuables objects. They conduct religious rites and are also centers of learning where young Lama novices as well as others study Buddhism and practice its canon. The number of Lamas in a monastery depends on its size, ranging from ten or twelve to hundreds. Some of the Lamas in these monasteries are believed to have been incarnates while some others are saints or perfect Buddhists.

The monasteries may also be called workshops of art. There the Lamas paint very fine portraits of the holy ones and make beautiful needlework pictures of them. These needle-works are rare works of art.

The religious and artistic fervor becomes all the more commendable when we consider that these Lamas, mostly living at the Monasteries, away from the urban amenities of the modern age keep the light of preaching of Buddhism alive.[13]

End Notes

1. Tsepon W.D. Shakabpa. *Tibet: A Political History*, New York: Potala Palace Publications, 1988, p. 24.
2. Min Bahadur Shakya. *Princess Bhrikuti Devi*, Delhi: Book Faith India, 1997, p. 33.
3. Chattopadhya, Alaka and Chimpa Lama: *Atisha and Tibet*. Delhi: Motilal Banarasidas, 1981, pp. 173-179.
4. Shakya, p. 33.
5. Ibid, p. 33.
6. Gyanamani Nepal. *Nepal Bhot Chin Sambandhka Kehi Samskritik Paksha (Some Cultural Aspects of Nepal Tibet China Relations)* Kathmandu: Royal Nepal Academy. 2045 B.S., pp. 8-9.
7. L. Austine Waddel. *The Buddhism of Tibet or Lamaism*. New Delhi: Asian Educational Services, 1991, p. 22.
8. Shakabpa, p. 34.
9. Ibid, pp. 36-38.
10. *Dalai Lama: Speech* at the 2500th Buddhajayanti Celebrations on 29th November 1956 in New Delhi. Shakabpa, p. 329.
11. Bhuban Lal Pradhan. *Buddhism in Nepal* (Unpublished) dfg Babarmahal, Kathmandu pp. 44, 46, 48-50.
12. Waddel, pp. 29-30.
13. Bhuban Lal Pradhan, pp. 35-36 and 39-41.

D. Buddhism in China

Introduction of Buddhism

During the reign of Maurya Emperor Asoka (273-252 B.C) Buddhism was adopted as the state religion of his empire, India. Asoka became a Buddhist himself and sent monks to proselytize through out India and the neighboring countries of Sri Lanka, Burma, Nepal and China.

During the Eastern (Later) Han Dynasty (25-220 A.D.), Indian monk Kayamudan went to the Han capital Luoyang to preach Buddhism. It is said that he informed his Chinese followers that late Indian Emperor Asoka had left 84,000 Buddhist relics of which 19 were located in China. The 19 Buddhist relics, it is said, were scattered over areas in the south of Xin jiang and west of Yunnan, both of which were gateways to India. It was there that the Buddhist scholars of the two countries began to visit each other and exchange their opinions. These visits of Buddhist scholars facilitated interactions and discourses on Buddhism.

In the year 242 B.C. 18 Buddhist monks from western regions brought Sanskrit scriptures to the city of XianYang in Shaanxi. However, their attempt at that time to gain a foothold for the religion in the heart land of China failed.

Asoka was also involved in founding the ancient state of the Keria Yuthian. Legend had it that Prince Kushana and, later, the Vizier of Emperor Asoka brought people there and founded the Yuthian state around the year 250 A.D.

It is said that the earliest success of Buddhism was in 80 B. C. when Kasmiri monk Vairochana obtained the approval of the Yuthian ruler to build a Buddhist shrine at a place several kilometers to the south of the city of Yuthian, which became the first historical Buddhist temple in Chinese territory.

The rulers of the Han Dynasty did not accept Buddhism until the middle of the first century. In 65 A.D. Prince Chu became a

Buddhist convert and followed the Buddhist doctrine of Shramana and Upasaka in daily life style. This caused a stir in the Han Imperial court, and even the Han Emperor Ming Ti was said to have seen a golden image of Buddha in his dream. As a result, an 18-man group of scholars led by Cai Yin and Qin- ting was sent by the Han court to study Buddhist religion in central Yuezhi. A Buddhist state was then founded in the region of former Scythia, Present Afghanistan and northern India. In 68 A.D the scholars returned to China, bringing with them Buddhist portraits, scriptures and two Indian scholar monks Kashyapa Matanga and Dharmaratna. Soon after, a Buddhist temple called Bai Ma Si (White Horse Temple) was built in Luoyang where the monks began their translation work of the scripture, symbolizing the first instance of an official approval of the religion. During the reign of Han Emperor Huan Ti (147 - 167) and Ling Ti (168 - 189), Buddhism became so popular in China that the statues of Buddha were even erected and worshipped in the Palace, while equal respect was paid to Buddha as to Huang Ti (yellow Emperor) and Lao-tse, the traditional Chinese saint. In the following years, Buddhist monks were invited from India and other places to Luoyang where they joined the translation work of Buddhist scriptures along with their Chinese colleagues, marking the beginning of the most magnificent translation venture seen in the history of cultural exchange between China and another country. With successive visits to China by many Buddhist scholars from India, Nepal and other countries, the doctrines of Buddhism began to be introduced more extensively in China, while Chinese scholars also began their study of Buddhism. This led to the writing of the first Chinese Buddhist book entitled "I Huo Lun" (On Truth and Doubts) in the third century by a Confucius writer Mou Rong,

The distinguished Buddhist scholar Buddhabhadra of Kapilvastu, Nepal was also invited in 4th century to visit China to teach philosophy of Buddha, explain Buddhist concepts to the Chinese Buddhists and answer their questions of them on Buddhism and help them to understand the preaching of Buddha, the Enlightened One.[1]

Translation of Buddhist Scriptures

In the earliest period, when Buddhist scriptures were introduced to China, they were in their Sanskrit version. In the year of 65 A. D., a Buddhist's group went to Yuechi where they copied 42 chapters of Buddhist scripture and brought them back to Luoyang in 68 A.D.

They translated it into Chinese with the title "Forty-two Chapters of Scripture." While this translation itself is no longer in existence, it was quoted in an introductory article written by Xiang Kai of the Han Dynasty, which said the translation had come from Futu, thereby indicating it was based on a Vernacular Indian version. Later, during the second to the third century, Xiyu monks came to China from Kangju, Anxi and great Yuezhi bringing with them a number of rare copies of the Buddhist scripture.

In the beginning of the fourth century, when Chinese monk Fa Xian visited India, Nepal, Sri Lanka and other places of pilgrimage related to the life, enlightenment, preaching and Nirvana of Buddha he found there that most of these Bhikshus depended on learning in oral tradition and related subjects were not available in the form of books. While the doctrines were conveyed orally, their understanding differed. As a result there were marked differences in Buddhist scriptures.

The Chinese Buddhists went on a pilgrimage to the west to find more and better copies of scripture on the spot. The earliest pioneer of the pilgrims was Zhu Shixing who visited Yuthian in 260 and returned with Buddhist scriptures. Dharmaraksha, a Yuczhi descendent whose family had lived in Tunhuang for generations followed the venture. In 265 he traveled deep into the north west of India and obtained 156 volumes of Buddhist scriptures. Having learned the languages, he translated the scriptures into Chinese during the journey and continued after arrival at Chang An. After that, copies of the scriptures were available in Luoyang and Chang An.

During the 400 years from the second half of the fourth to the mid eighth century, the search for and collection of Sanskrit Buddhist scriptures continued with growing enthusiasm in China. Such noted monks as Kumarjiva and Buddhabhadra went to China. Fa Xian, Dao Tai, Zhi Meng, Bao Xian, Xuan Tsang, Yi Jing and Bu Kong traveled to India and China one after another with the objective to promote understanding of Buddhism in China. Xuan Zsang was most successful in collecting 657 volumes of Sanskrit scriptures including Mahayana scriptures and Mahayana Theories.

As a result of the efforts of these pilgrims, the city of Chang-An became virtually a center of Buddhist literature in China. During the years when the famous translator Kumarajiva (334 - 409) from Quici, Buddhabhadra (358 - 429) from Kapilavastu, Nepal and Konarods of west India were engaged in the translation of Buddhist scriptures in Chang An. Fa Xian and other noted pilgrims returned to Chang An to join them in their translation works. The tradition continued for centuries, 700 years, to make China rich with ancient Buddhist scriptures and literature through the translations, which were essential for the compilation of a complete volume of Buddhist doctrines called Tripitaka. It was later introduced to and reproduced in other Asian countries including Xinluo, Korea and Japan. [2]

Buddhist Arts in China

Buddhist art, as an important part of the religious arm, was introduced to Yutian in Xinjiang from Kashmir. The gypsum inset statue of Buddha and red pottery with sitting Buddha unearthed from a ruin dated to the first century B.C. in Malikawati south of Yutian in 1979 were the oldest Buddhist art symbols found in China. Apart from these, the earliest Buddhist painting known in China was a portrait of Shakyamuni drawn on cotton fabric, which was brought from the great Yuezhi to Luoyang by Cai Yin in the eastern (later) Han Dynasty upon the order of Han Emperor Ming Ti. After the Bai Ma Si (White Horse Temple) was built in Luoyang in 68 A.D., a mural called "Thousands on horseback pay tribute to the Stupa" based on an original sample from India, was painted on the temple wall. This was also the first known mural in a Chinese Buddhist temple. However, the Chinese artists also drew their earliest Buddhist paintings or scriptures during the Han Dynasty from their own imagination, which thus resembled supernatural images in Chinese fables or fairy tales. Such examples were seen in the wall painting of an "Immortal on white Elephant" discovered in a late eastern Han tomb unearthed in Horinger of inner Magnolia in 1971.

Following the arrival of more and more Buddhist monks from India since the third century, Buddhist paintings were introduced through either the visiting Indian monks or Chinese pilgrims returning from abroad to inland China. As Buddhism grew more popular during the Jin Dynasty (265-420), many Chinese artists who engaged in Buddhist painting were themselves Buddhists. Another Buddhist artwork was a 1.4-meter high jade Buddha statue presented to China by Sri Lanka. The Buddhist art of mural painting became even more popular during the Tang Dynasty, when examples from India and Qiuci were widely initiated. The contents of such murals were no longer confined to the life or teaching of the Buddha, but focused on stories from Buddhist scriptures then in the late Tang

Dynasty. It became more fashionable to paint portraits of Buddha on tough silk and hang them on walls.

The lion pattern was first introduced into north China before Han Dynasty, as a winged animal called Tian Lu (Heavenly gift) or Buxie (guardian against evils). At the time, lion was idolized in Persia and northern India as the symbol of power. The memorial monument of Indian Emperor Asoka in Lauriya Nandangarh had lion symbols on the pillar capitals while the stone pillars of Sanchi had capitals bearings four lions.

Another decorative art introduced from the western regions, which became popular during the Han Dynasty, was the grape and honey suckle pattern. Grape pattern was widely used in the design of both silk textile and polished bronze mirrors.

The image of winged immortals appeared widely in the stone murals of the Han Dynasty, primarily under the auspices of Qin and Han rulers who favored Taoist philosophy. It became popular as the symbol of paradise advocated by Buddhists and as the winged angels introduced from Greco-Roman fables.

The most astonishing discovery of the Greco-Roman time art in Xinjiang was the Roman angelic paintings found in the ruins of a Buddhist temple in Miran west of Lop Nur.

During the Han and Jin Dynasties the Buddhist fine art, which absorbed the art style of Greco-Roman paintings to form its own ethnic culture with Gandhara as its geographical center, gradually spread into Xinjiang region. It followed the Buddhist religious influence and flourished in a new cultural boom, first in the areas inhabited by Indian immigrants and the people speaking Tukhara language. The birth of Gandhara fine art marked the beginning of a new epoch in the history of art, glorifying the vast central and East Asian region with its brilliant feats through the centuries. In the south of Thian- Shan Mountains, the boom of the Buddhist art spread along both the south and north edges of the Tarim Basin with Yutian and Quici as its center.

This tradition has continued and developed in accordance with the facilities available for the enhancement of Buddhism in China all along with the time.[3]

Buddhist Architectures in China

In the history of architecture, the design of religious structure had been the most ambitious development in China. Most of the new structures belonged to the religions of foreign origin, especially

Buddhism. Ever since Buddhism was introduced to China, the construction of grottoes became the rage in Xinjiang as well as in northern China. These cave structures, which could last for a long time in dry desert or hilly regions, comprised mainly two kinds: the Shrine (Chaitya) and the Monastery (Vihara). The design of temple buildings had also followed the Indian pattern in the beginning. However, the structure of pagodas, which had originated from the Indian Stupa, had seen remarkable developments. The Indian Stupa (Thupa in Pali language) was originally built to preserve Buddhist relics.

For the first time the Stupas were erected in the period after the Nirvana of Buddha at Kapilavastu, Lumbini, Kushinagar and nearby places to preserve the relics of former and historic Buddhas. Then Stupas were built at Sanchi. In the first century B.C., a huge stupa was built at the site of Shakyamuni's enlightenment in Bodhgaya.

The earliest type of Chinese-style tower structures was the multi-storied wooden pagoda, represented by the Bai Ma Si (White Horse Temple) Pagoda in Loyang built in the Eastern Han Dynasty, the Yongning Temple's seven-storied pagoda in Da-tong built in 467 during the Northern Wei Dynasty and the Yongning Temple's nine-storied pagoda in Loyang built also during the Northern Wei Dynasty in 516.The Yongning Temple Pagoda in Loyang which totaled 1000 Chinese Chi (330 meters) high. Brick pagodas began to appear in China during the sixth century. The oldest and most spectacular structure was the Songyu Temple pagoda built at Mount Songshan of Henan in 524A.D. The 15 storied, multi-caved polygonal brick pagoda was built in the form of a curvaceous skyscraping spire.

The Buddhist pagodas built in the Tang Dynasty included both the stupa-type and the multi-storied pavilion-type or multi-caved brick structure. Existing examples of the Stupa-type Buddhist structures included The HsuanTsang Pagoda in the Xingjiao Temple in Xi-an. In later development, Buddhist pagodas of the octagonal shape began to appear in the ninth century, as were represented by the several pagodas built during the Liao Dynasty in north China, and by the tilted-caved twin pagodas found in Guanzhou of Fujian.

In this context it will not be inordinate to mention the contributions made by the Nepali artist Araniko in the 13th century during the Yuan Dynasty. He went to build golden chaitya, arts and architecture, including monasteries and other objects required for ritual worships in Tibet. After completion of the assigned works there, Phagpa, impressed with his genius, took him to Imperial court in

Beijing. During the 40 years of services to Emperor Kublai Khan in China he built three white Chaityas, many monasteries, and temples, hundreds of images, engraved or caste, of Buddhist, Taoist and Confucius religion, various kinds of paintings and portraits, decorations, and jewelleries for them. He also trained many Chinese, Nepali, Tibetan and Mongolian novices to continue the style and tradition of the Art, which encompassed all of China and nearby countries with the influence of his artistic skill and genius. [4]

Spread of Buddhism

Buddhist monasteries first appeared in China during the Eastern Han dynasty but it was only after the Western Tsin dynasty (255-316) that Buddhism began to spread in this country and flourished in the Southern Dynasties. At its heyday in the Northern Dynasties, Buddhism boasted thirty thousand monasteries and over two million monks and nuns throughout the country.

The propagation of Buddhism and translation of a large number of Buddhist scriptures exercised a great influence on the culture of China. Buddhist scriptures embody the culture of ancient India, including knowledge about nature, views on human life, as well as historical records of India. They also contain beautiful literary works, such as tales, fables, long poems and songs. These constituted a rich source of inspiration for the science, philosophy and literature of China. It was also to the influence of Indian and Nepali art, architect, sculpture and painting that Chinese art owed its unique style.

At that time, there were three famous Buddhist translators, the Venerable Tao An (312-385) a Chinese, Kumarajiva (343-413) an Indian and Buddhbhadra (358 - 429) a Nepali who spent many years in China and translated more than three hundred volumes of Buddhist scriptures.

By the first half of the sixth century, everywhere in north and south China temples and pagodas were built and Buddhist statues sculptured, cast and molded. These works of art are a tribute to the great achievements in the field of art made by the people of the time.

In Northern Wei it took more than one hundred years to complete the many grottoes and temples on Yunkang Hill (near Tatung, Shansi Province). An image of Buddha carved of stone is still intact. It is 50 feet tall and is in a grotto measuring 70 feet wide and 50 feet deep. The Buddha sits on a pedestal measuring 50 feet across and is surrounded by four smaller Buddhas. The pedestal, column and walls are richly carved. There is also a big image of Manjushree seated on a lion, carved in the mountain.

Next to this there are three more caves, which are differently constructed. In one of them is a bas-relief depicting the story of Sakyamuni mounting a horse in the night to leave his home to become a monk. Four gods support the four hoofs of the horse as if to prevent the household being awakened by the sound of the hoof. In almost all the grottoes there are bas-reliefs of flying angels performing exquisite dances. These figures are supple and graceful and their garments are exquisitely carved. There is also a big image of Manjushree seated on a lion, carved in the mountain. [5]

This process continues till today. And thus China has become a prominent Buddhist country equipped with a great collection of Buddhist script, sculptures, arts and architects. Like in other areas it has also become a source of Buddhistic matters for which scholars and artists from different countries solicit their cooperation.

Thus it could be seen how the Chinese people appreciated Buddhism as an agreeable way for mental peace and also for harmonious social relations. This popular opinion helped Buddhism to secure an important place among the guiding principles of Chinese life like Taoism and Confucianism. This concept remains till today to be a special characteristic of Chinese life.

The Chinese Buddhist scholars have compiled a huge book (approximately 2' long 1.5' broad and about 8" thick) on the development of Buddhism in China. It deals with the major events and important developments in philosophic approaches, processes and procedures of rites and rituals of worshipping the Buddha. It is furnished with relevant photos and sketches of images and scenes. It covers a period of two thousand years from the time the story of the Buddha reached to China up to the present. Publication of this book has become a very helpful means to study and popularize Buddhism among the devotees and persons interested in Buddha's preaching. A copy of this book is kept in the Chinese Temple in Lumbini Nepal, and can be seen upon request.

Tooth Relic of Buddha

The Holy Tooth Relic Of Shakyamuni Buddha is enshrined in a new pagoda constructed by Buddhists of China. The pagoda is located at the original site of the Ling Kuang Monastery, at the western hills in the suburbs of Beijing. This Holy Tooth Relic has been preserved in China for more than fifteen hundred years.[6]

According to Buddhist historical records, the Buddha left two teeth in the world when his body was cremated after his Nirvana. One of them was taken to Ceylon (now Sri Lanka), the other one to the ancient kingdom of Udayana (at present the Swat Province of Pakistan). From Udayana it was brought to Khotan (at present in the Xinjiang Autonomous Region of China). During the 5th century, a Chinese monk scholar of southern Chi Dynasty, named Fa-Hsien (not the famous traveler Fa-Hsien) traveled to Khotan and brought the relic to Nanking, which was then taken to southern capital of Chi. Following the reunification of China under the Sui Dynasty, the Tooth Relic was sent to the new Capital Chang An. During the five dynasties when central China fell into a Chaotic State, the Tooth Relic was taken from one place to another until it reached Yen-Ching (present Beijing), the Capital of Liao Dynasty in the North. The "Chronicle of Emperor Tao-Tsung" in the history of the Liao Dynasty, vol. XXII, contains a record related to the enshrinement of the Buddha's Tooth Relic in the Chao-Hsien Pagoda in the 8th month of the 7th year of Hsien-yang (1071). This is how the Buddha's Tooth-Relic was brought to Beijing.

The Ling-Kuang Monastery, enclosing the Chao-hsien Pagoda, was founded in the 8th century, and the pagoda, which was an octagonal brick construction of ten stories, was built at the Southeast corner of the premises. Because the brick bore stamped pictures of Buddha and Pagodas, this pagoda was generally known as the "Pagoda with pictures (images) of one thousand Buddhas", The Ling-Kuang Monastery had been a famous place for pilgrimage and tourism in Beijing for several hundred years.

In 1900, when the foreign forces attacked Beijing, the monastery and the Chao-hsien Pagoda situated far in the suburbs of Beijing were also reduced to the ruins. After the catastrophe, the monks of the monastery when clearing the rubble found in the basement of the Pagoda a stone casket in which the Tooth-Relic was preserved. In the casket there was an aloes-wood box, on which the words "The Holy Tooth-Relic of Shakyamuni Buddha" were written. These words were written by Shan-Hui on the 23rd day of the 4th month in the 7th year of Thien-Hui" (963 A.C.). Fortunately, the stone "dew-basin" originally set on the top of the Pagoda still remains intact. The date of construction inscribed on it agrees with the record in the "History of the Liao Dynasty".

During the half-century after the discovery of the Tooth-Relic in 1900, the prevailing conditions at that time in the country made it impossible for the monks and devotees to worship the Holy-Relic in accordance with the Buddhist rituals.

After the establishment of the Peoples Republic, the Tooth-Relic was brought to Kuang-Chi Shi monastery in 1955, where the Tooth-Relic was enshrined in a golden stupa inlaid with seven kinds of jewels kept in the Sharira Pavilion, for the worship of Buddha by the devotees both at home and from abroad.

At the request of the Buddhists of Burma and Ceylon, the Tooth-Relic was taken to these countries on two different occasions, where the people there worshiped it with great devotion.

In 1957, the Buddhists of China proposed to construct a new Pagoda according to the Buddhist tradition for the purpose of providing a permanent place for the worship of the Holy Tooth-Relic, as well as for restoring the magnificence of all the historical sites of renown. Construction work had started from summer 1958 and, together with its accessory buildings, it was completed in spring 1964.

On June 25, 1964, the Buddhist Association of China performed in a solemn way the inauguration Ceremony when the Holy Tooth was enshrined in the Tooth-Relic Pagoda. Buddhist delegations from Cambodia, Ceylon, Indonesia, Japan, Laos, Mongolia, Nepal, Pakistan, Vietnam and Southern Vietnam attended the ceremony on invitations. The Buddhist delegates of these countries expressed their pleasure and praise for the significant occasion in the history of Buddhism in China.[7]

END NOTES

1. Shen Fuwei: *Cultural Flow Between China and Outside world Throughout History*: Foreign Languages Press Beijing 1997, p. 47.
2. Ibid., pp. 100-102
3. Ibid., pp. 59-65
4. Ibid., p. 126
5. *An Outline History of China*: Foreign Languages Press, Beijing 1958, pp. 96-98.
6. *The Buddhist Tooth Relic Pagoda,* The Buddhist Association of China Beijing, 1969, pp. 5-6.
7. Ibid., pp. 8-10.

Bibliography

English Books

Anning Jing: Anige (1245-1306) A Nepali Artist at Yuan Court: A thesis Presented by for the degree, Master of Arts, Graduate School of The Ohio State University, Department of History of Art 1989 (not yet published).

Assad Husain: British India's relations with the Kingdom of Nepal, George Allen and Unwin Ltd, London 1970.

Asharam Shakya: Araniko, the Pride of Nepal, Buddha Jayanti Souvenir Yampi Mahavihar Lalitpur 2002.

Avtar Singh Bhasin: Nepal's relations with India and China, SIBA EXIM Pvt. Ltd. Delhi 1994.

Bachelor Stephen: The Tibet guide, wisdom Publication, London W.I. 1987.

Bai Shouyi: An Outline History of China, foreign Languages Press, Beijing 2002.

Beal Samuel: Buddhist Literature in China, Sri Satguru Publication, Delhi, India 1988.

The life of Huen Tsang, Buddhism in China,

London 1884, Buddhist Records of Western World 1884, and Fahien's Travel in India 1869.Published From London and India

Bell Charles: Tibet Past and Present, Low Price Publications Delhi, India First Published in 1924 Reproduced 1997.

The people of Tibet, Religion of Tibet and Portrait of a Dalai Lama, Motilal Banarasi Das Publishers P.Ltd, Delhi

Beijing White Pagoda

Temple Administrative

Office: A brief Picture - Biography of Arniger, 2008.

Bhuban Lal Pradhan: Lumbini, Kapilavastu Devadaha, Research Center for Nepal and Asian Studies, Tribhuvan University, Kathmandu 1978.

Buddhism in Nepal, Unpublished book Babarmahal Kathmandu.

Blofeld John: The Wheel of life the Autobiography of a western Buddhist Century, and London Melbourne Auckland Johannesburg 1972.

Bohra K. And Saha B.P: Ancient History of India, Vikash Publishing House P. Ltd Delhi 1988.

Chang Jung: Wild Swans, Flamingo, an imprint of Harper and Collins Publishers, London. W6 18JB.1993.

Chattopadhya Alaka and Chimpa Lama: Atisha and Tibet, Motilal Banarasidas, Delhi 1981.

Ch'en Kenneth: Buddhism in China A Historical survey, Princeton University Press, Princeton, New Jersey 1973.

China Relics Publishing House: Potala Palace, Beijing Xinhua color Printing House, Beijing 1994.

Committee of Nationality and Religious Affairs of the Department of Civil Affairs of Shansi Province: A List of Buddhist Monasteries on the Wu T 'ai Mountain, 1959.

Dalai Lama: i) My Land My People, 1962,

ii) and Speech at the 2500th Buddhajayanti Celebrations on 29th November 1956 in New Delhi

Dawson Raymond: The Chinese Experience, Weidenfeld and Nicolson London SW11. 1978.

Deng Xiaoping: Fundamental Issues in Present day China 1987, Foreign Language press Beijing, China.

Dharmodaya Sabha: Report of International Buddhist Conference, Kathmandu 1956.

D.R. Regmi: Ancient Nepal, Calcutta 6/1A Banchharam, Arkur Lane 1960.

Dr. T.R. Ghoble: China Nepal Relation and India, Deep and Deep Publication, Delthi 1991.

Eastman Roger: The way of Religion, Harper and Raw Publishers 10 east, 53rd street, New York 10022.

Edited by Sankarnarayan KalpakamYorifomy Motohiro

Josh Shubhada A . Buddhism in India and Abroad, Somaiya Publications Pvt. Ltd. Mumbai, New Delhi 1996.

Edward J.Thomas: The life of Buddha, Vanarasidass Publications Private Limited, Delhi 1997.

Encyclopedia of Buddhism: Published in Japan.

Ennin: A Record of Travels in China to seek for the Dharma.

Fa Xien:A Record of Buddhist Kingdoms, translated and published by Foreign Languages Press Beijing, China.

Foreign Language Press China: An Outline History of China Beijing. 1958.

Gao Sheng Zhuan : Collection of life Stories of eminent Buddhists published in China.

Gernet Jacques: A History of Chinese Civilizations, Cambridge University Press U.K. Australia 1999.

Ghobble T.R.: Nepal China Relation and India, Deep and Deep Publication, Delhi.1991

Goldstein Malvin C : A History of Modern Tibet, 1913- 1951 University of California Press, Berkeley Los Angeles London 1991.

Hai Lan: Araniko's Architectural Legacy, Nepal-China Cultural Council Souvenir 3, 1982

Han Nienlung: Beijing Diplomacy of Contemporary China, New Horizon Press,1990 pp.182-184.

Harrier Heinrich: Seven years in Tibet, INDUS, 1995, and Return to Tibet. Penguin Books, 27 Wrights lane, London 1985 Return to Tibet Penguin Books.

Harishchandra Lal Singh: Modern Interpretation of Buddhism, Shirish Singh Lalitpur, Nepal 1994.

Hoffman H: The Religion of Tibet, 1961.

Hopkirk, Peter: The Great Game, Oxford University Press, Oxford, 1990.

Hsuan-Tsang: The records of the Western Region in the Tang Dynasty or records of western Travels translated and Published by foreign languages press, Beijing.

Hussein, Asad: British India's Relations with the Kingdom of Nepal, George Allen and unwinds Ltd London, 1970.

Institute of Foreign Affairs: Nepal China Relation Kathmandu 2005.

IUCN Office: A Report prepared by The World Conservation Union, Lalitpur Nepal,1998.

Jojin: A Record of Visits to the T'ien'-t'ai and Wu T'ai Mountains. Both this and Ennin's works are included in the encyclopedia of Buddhism Published in Japan.

Kawaguchi, Ekai: Three Years in Tibet. Book Faith India, Delhi 110033,1995.

Kenneth Ch'en: Buddhism in China. A Historical Survey, Princeton University Press, Princeton and New Jersey 1973.

Khadka, Narayan: Foreign Aid and Foreign Policy Major Powers and Nepal, Vikash Publishing House, Delhi 110014.

Khanal, Yadu Nath : Nepal's Non-Isolationist Foreign Policy, Satyal Publications, Delhibazar, Kathmandu, 2000.

Lamb Alistair: Britain And Chinese Central Asia, British India and Tibet, also Tibet, China and India.

Lan Hai: Beijing's White Dagoba: A link with the past, a symbol of friendship. Araniko's Architectural legacy, Nepal China Cultural Council souvenir 1980 and 1987 respectively

L. Austine Waddel: The Buddhism of Tibet or Lamaism, Asian Educational Services, New Delhi 1991.

Levi Sylvain: Le Nepal, Asian Education Services, New Delhi.

Li Tieh-Tseng: Tibet, Today and Yesterday, Bookman Associates New York 1954.

Liu Xinru: Ancient India and Ancient China, Trade and Religious Exchanges, AD 1-600 Oxford University Press, Delhi, 1994.

Majumdar, Kanchanmoy: Political Relations Between Nepal and India 1877-1923, Munsiram Manohar Lal Publishers Pvt.Ltd. S.S. Rani Jhansi Road, Delhi, 1971.

Manadhar, Triratna and Mishra Tirtha: Nepal's Quinquennial Missions to China, Published by Mrs.Purna devi Mananadhar and Mrs.Pushpa Mishra, Kathmandu, Nepal 1986.

Manandhar,Vijay Kumar:A Comprehensive History of Nepal-China Relations, (Vol. 1,2.) Adroit Publishers, New Delhi 2004.

Marsha Smith Weinder: Aspect of Painting and Patronage at the Mongol Court: 1260-1368, a Dissertation Presented for Ph.D.in California University 1982, (Not yet Published)

Maxwell Neville: India's China War Anchor Books, Garden Life, New York 1972

Mikinosuke Ishida: Gendai no kogeika Neparu no ozoku a-ni-ko no den si tsuite (on the life of the Nepali Craftsman A-ni-ko of Yuan Times). Moko Gakuho Vol. 2 (1941) P. 244-260.

Min Bahadur Shakya: Princess Bhrikuti Devi Book Faith India, Delhi, 1997.

Nepal China Nongovernmental forum: Report of the 9th meeting 12-13 June 2007.

Pai Huan-ts'ai The Cultural Objects of the Wu T'ai Mountain, Published by the Shansi People's Publishing House, 1957.

Panikkar K.M.: In Two Chinas, Hyperion Press, INC. Westport Connecticut 1961.

Percival Landon: Nepal, Asian Education Services, New Delhi 1993.

Pradhan Bhuban Lal: Bhrikuti is not the Daughter of Amshu Barma, Rolamba, Volume 1 issue 2, 1997.

Prem Raman Upreti: Nepal Tibet Relation 1850-1930 Nara Publications, Kathmandu 1980.

Rajbhandari Bharat Lall: Foreign Assistance in Nepal, Kualakhu Tol, Lalitpur, Nepal 1973.

Ram Rajendra: History of Buddhism in Nepal. Moti Lal Banarasidas Delhi, Patna, 1978.

Research and Information Division of FNCCI : Charts, Compliled from various publications of trade promotion center and Nepal Rastra Bank.

Rhys David T.W: Buddhism, London 1912.

Richardson H. E.: Tibet And its History, Oxford University Press, London 1962.

Rose Leo E.: Nepal Strategy for Survival. Center for South Asian studies, University of California Press, Berkley Los Angeles.1971

Rossabi Morris: Khubilai Khan His life and Times, University of Califormia Press, Berkeley California 1988.

SAARC Summit (14th): 29th clause of Delhi Declaration, 2007.

Salu Association, Salu Monastery: Paintings of Araniko Style, Nyangro, near Sigatse Tibet China.

Samuel Beal: Life of Shuan-tsuang, Munsiram Manohar Lal, Delhi 1973.

Schlagintweit E.: Buddhism in Tibet Book faith India Delhi 1999.

Scott Kenneith: The Chinese Their History and Culture. Mac Million Company, New York 1964.

Shah Rishikesh: Modern Nepal A Political History 1769-1955, 1996

Shakabpa Tsepon W.D: Tibet: A political History, Potala Publication, New York, 1992.

Shakya Min Bahadur: Princess Bhrikuti Devi, Book Faith India, and Delhi, 1997

Shen Fuwei: Cultural Flow Between China and outside world throughout History, foreign Languages Press, Beijing, China 1996.

Singh Shanker Man: Boosting Nepal-China Economic Tie, Kathmandu Post, December 1993.

Smith Charles: Training the links. Far Eastern Economic Review, 10 may 1987.

Smith Huston: Religion of Man, Harper and Raw Publishers 10 East. 53rd street. NY 10022.

Snellgrove David and Richardson Hugh: A Cultural History of Tibet, Shambhala, 300 Massachusetts Avenue Boston, and Massachusetts 02115 U.S.A.

Snellgrove David: Buddhist Himalaya. London 1957.

Soot hill William Edward and Hodous Lewis: A dictionary of Chinese Buddhist Terms, Moti Lal Banarasidas Publishers P.Ltd, Delhi, 110007.

Taring Rinch'en Dolma: Daughter of Tibet, Allied Publishers P.Ltd. 1978, New Delhi 10064.

The Buddhist Association of China: The Buddhist Tooth Relic Pagoda, Beijing 1969.

Thomas Edward J.: The life of Buddha as legend and history Motitlal Banarasidass Publishers Private Limited, Delhi, India 1997.

Thomas Watus: On Yuan Chuan's Travel in India London.

Tieh-tsheng Li: Tibet Today and Yesterday, Bookman Associates, New York, 1960.

Triratna Manandhar and Tirth Prasad Mishra: Nepal's Quin Quennial Missions to China, published by Mrs. Purna Devi Manandhara and Mrs. Pushpa Mishra, Kathmandu 1986.

Tripathi Rama Shankar: History of Ancient India, Moti Lal Banarasidas Delhi. 1967.

Tsepon W.D. Shakabpa: Tibet a political history, Potala Publications New york.

Tuker Francis: Gorkha, Constable and Company Limited, London 1957.

Uprety Prem Raman: Nepal Tibet Relation 1850-1930.Puga Nara Publication, Kathmandu, 1980.

Vasin Avatar Singh: Nepal's Relation with India and '"China. SIBA Exim Pvt. Ltd. Delhi, 1994.

Vijaya Kumar Manandhar: Nepal-China Relations Vll.IandII Adroit Publishers, 4675/21, Daryaganj, New Delhi -110 002

Waddel L. Austine: The Buddhism of Tibet, Asian Educational Services, New Delhi Madras 1991.

Wang Hung-wei: Some thoughts on Nepal China Relations, Friendship Journal of china Study Center December Issue, 2000.

Warren W. Smith Jr.: Tibetan Nation, Harper Collins, Publishers, and Delhi India 1997

Wang Huang-Wei: Some Thoughts on Nepal China Relations, Friendship, December Issue, China Study Center, Kathmandu, 2000.

Wu Cheng'en: Journey to the west (the story of Hsuan tsang's travel in the form of a novel) in three volumes translated by W.J.F. Jenner Foreign Languages Press, Beijing 1995.

Younghusband Francis: India and Tibet, 1993. Asian Educational services, New Delhi.

Yunus Mohammed: Reflections on China. Wajed Alis Lahore, Pakistan 1986.

Chinese Books

Beijing University Library: Thang Dai Yu Xizhang Weuming. Beijing University Library

Chao Hsien-chung : T'ang-kuo Hsiu-Ho Chi-Lueh {Summary Narrative of the Peace Settlement of the Nepal-Tibet Dispute (1883)} Preface dated May 12, 1888, Published Privately by author.

Chao I: P'ing-Ting K'uo-Er-K'a Shu-Lueh (Summary Narrative of the Subjection of the Gorkhas). From Chuan IV of "Huang-Chao-Wu-Kung Chi-Shang.Yangchow, 1792.

Chou Yiliang: Zhog guo He Ya Chou Ge Guo Renmin de Heping Youhao Zheng Shi, Beijing University Library

Compiled by Chang Ting-yu and others: Ming- Shi (History of the Ming). 1739. Chuan 331 concerns Nepal.

Compiled by Hsiu Ouyang : Hsin t;ang Shu (New History of the T'ang) completed in 1060 A.D. Vol.39, chuan 221 concerns Nepal.

Compiled by Hsuan Tsang and edited by Pien-Chi: Ta- tang-Hsi Yu- Chu (Records of the Western Countries in the Great T'ang Period). Compiled by Hsuan-chuang and edited by Pien-chi; completed in 648 A.D

Compiled by Liu Hsu and others: Chiu t'ang Shu (Old History of the T'ang Dynasty) in the period from 936 to 946 A.D. Vol.40, Chuan 198, concerns Nepal.

Compiled by Long Wen -pin: Ming Hui-Yao (Classified Records of the Ming Dynasty), no date. Chuan 78 concerns Nepal.

Compiled by Tao hsuan: a Monk : Chi-Chia-Fag- Chi (Description of the Lands of Shakkyamuni Completed in 650.

Compiled by Wang Hong-hsu: Ming- Shi- Kao (Draft History of the Ming) 1714. Chuan 309 concerns Nepal.

Encyclopedia of Buddhism, Published in Japan.

Ershisi shi : 24 History Books of China, Wei Lue, Xizhang, 3rd Part 30th Zuan, Zhong Hua Shu Zhu, Xin Hua Shu Dian, Beijing, 1975.

Fan Wenlan Zhong Guo Tong Shi (Comprehensive History of China) Renmin Chupan Shi 1-7 Vols, Xinhuashu Dian1949 5th print 1978.

Gao Sheng Zhuan (Collection of life stories of eminent Buddhists Published in China).

Hsuan Tsang: Records of the western Regions in the Tang Dynasty, Foreign Languages Press, Beijing.

Hu Zhizan: Zhongguo He Nepoer Renmin de Shenhuo Youyi, Guang Ming Ribao, 27-9-1956.

Huan Shang Zang: Zhog guo He Nepoerde Quantong Youyi People's Daily 20-11-1955.

I-tsing: Ta-T'ang-hsi-Yu-Chiu-Fa-Kao-Seng-Ch'uan (Life of the Eminent Monks who traveled to the Western World for Research in Buddhist Law in the Great T'ang Period). Completed about 692 A.D.

Li Yachou: Xizhang Guo Wenlun. Beijing University Library

Luo Zhuchen : Present Nepal, Siquan Renmin Chupan Shi ISBN 7-220-04936-6D.690.

Sahaja Shri : "Qi-jie" and "Instruction words" 3 Vols."Wu Thai

Shan Yanjiu" Wu Thai Shan Research Committee, Shanshi, China.1997 P40

Suzuki Nakamasa: China, Tibet and India- Their Early International Relations. Tokyo: Hitotsubashi Shobo, 1962(Japanese).

Tao- Shi: Fa-Yuan-Chu-Lin (Forest of the pearls of the Garden of Buddhist Law) completed in 668 A.D. (Japanese edition, Ta-Tsang-Chin, Vol. 53.)

Tu Yu: T'ong tien (Encyclopedia of Source Material on Political and Social History). Completed around the end of the 8th century. Volume 46, chuan 190, and volume 47, chuan 193, concern Nepal.

Wang Chin Huan : Xizhang Wang Tongji (Annuals of Tibetan Kings) Shang Wu Yin shuguan, shanghai, China 1949

Wang Hungwei and Liu Zheng-hua : Nipo-er Minzhu Zhi, Xinhua Shudian 15BN 7-80057-027-4/2- 16

Wei Yuan: Ch'ien-Lung Cheng K'uo-er-k'a Chi) Narrative of the Conquest of the Gorkhas under Ch'ien-lung), from "Sheng-Wu-Chi"(Military Exploits of the Ch'ing Imperial Period), Beijing.

Wu Tai Shan Yanjiu Hui (Wutai Shan Research Committee) : Wu T'ai Shan Yanjiu (Mt Wu t'ai Research Containts) A Magazine first issue of 1997 Shan-xi China.Distributed by China Interpational Maps and Books Trading Corporation, Beijing 1997, p.40

Yang Gungshu: Yige Wyjiao teshide Huiyi :(A Memoir of a Diplomat Hainan chu pan shi 1995 page 223)

Yin Falu: Zhongguo He Nepoer de Quantong Youyi People's Daily 4-8-1957.

(The Writers name of the following books were not available so the titles)

Ch'ing-Chi-Chou-Tsang-tsou-Tu: Memorials and Correspondence Concerning the Arrangement of Affairs during the latter part of the Ch'ing Dynasty, Peiping, National Academy, 1938, 3 volumes.

Chin-ting K'ou-er k'a Chi-Lueh.: Official Summary Account of the Pacification of the Gorkhas. Peking. , 1796. 54 Plus 4 Chuan in 8 vols.

Hsu Chi-yu (Ch'ing Dynasty): A new record of the Wut'ai Mountain.

Hua Yuan Ching: Abatamsaka sutra 1-8 Volums, Beijing University Library

Ming- Shi- Lu: Veritable Records of the Ming Dynasty. Nanking, 1940.

Qing Shi Gao: Draft of the History of the Qing Dynasty, Beijing University Library

Qing Shi Lu: Unpublished records of the Ching Dynasty Beijing University Library

Thang-dai Yu Xizhang Wenming: Beijing University Library

Yang Kungshu A Diplomat's Memoir, Hainan Chu Pan She, China. 1995

Yapian Zanaheng: Opium war, Xin hua Shu Dian, Beijing.

Zhon Guo Ershisi Shi 24 History Books of China, Zhoug Hua Shu zhu, Xinhua Shu Dian Beijing 1975.

Zhue Xian Zuan: Biography of Buddhabhadra, Beijig University Library

Zhung Guo: Xiantai Shi Ze Yuekan (Modern History of China) 1-6 Volums Beijing

Nepali, Hindi and Sanskrit Books

Acharya Baburam: Chou Enlai Welcome-Special Issue Gorakhapatra 1957.

Nepal-Tibet Sambandha. Pragati Year 2 and 4 Vol. 4 Balbahu Araniko Sharada Monthly Bhotko Raja Ra Tinko Samaya (Kings of Tibet and their time) Sharda, Varsha 12 Sankhya 9-2003

Cheen Tibet Ra Nepal, Edited and Published by Shrikrishna Acharya, Kathmandu 2059 B.S.

Bajracharya Dhanabajra : Lichchabi Kaleen Nepalka Abhilekha Nepal, (Records of Lichchavi Piriod) Asiyali Adhyayan Samdthan (CINAS) Tribhuban University Kathmandu 2030 B.S.

Lichchabi Kaleen Nepalko Aitihasik Patra Masangali, Kathmandu.

Bhattarai Niranjan: Cheen Ra Tyasasita Nepalko Sambandha, Royal Nepal Academy, Nepal. 1961

Cheen Nepal Sambandha, Sajha Prakashan, Kathmandu, 2001.

Gyanamani Nepal: Nepal Bhot Chin Sambandhaka Kehi Samskritik Pakhsa Nepal Academy Kathmandu 2045 B.S. .

Joshi Satya Mohan: Kalakar Araniko (Artist Araniko) Shajha Prakashan Kathmandu 2044 B.S

Nepali Kalakar Araniko sambandhi Chiniyan Samiti ankit Vivaranharu, Nepal Chin Samskritic Parishad 1982.

Prajhaparamita Sutrama Samskritik Manyataharu, Gorakha Patra 2048 B.S.

Khanal Mohan Prasad: Nepalma Bhot yuddhako Tayari, Preparation for war with Tibet in Nepal, Katyayani tole, Baneshwar, Kathmandu, 2036 B.S.

Bajracharya Bhikshu Dharma Milra : Manjushree Guru: 2038 B.S.

Nepal Gyanamani: Nepal, Bhot Cheen Smbandhaka Kehi Samskritik Paksha (Some cultural Aspects of Nepal's relations with Tibet and China) Nepal Rajakeeya Prajna Pratisthan, Kathmandu 2045 B.S. 2) Lichchabikalma Nepalko Chinsanga Sambandha, Souvenir, Nepal China Samskritik Parishad 1980.

Nepali Chittaranjan: General Bhimsen Thapa, Ratna Pustak Bhandar, Kathmandu.2035 B.S

Nepal-China Yuddha (Nepal China war) Sharada Monthly 21-1- 1956.

Nepal-Tibet Sambandha. Pragati year2and4 Vol.4

Pradhan Bhuban Lal: Nepalma Bouddha Dharma, (Buddhist Religion in Nepal) Royal Nepal Academy, Kathmandu, 2045 B.S.

Bodhisattwa Manjushree Pauranik or Aitihasik (Is Manjushree Mythological Deity or Historical Personality) Gorakhapatra 2048-2-11 B.S.

Shakya Hemaraj: Swayambhu Maha chaitya, Swayambhu Vikas Mandal, Kathmandu 2035 B.S.

Sharma Balchandra: Nepalko Aitihasik Ruparekha (Historical Outline of Nepal). Dudhvinayak, Varanasi, India 2008 B.S.

Sharma B.L.: Rashtrapita Ra Ma (Father of the Nation: King Tribhuvan and Me) Indra chauk, Kathmandu 2041 B.S.

Nagari Pracharini Sabha: Fa Hsien Yatra Vibaran, (In Hindi) Language) Banaras, India.1961, pp 48

Mnjushree Mulakalpa (In Sanskrit), Trivendram- edition,1920 p 137

Index